Landscape
Architecture

Landscape
Architecture

Meaghan Kombol

$$\frac{30}{30}$$

Φ

Introduction

In a world where more than half the population lives within an urban environment – which, according to the United Nations, is likely to increase to nearly 70 per cent by 2050 – an understanding of the importance of landscape architecture has never been more relevant. Even now, from the moment you step out of your front door there is an increasing chance that much of your journey will have been strongly shaped by the work of landscape architects. Whether it's the route you take to the bus stop or the train station, the water feature your children run through in the park on a hot summer day, or even the playground that helps them develop their motor skills, landscape architects may well have played an essential role in making these experiences safe, inspiring and ecologically sound.

As a practising landscape architect, I have a keen understanding of the profession's many intricacies. When I visit projects and admire the work of others, I can imagine the problems they faced when designing and I can see how they have attempted to address important concerns such as managing light conditions or maintaining a cultural narrative. Yet my curiosity about their method and the technical skill with which they have overcome site-specific obstacles – my professional fascination, if you like – does not prevent me from experiencing the space in the same way as any other member of the public. All around me, I see how landscape architects are finding intelligent and beautiful ways of enhancing the modern world.

My appreciation for the way we can manipulate the landscape has existed since childhood, growing up in the United States amid the foothills of the Cascade Mountains, Washington, at the doorstep of the breathtakingly beautiful Mount Rainier. I have fond memories of sitting with my father at the wheel of a backhoe, observing him as he moulded the land around each one of the six houses in which I grew up. Equally fond are my memories of trekking with my mother on weekends, forging paths through thick Douglas fir forests. I was always impressed by my father's skill in defining spaces, enabling privacy by shaping the existing land, and by my mother's ability to create journeys through centuries of woodland growth. Through my parents I was introduced to the idea that, with respect and care, the landscape could be sculpted and its beauty enhanced for a practical benefit. Combined with forest treks and swims in glacier-fed lakes, these early experiences and the joy that they brought would play a major role in shaping my view of the landscape as a journey through space and time, creating a deep understanding of the value of landscape architecture to health and well-being.

I moved to New York City in my early twenties and was fortunate to find a job with the ingenious graphic design firm M&Co. Working both with the maverick graphic designer, Tibor Kalman, and also with Maira Kalman, the sublimely talented designer, illustrator and writer, I gained further insight into the value of good design. Just as importantly, they brought out the flâneur in me and reawakened my childhood appreciation for evocative spaces and experiences. Next, armed with an inspired design aesthetic, I moved to the UK and found myself drawn to the profession of landscape architecture.

So what exactly is landscape architecture? Prior to the 1800s, professionals were dedicated to the planning of large-scale landscapes for aristocrats, churches, governments and royalty. In France this was demonstrated when Louis XIV commissioned André Le Nôtre's exquisite designs for the Gardens of Versailles and Vaux-le-Vicomte. In England, a hundred years later, 'Capability' Brown would depart from such formality when creating landscapes to surround large estates and properties, such as Blenheim Palace. But it wasn't until the early nineteenth century that the term 'landscape architecture' was coined to define a 'modern' profession, and Frederick Law Olmsted's Central Park in New York City provided one example of what landscape architecture would become.

With an emphasis on creating a dedicated space for the benefit of the wider community, the park incorporated existing elements while providing unobtrusive through routes for people and traffic. While areas of the landscape were adapted over time, responding to users' needs, the importance of maintaining the park for the health of both the city and its inhabitants has remained a priority. The creation of a professional organization, the American Society of Landscape Architects (ASLA) – established in 1899, was soon followed by other countries recognizing landscape architecture through their own professional associations. Having evolved greatly since the creation of large-scale parks and flower gardens for the privileged elite, today landscape architecture stands at the forefront of design for social, cultural and environmental health worldwide, creating spaces within our natural and built environments that respect and enhance our interaction with the landscape.

Contemporary landscape architecture goes much further than designing within the four walls of a flower garden or planting trees on either side of a building. The densification of the twenty-first century world means that landscape architects must play an ever more decisive role in forming the space around us, influencing how we live, work and play, and in defining our relationship with the land. It has become increasingly important that landscapes are designed to deal with the consequence of urban growth, such as creating 'floodable' landscapes in areas with high rainfall or incorporating systems that minimize water evaporation in drier climates. Furthermore, where our natural habitat might concede to urban sprawl, the necessity of maintaining a cultural and historical narrative is an important consideration when designing. Sustainable environmental and contextual decisions need to be made by qualified professionals who are passionate about maintaining an ideal symbiosis between the natural and the built environments, and landscape architects are constantly devising creative ways to sustain urban growth while ensuring the improvement of natural habitats across the world. Indeed, as a multidisciplinary profession, landscape architects are perhaps best situated to effectively manage the complex decisions necessary for new urban developments.

With this in mind, it might seem strange that the landscape architect's expertise has often not been considered during the initial process when key decisions have been made between planners, architects, landowners and developers. However, the more intense our urban habitation becomes, the more extensive the need for interdisciplinary collaboration when designing. Whereas the landscape might once have been an afterthought – an attempt to neatly tie up a piece of architecture or a renovated streetscape – the need for a collaborative approach from the beginning is now becoming better understood. Broader landscape issues are more frequently addressed beforehand, anticipated and planned for. The landscape architect's ability to provide effective connectivity – connecting people to the places they inhabit, both physically and emotionally – is now increasingly reflected in a greater sense of connectivity and cooperation during the initial design process. Professionals from the diverse disciplines responsible for determining our interaction with the environment are beginning to listen to one another, and this communication of ideas holds the key to future success. As communication and collaboration form the basis for a successful society, so too must they provide the foundation for a successful society's infrastructure.

As well as establishing a dialogue with architects and other professionals across diverse disciplines, collaboration – both within their own firms and with others in the field – forms an important part of the landscape architect's design process, as they aim to create an optimal balance between environmental, social, economic and aesthetic needs. Indeed, the format of this book aims to highlight the collaborative aspect of landscape architecture, while at the same time shining a spotlight on the work of some of today's most exciting and inspiring practitioners from around the world.

Landscape architects are united in their aims of improving our quality of life and improving our interaction with the natural environment, not just for now, but also for the future. With this in mind, they collaborate to improve their practice and to achieve these aims, teaching and mentoring others, and often lecturing at the same universities and appearing on design review panels together to review and judge the latest projects from around the world. Professional relationships arise from these situations, and many lead inevitably to further collaboration.

As a result of these relationships, a selection of thirty of the world's most celebrated landscape architects were invited to recommend one practitioner whom they feel to be particularly inspiring in their design approach, someone they believe to be delivering some of today's most innovative or forward-thinking designs. In this way, the book provides an extensive list of sixty cutting-edge landscape architects, comprising thirty well-known designers and thirty names we should know more about. With each designer responding to the same questions regarding their work, their design process and their inspiration, we gain a fascinating insight into their thoughts and feelings about the profession as a whole, its role in the world today and the future of the industry. The resulting answers contain challenging ideas, thought-provoking philosophies and the stimulating mix of wit and wisdom that comes only from extensive experience and boundless creativity.

The book is organized alphabetically according to the thirty invited landscape architects, with each of their pages directly followed by their recommended practitioner. Taken as a whole, the book presents work from sixty of the world's most interesting and significant landscape architects, brought together from twenty countries, spanning six continents and offering a unique global perspective of exactly who is shaping our landscape today – and how. Each of the landscape architects' pages features a handpicked selection of their work, representing past, present and future projects. Past projects highlight work built throughout the past decade, while present projects highlight work recently completed or still in progress, while future projects are yet to break ground. From Laurie Olin to Toru Mitani, and Martha Schwartz to Claudia Harari, each page reveals fascinating and personal details about creations, inspirations and design processes, as well as setting out the key issues facing landscape architects today and discussing what the future holds for the industry. This insight, together with full-colour photographs, sketches and drawings, aims to highlight the latest trends in landscape architecture and reveals how designs are evolving to create ever more sustainable, sophisticated and enjoyable landscapes.

One trend, illustrated throughout the book, is that regardless of how designs are developed – whether from handmade clay models or the latest parametric software – landscape architects create work that constantly redefines the way we interact with the world – both built and natural. Designed to function for a wide spectrum of uses, users and weather systems, these landscapes are also built to endure and adapt, accommodating fluctuations in use over time as well as working and evolving through the seasons. Another common trend that emerges is a demand for better university training for landscape architects, calling for improved tuition which not only provides graduates with the necessary skills for dealing with the profession's increasing complexities, but also empowers them to find their own voice and challenge the status quo. A final clear trend is the recognition that the role of landscape architects needs to be readdressed. The profession needs to be brought to the forefront of new development in order to moderate between the natural and built environments. The landscape architect's expertise in looking at the overall site context so as to best develop logical, sustainable spaces, best suited for a project, must be routinely acknowledged.

Not only do I hope that this book will offer students, practitioners and enthusiasts an inspiring and insightful look at global landscape architecture today, but I also hope it will document, and in some way accompany, a necessary change in how we view this constantly evolving and increasingly important profession. The work of the landscape architect affects how we exist socially within the modern natural world; it brings us together, regardless of our status or background, by providing a shared experience of an environment. It is the landscape architect's skill that ensures a positive experience that is both highly functional and aesthetic, made subjective through innumerable personal interpretations.

Meaghan Kombol

Stig L Andersson, SLA
Copenhagen, Denmark

Having studied nuclear physics, Japanese culture and chemistry before becoming an architect, Stig L Andersson has developed his interest in Japanese culture's relationship with substance, space and changeability through his own practice, SLA Architects. A founding partner and creative director, Andersson began SLA in 1994 as a landscape architectural practice, and it has since developed into an international interdisciplinary organization working with urban design, landscape and city planning. Renowned for his sensory and poetic work, Andersson merges a site's unique amenity values with cutting-edge climate adaption and resilient urban design. Andersson is a Professor in Aesthetic Urban Design at the University of Copenhagen and is a sought-after lecturer and teacher at universities and architecture schools, receiving numerous national and international awards, including the C F Hansen Medal – the highest national honour given to a Danish architect. In 2014, Andersson curated the Danish Pavilion's exhibition at the 14th Venice Architecture Biennale under the title: *Empowerment of Aesthetics.*

Andersson lists snow, states of water, rapid changes in weather – and Iceland – among his favourite natural landscapes, and one of his more recent projects, Cloud, situated in Copenhagen, responds to these natural inspirations in a way that typifies SLA's method 'by designing physical matter in a way that creates the foundation for an atmosphere'. His choice of one of his own projects in which to spend the day, Cloud uses and enhances the site's microclimate while allowing visitors to experience three states of water – liquid, solid and gas – simultaneously. The urban space deals functionally with water, by recycling rainwater and dealing effectively with torrential rain, while also providing aesthetic value. This entrance plaza for the Crystal building, housing the new headquarters of a major Danish bank, takes Copenhagen's grey climate and converts it into an experiential space. As Andersson explains, by using 'the principle of the Bose-Einstein condensate in creating a "fourth state" of water, where all states are visible at the same time, everything except the building fluctuates in water, fog, clouds, light and rain'. Asked what 'tools' he uses when designing, Andersson responds, 'my senses and my brain'. By way of clarification he continues: 'To use the senses, to experience something, to wonder. That is the beginning. The tools to solve a given problem are always a combination of education and culture.' His designs do not depend on 'inspiration', but rather, 'on the fact that the world is complementary', comprising two paradigms, dominated by one, the rational, while the other, the aesthetic, he believes is 'vastly misrepresented'. He explains: 'By

aesthetic I do not mean "beautiful" or "visually pleasing", but that which speaks to all our senses ... and which is the foundation for wonder, reflection [and] new knowledge.' Andersson states the desire to equalize the aesthetic with the rational as 'my drive, my reason to get up in the morning, and – yes – my inspiration'. It is also something he feels is an important issue facing the profession today, believing that landscape architects need to 'develop a new kind of architectural design language that lets us equate the repressed paradigm of the grown environment with the dominant paradigm of the built environment'.

Exhibited as one of ten designers in the Xi'an China International Horticultural Exhibition in 2011 in Shanxi Province, Andersson's Yellow Mud Garden explores the sensuous side of nature. Paying homage to the Yellow River and its rich clay, which 3,000 years ago helped support the Chinese civilization through its use as a material for building, pottery and art, the site features large figures of clay and mud of varying colours. A re-creation of the area's original plantation and a cross-cultural and socially inclusive landscape design, SLA created a distinct and highly site-specific public park at the edge of the Yellow River. Exploring mud, here in its various forms, states and colours, the design plays with our perception of this abundant, yet rarely celebrated material. Contrastingly, his City Dune project – located in an urban setting on the Copenhagen harbour – features a fully accessible 'green tract' that connects pedestrians and cyclists with the harbour, the Swedish SEB bank and the Tivoli Congress Centre. Sustainably driven, the plaza is designed so as to attenuate and re-use all of the site's rainwater for irrigation and, on hot summer nights, be emitted as cool moist air.

Discussing the future of landscape architecture, Andersson thinks that 'the connotation of "landscape" dates back several hundred years' and that the profession is therefore stuck with an image of what it's about, 'usually something about plants, and usually something that is subordinated to "building architecture"'. He believes a 'quantum leap' is needed to change this perception and gain more influence in the world. While his reminder that the 'grown environment' should not be used 'merely as building blocks in the built environment's agenda', but instead its 'inherent and distinct nature' uniquely harnessed, goes some way to making this change, it is essential for Andersson that we address this balance, both between the built and the grown, and between the rational and the aesthetic, as he explains, 'Recently, there has been a growing belief that landscape architecture can solve many of our future problems. We can. But by primarily focusing on the problem-solving aspect of the profession we risk being solely utility-oriented. And that is only half the solution. The other half is the aesthetic. The future of landscape architecture must thus encompass both.'

Favourite plants and materials

'Form, growth and texture are what interests me in plants and materials.'

Favourite artists

1 Cy Twombly
2 Du Fu
3 Ikeda
4 Eduardo Chillida
5 Asger Jorn

Inspiration

1 Physicist Niels Bohr
2 Physicist/chemist
  Hans Christian Ørsted
3 Artist Johan Thomas Lundbye
4 Author Inger Christensen
5 Chef Ferran Adrià

Favourite natural landscapes

1 Snow and states of water
2 Rapid changes of weather
3 Fluctuations, and Iceland

Yellow Mud Garden, Xi'an, Shanxi Province, China (2010–11)

Part of the 2011 Xi'an China International Horticultural Exhibition, this garden was created as a tribute to the Yellow River's rich history of clay – historically used as a building material, in pottery and art. Here, SLA designed large clay figures and used mud of various colours to create an exploratory public park at the edge of the Yellow River.

This sustainable project links the public spaces around the Swedish SEB bank headquarters with the surrounding area and the harbour. Drawing inspiration from the lush hillsides of the Scandinavian landscape, the design creates a welcoming urban green space. The terrain's contours both accommodate technical and functional demands – from drainage and lighting to planting areas – while creating routes suitable for all.

Cloud provides Copenhagen with a sensuous urban space that offers visitors the chance to enjoy some of the city's most characteristic weather traits – clouds, rain and mist. This is represented in both the grey shades of paving, and in the water, visible as water jets, a circular water feature that reflects the sky, and dividing the plaza into various spaces.

The Delta District, Vinge, Frederikssund, Denmark (2025)

In the future city of Vinge, the Delta District is transformed into a lush cityscape where meadow, fruit trees and streams form the basis of this harmonious new development. The design unites urban life and nature to create a sustainable neighbourhood. The project is exemplar of how nature can have a dual function: manmade elements that absorb rainwater, preventing flooding, while creating enjoyable amenity landscapes.

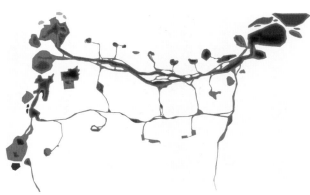

Favourite plants

1 Air plants such as *Tillandsias*
2 Colombian orchids
3 Giant mafafa
  (*Xanthosoma robustum*)
4 Jaboticaba (*Myrciaria cauliflora*)

Favourite trees

1 Kapok (*Ceiba pentandra*)
2 Araguaney (*Tabebuia chrysantha*)
3 Pink trumpet (*Tabebuia rosea*)
4 Black olive (*Bucida buceras*)

Favourite materials

1 Water
2 Vapour
3 Ice
4 Fog
5 Concrete

Favourite natural landscape

Páramo – a South American
treeless plateau

Inspiration

Architect Cedric Price

Sitting at the crossroads of architecture, landscape architecture and urbanism, Luis Callejas's projects push the boundaries of design to create highly celebrated, articulated projects. Former partner and director of Paisajes Emergentes, Callejas set up LCLA office in 2011. Now based in Boston, Massachusetts, and Medellín, Colombia, Callejas dedicates himself to deploying landscape architecture as a medium for design in Latin America, where the field has not yet been widely established. In 2010, Paisajes Emergentes, comprising Callejas, Sebastian Mejia and Edgar Mazo, was selected as one of the world's ten best young practices by the Iakov Chernikhov International Foundation. And in 2013, Callejas received the Architectural League Prize for Young Architects from the Architectural League of New York. Callejas is a Lecturer of Architecture and Landscape Architecture at the Harvard Graduate School of Design.

Citing his creative inspirations as 'geography and extreme landscapes, strong weather events and Brazilian Modernism', and armed with a camera and a computer, Callejas's designs evolve in the forms of plans and collages. Callejas explains that he often looks 'for projects and competitions that can potentially serve as a vehicle for specific research agendas that I'm exploring at the moment'. The explorative nature of his works can be seen in the numerous studies he creates and the resulting experimental concepts. With his design for the competition Tropicarium, in Bogotá, Callejas examined the concept of the *jardin d'hiver* (winter garden). Normally constructed within the confines of structure to protect plants from cold weather, when created in a warm tropical environment, open-air courtyards can be created without the need for climate control. Featuring tropical vegetation typical of Bogotá, this project explores different ecosystems through a series of 'landscape-curated' rooms divided by PVC curtains.

In regard to collaborations, Callejas appreciates the specialist knowledge of individual disciplines and recognizes that, when working with people from such fields as botany, he often finds interesting ideas emerge from conflicting opinions. In addition to working with architects, engineers and botanists, in the future Callejas would like to work more with media artists and video-game artists, a combination that would surely add another exciting dimension to his work.

When asked about global issues facing landscape architects today, Callejas is an advocate for giving more presence to the field of landscape architecture in Latin America. Yet he explains that when working in Latin America, 'I still have to present myself as an architect and leave the conversation about landscape as

something internal to the studio.' Callejas believes it will be some time before landscape architecture is developed as a 'robust field' in Latin America. This lack of professional definition didn't stop him creating the highly celebrated Aquatic Centre, located in his hometown of Medellín. Even though the competition brief called for an enclosed building, Callejas provided a design that fittingly reflected Medellin's tropical location. Located in the middle of the Andes Mountains, and created for the 9th South American Games, this project incorporates professional and recreational aquatic sports within a space that also transforms into an aquatic park for public use. Enabling year-round views of the surrounding terrain and taking full advantage of the constant temperate climate, the four pools are completely open to the air.

The project includes public swimming and swimming lesson facilities interconnected by a flooded garden landscape comprising tropical wetland species, while separate bathroom and changing facilities are located below ground. Seemingly carved into the ground, a series of courtyards provide natural light below. The planting presents the expansive 16,000-square metre (172,223-square feet) facilities as an extension of the surrounding landscape, while sunken concrete walkways offer shade and mirror the raised rail track running parallel to the site. A pool used for synchronized swimming is positioned above the gardens, while windows below ground allow pedestrians a glimpse of the swimmers from ground level. Ultimately, the new Aquatic Centre behaves as an unsolicited landscape and public space where water becomes the main asset to catalyze vibrant public occupation. It responds to the need for a professional swimming facility, yet the driving force behind the project was to re-frame the aquatic activities as a public event open to the city.

When looking towards the future of landscape architecture, Callejas feels that 'addressing the problems of urbanization both in cities and outside of them is already the present and most immediate future'. Wishing to see 'strong alliances' between art and landscape architecture, he feels that 'new generations of students from top schools will create art practices in a way that we haven't seen before'. In fact, Callejas reflects, he enjoys it when his own students at the Harvard Graduate School of Design 'feel liberated from using the moral weight of ecology as a design medium', and instead 'take fiction and narrative with the same degree of seriousness as ecology'.

For his next research project Callejas would like to add a second public pool to his repertoire. Only this time he'd like to construct an oceanic version. As he explains, 'I've been chasing and photographing oceanic pools all over the world since finishing the Aquatic Centre.' The ideal of creating a project based on his own vision, extensive research and concept development is destined to create another inspiring design.

Luis Callejas,
LCLA office
Cambridge, MA, USA / Medellín, Colombia

'It is crucial for our profession that one is able to express one's ideas and aesthetic perceptions of the material in drawings that communicate with the recipient, rather than to the recipient. Luis Callejas is able to achieve this in a way so others can learn from him.' Stig L Andersson on Luis Callejas

Luis Callejas, LCLA office

Tropicarium, Bogotá, Colombia (2014)
Done in association with Giancarlo Mazzanti, this competition design uses the concept of a winter garden to create a collection of 'curated' rooms highlighting the exotic plants typical of its tropical location in the Andes Mountains. Bogotá's warm weather allows for open-air courtyards, defined by PVC curtains; visitors pass through the spaces at ground level and over arcing bridges.

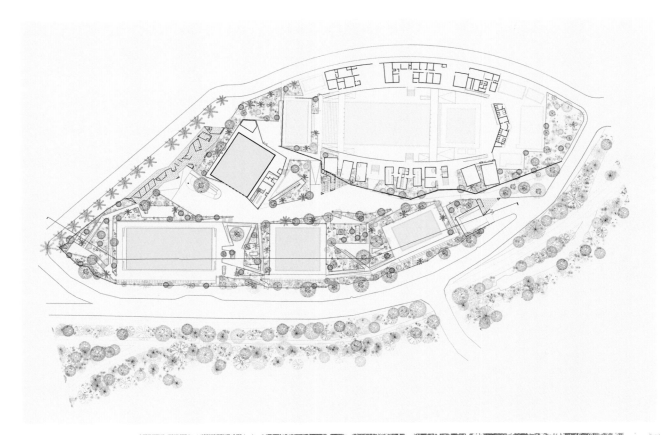

Luis Callejas, LCLA office

<u>Aquatic Centre</u>, Medellín, Colombia (2012)

Designed in association with Edgar Mazo and Sebastián Mejía, this project is an open-air swimming complex that also functions as a public park. The design is articulated as a system of gardens, planted with species typical of tropical wetlands, through which the centre's four pools are connected. A set of courtyards below ground provides meeting spaces, while submerged windows give passers-by underwater pool views.

Thorbjörn Andersson, Sweco Architects Stockholm, Sweden

Thorbjörn Andersson has practised landscape architecture since 1981, having studied landscape architecture, architecture and art history in Sweden and the United States. He is probably best known for his work in the planning and design of public spaces in the city. In addition to his continuing practice, he is also the founder and editor of the journal *Utblick Landskap*, an author and a professor. He has received numerous accolades, including the Prince Eugene Medal from His Majesty, the King of Sweden for his contribution to the field of landscape architecture in 2009.

Andersson states that 'in Scandinavia there is a tradition of using what you have rather than what you want,' and indeed this philosophy clearly provides inspiration for his own projects, which cooperate with their natural environment in this way. As Andersson explains, 'The idea is to get the most for the least, which also is a sustainable attitude.'

He finds further inspiration from disciplines outside of the field of landscape architecture, such as gastronomy, dance and film. Pina Bausch's German dance company is one such example. He explains that he is inspired by 'the way they colonize places with their bodies and gestures'. Similarly, with gastronomy, it's less about the food and more about the presentation. His Physic Garden at the Novartis Campus in Basel, Switzerland reveals a choreographed relationship between the plants and the visitors. Organized as a semi-enclosed theatre, one enters via a zigzag movement between backdrops of yew and hornbeam hedges. Arriving at the centre, sunken planting beds open up to reveal thirty-two of the most important pharmaceutical plants organized in a striped pattern, while bridges without railings seemingly 'float' visitors through the space.

02 / 02

He also experiences 'an uplifting spirit by watching the work of the Russian film director Andrej Tarkovskij and how he deals with abandoned land, mystical places, and what he finds there'.

Having started out wanting to be a journalist, and written extensively over the years, it's no surprise that Andersson's creative process starts with writing. 'Sketching is scary because the minute you draw a line, you have taken a decision,' he explains, adding that 'words are much more open'. So by the time he is ready to draw, the design has been more or less resolved through words. The design then moves fairly quickly, and when asked what tools he prefers, his response appears to echo his propensity for making use of what you find: 'I am not fetishist about tools ... sometimes I would even use those short pencils that you get for free at IKEA ... but I do like models, they are good for rhetoric.'

Favourite plants

1 Oriental poppy (*Papaver orientale*)
2 Wild thyme (*Thymus serpyllum*)
3 Male fern (*Dryopteris filix-mas*)
4 Alpine columbine (*Aquilegia alpina*)
5 Butterbur (*Petasites hybridus*)

Favourite trees

1 Common beech (*Fagus sylvatica*)
2 Downy birch (*Betula pubescens*)
3 Italian alder (*Alnus cordata*)
4 Black pine (*Pinus nigra*)
5 Honey locust (*Gleditsia triacanthos*)

Favourite materials

1 Water
2 Granite
3 Wood
4 Light and shadow

Favourite natural landscapes

1 Deserts and glaciers for contemplation
2 Meadows and forest paths for motivation

Andersson says that his early career often involved working with architects who expected him to simply place plants around buildings and lay out parking lots. Explaining, 'Those were not happy days ... at that point, I set my mind not to work with architects in the future, but try to create a client's interest for independent landscape architecture.'

Yet, with University Campus Park, Umeå, Sweden, Andersson clearly had collaboration and cooperation in mind, having created a park that supplies a variety of designated places with the ability to foster informal discussions and encourage knowledge exchanges. It comprises sun decks, jetties, open lawns, walking trails and terraces organized around an artificial lake with a central island acting as the departure point for a small archipelago. Promenades move through the site between nodes of social interest.

Albeit a campus, this project responds to what Andersson feels is one of today's most pressing design issues: how to 'live in tolerance and mutual respect' in densely populated urban areas. He sees parks and squares as 'training fields' for improving social skills as people 'interact with strangers, create kinship and respond to encounters'. 'As a designer,' he explains, 'I take part in this simply because that is the only kind of landscape architecture that I do; public space.' To do this he minimizes programming, 'making the design humble', and limits the number of 'dead things' in order to maximize social interactions.

His design of an observation deck in Rinkeby, a suburb north of Stockholm, is located in a district, which, according to Andersson, has 'high unemployment, high immigration ratio and low self-esteem'. The challenge for this design is to connect Rinkeby to the recreational areas set within a nature reserve. Separated by a freeway and a 15-metre (49-feet) level change, this design reconnects the area by placing the freeway in a tunnel and creating an observation deck on top. In explaining his design, Andersson states that 'Only restoring pavements, trees and lighting would demand twice the budget we have. So we decided to put everything into a spectacular viewing point' and in doing so, he provides physical access to the field below, while creating a significant landmark for the community.

In discussing the future of landscape architecture, Andersson provides a suitably idiosyncratic response: 'Probably less about design, and more about planning, less about decoration, and more about processes, less about taste, and more about politics, less about statements, and more about social understanding, less about the picturesque, and more about the usable, less about result, and more about change, less about what you see, and more about what you feel.'

Physic Garden at Novartis Campus, Basel, Switzerland (2012)
This project's name references monastery gardens where medieval monks developed their knowledge of the pharmaceutical properties of plants. Walkways span sunken gardens, framed by a low granite wall. On the sides of the sunken beds are four log racks comprising wood selected to represent species from which chemical substances have been extracted for use in the pharmaceutical industry.

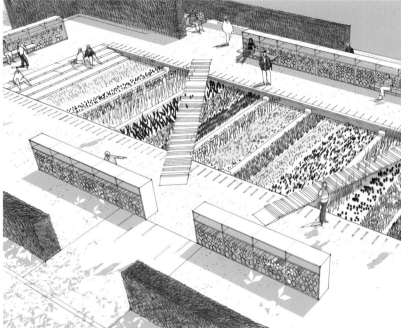

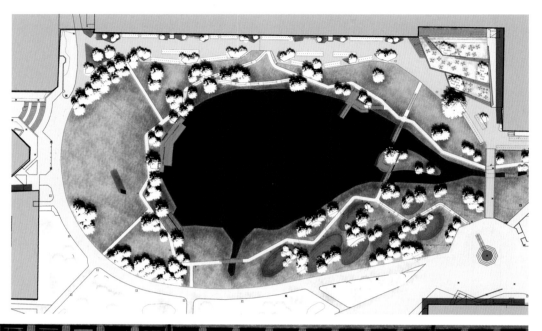

University Campus Park, Umeå, Sweden (2010)

This campus park offers various spaces for informal encounters and academic discussion, including promenades, jetties, open lawns, walking trails and terraces arranged around an artificial lake within a small archipelago. In front of the lively student union, an outdoor lounge is orientated over a series of fan-shaped, gravel terraces featuring seating areas and multi-stemmed trees.

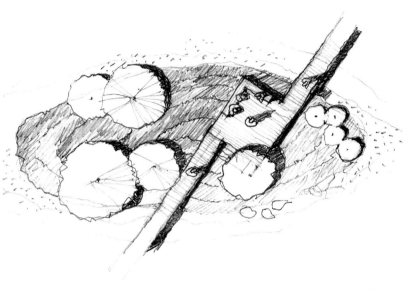

Hyllie Plaza, Malmö, Sweden (2010)

This plaza's trees are arranged in a series of glades, within which seating areas are located on surfaces paved with wood block. Framing the plaza's edges are tall masts between which stretch steel cables arranged in a certain disorder resembling a spider's web. The cables support a field of light-emitting diodes (LEDs) programmed to create a night-time digital sky for four seasonal scenarios.

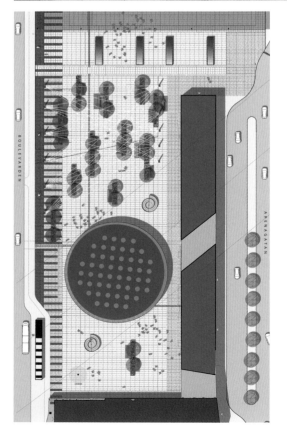

Observation Deck at Rinkeby, Rinkeby (2015)

This project connects Rinkeby to a recreational area located within a nature reserve. Separated by freeway and a 15-metre (49-feet) level change, this design relocates the road inside a tunnel and features an observation deck clad with boards, allowing light to permeate at night. The descent from the deck to the field is along a ramp featuring seating areas, trees and sculptures.

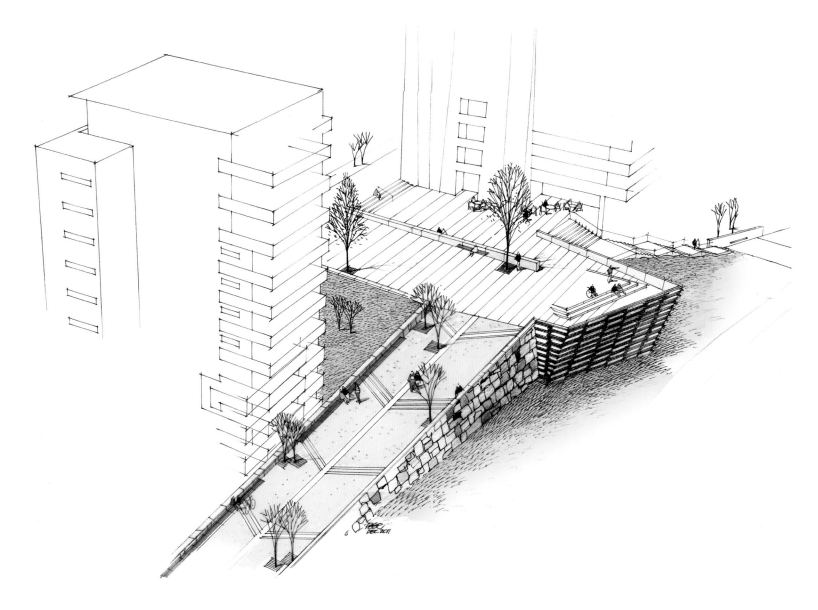

Sounds such as the 'common swift in June' together with the desire that his studio's realized projects 'inform and influence the built environment and planning process' give Mattias Gustafsson direction and momentum to create designs which improve the lives of city dwellers. Since establishing URBIO, his projects have sought to give nature a place within the city while also giving city dwellers a place to re-establish their bond with nature. Gustafsson's work explores urban development issues from a landscape architectonic perspective, with particular regard to biological and social relationships. Having studied landscape architecture, urban design, landscape ecology, human geography and garden history, Gustafsson is well equipped to work on projects that examine landscape architecture's role in sustainable urban development. Gustafsson lectures frequently on the subject, and his firm, URBIO, was given the Innovator of the Year award in 2012 by the Association of Swedish Architects for their sustainable work within cities.

Citing 'blue and green and all in between' as his favourite colours, Gustafsson sets out to create landscapes that enhance flora and fauna (green), water management (blue) and society (red). These colour concepts run through his designs and his desire to create landscapes that enhance urban ecosystems whereby the blue/green systems form symbiotic relationships with humans and their activities. 'Through this RGB mixture an enriched urban environment is created where users interact directly with urban nature.' The RGB elements, together with programming, provide a platform from which 'smart urban habitats together with sustainable, experiential and ecologically interesting urban environments are created'.

Although modern in his approach, some of Gustafsson's inspiration comes from a book entitled *Die Welt in der wir leben* (*The World We Live In*), part of a thirteen-part series from *LIFE* magazine first printed between 1952 and 1954, which was given to him as a child by his grandmother and is filled with old-fashioned pictures of landscapes, habitats, prehistoric animals and geological studies. 'This was where my interest in the perception of nature was born', he states. And it's clear that the book's panoramic pictures still inspire Gustafsson's designs today. Gustafsson and a team of talented employees work in keeping with URBIO's RGB urban design principles and their vision for creating landscapes that celebrate biophilia – human beings' intrinsic affinity with nature. Educational trips to sites within Sweden and abroad enhance this creative process: 'By constantly developing our toolbox of creative ways in which to weave sustainable ideas into the urban fabric, we retain a deep well of ideas from which inspiration may be drawn.'

URBIO'S Butterfly Biotopes Roof and Streetscape in southern Stockholm is an example of a project that features an ecological thread knit into an urban fabric. In this case the roof of a 750-vehicle, multistorey car park has been converted into a lush backdrop for visitors while enhancing ecology. The planting includes blossoming and fruit-bearing trees, a 'butterfly restaurant' made up of planting beds filled with perennials and an extensive biotope roof garden – all constructed so as to attract nectar-seeking insects and, in turn, supporting the native fauna.

In URBIO's Phase Brofästet courtyard project, set to be constructed in the Royal Seaport expansion (Norra Djurgårdsstaden), Stockholm, in 2018, the design aims to reconnect the two 'contrasting environments' in which the landscape is located: an old industrial grounds on one side and the Royal National City Park featuring hardwood forests, on the other. The proposals seek to create spaces that are true to the concept of biophilia and include forests, rainwater gardens and tree groves – reconnecting visitors to nature and establishing connection routes for nature across the new development.

His principles of urban sustainability run deep and are paramount to his design and his practice. Gustafsson is 'convinced that it will be fundamental to include urban ecosystem services in future landscape architectural projects ... as landscape architecture, like no other discipline, has a key role in the creation of sustainable urban structures'. Gustafsson believes that the demand for sustainable and high-quality landscape projects has increased greatly in Sweden over the last five years, inevitably enhancing the city's quality of life.

Rather than separating the concepts of nature and the built environment, URBIO's designs form landscapes that enhance ecological relationships while connecting those who use them. In this way, 'urban environments are established where the quality of life is higher, health and well-being among the users is strengthened and climate adaption goals achieved'. By placing great value on the importance of biophilia in their design, URBIO pushes the boundaries of what is possible through the integration of nature within cities. As Gustafsson concludes, 'In order to create a resilient city there is a need to plan for all scenarios. It is through the knowledge and awareness of how we affect the climate and the climate affects us that we can start planning for a new and improved urban landscape.'

Mattias Gustafsson, URBIO
Stockholm, Sweden

'While everyone is talking about ecology and sustainability, but rarely get further than abstract statements, Mattias Gustafsson and his office URBIO make efforts to transform these ideas into concrete design. They have an ideology that feels real. This is biodiversity in factual terms.'

Thorbjörn Andersson on Mattias Gustafsson

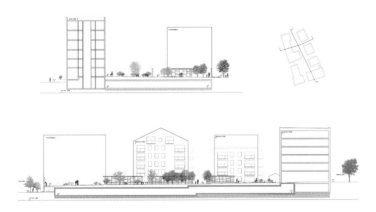

Western Quarter, Phase Brofästet, Royal Seaport, Stockhom, Sweden (2018)

This neighbourhood courtyard's outdoor environment is enriched with landscape features such as tree groves, ecologically rich planting areas and rain gardens. The courtyard lies in an open block with a path that leads across the yard. In one of the buildings a kindergarten is situated on the ground floor with a small outdoor space where children can play when not in the forest or park.

Mattias Gustafsson, URBIO

Mattias Gustafsson, URBIO

Butterfly Biotopes Roof and Streetscape, Stockholm, Sweden (2012)

This project converts a multistorey car park into a green and relaxing oasis for hospital visitors while boosting local fauna. To achieve this goal, a street 400 metres (1,312 feet) long has been planted with vegetation groves and fruit-bearing tree species, while the car park's roof has been made into a 'butterfly restaurant' in the form of an extensive biotope roof garden.

Vasagatan RGB, Vasagatan, Stockholm, Sweden (2014)

This speculative proposal aims to transform parts of Stockholm's central street Vasagatan into a highly valued link in the city-street network, by converting the hardscape into a platform for social interaction combined with sunken areas for large-scale rainwater infiltration and new tree planting. The illustration highlights the relationship between humans and their environment and the need to create resilient cities.

Enric Batlle,
Batlle i Roig Arquitectes
Barcelona, Spain

Together with Joan Roig i Durán, Enric Batlle founded the firm Batlle i Roig Arquitectes in 1981, an office creating internationally recognized works covering a wide range of projects mainly focusing on landscape architecture and the environment. Based in Barcelona, their frequently shortlisted work has received various awards as well as featuring in the 8th European Landscape Biennial in 2014. Coordinator and teacher of the Polytechnic University of Catalonia's Master in Landscape Architecture programme, Batlle also teaches and runs landscape-themed workshops at Polytechnic University of Catalonia's School of Architecture.

As his choice for one of his recent park projects in which to spend the day, Batlle cites the Environmental Recovery of the Llobregat River in Barcelona, not only because of its proximity to where he lives, but because, with extensive pathways offering beach access and meandering through metropolitan farmland, it enables him to view 'nature in the city'. Indeed, with over 30 kilometres (19 miles) of paths, it seems that – outside of his own garden – this is the most likely location for Batlle to hear some of his favourite sounds: rustling leaves, nesting birds and pond frogs. With an ability to create spaces that are both aesthetically strong and ecologically rich, his designs incorporate existing obstacles – a landfill, unique watercourse or topography – transforming the site into a graphic landscape that appears to be peeled back to best reveal its most visually pleasing and ecologically enhancing layers. This often means working with a site's acquired features: for the Environmental Recovery of the Llobregat River, and also for Atlantic Park in Santander, it was the riverbed topography; for the Garraf Waste Landfill in Begues it was the existing farmland and landfill topography; and with Marina Park in Viladecans southwest of Barcelona, it was the site's under-utilized stream.

After establishing the base layers of the site's natural setting, the design for Llobregat River Park moved forward on a more detailed level. For the stretch of the Llobregat River between the towns of Sant Boi and El Prat de Llobregat, Batlle i Roig devised a landscape that redefines its riverfront edge for both social and leisure activities. Batlle explains that it was 'the meandering lines of water' and 'nature's formal systems' that influenced and located paths and bridges. The result is a new peri-urban park that improves connectivity between the river's embankments and the towns along the river.

In addition to layers of vegetation and connectivity, Atlantic Park in Santander, used the 'power of metaphor' to manipulate the existing topography and water. This park's site was a large tract of open space on the outskirts of Santander zoned by the city's masterplan as a public park. Its location, at the centre of major urban growth perpendicular to the Atlantic Ocean, combined with its riverbed topography, offered Batlle i Roig a chance to experiment with geographical and botanical parameters while influencing the site's morphology.

At Marina Park the aim was to conserve as much of the natural landscape as possible. As Batlle explains, the project 'simply superimposed ecological value and social connectivity to the site' incorporating an existing waterway and 'endless paths'. Marina Park was the culmination of the Riera de Sant Climent project that saw the restoration of an under-utilized stream into a linear green park, also designed by Batlle i Roig. Basins positioned on the side of the park's central watercourse allow for temporary flood control in the event of high water volume. The revised park system created a natural corridor connecting the surrounding hills, the city, the Baix Llobregat Agricultural Park and the sea.

When asked about his design process for the Garraf Waste Landfill site, located southwest of Barcelona, Batlle explained it meant looking at 'agriculture as a system', and how individual systems worked within that framework: topography, water and vegetation versus fields, terraces and channels. These influences helped shape the site, which saw the restoration and re-integration of a former landfill within the existing Garraf Natural Park. The rejuvenated landscape is formed of terraces and vegetation set within a complex topography that integrates slopes and drainage solutions in order to enhance the accessible open space while also creating a new gateway into the park.

Dealing with complex sites in terms of remediation and structure, Batlle i Roig develop projects in coordination with diverse disciplines in order to produce insightful and cutting-edge designs. Beyond employing architects and landscape architects, their team also includes full-time agronomists and engineers, as well as working with specialists, such as environmentalists, geologists and biologists. However, these collaborations can lead to what Batlle sees as today's most pressing design issues, 'integrating the proposals offered by different disciplines into a single solution'. In fact, he believes the key to the future of landscape architecture is to integrate the disciplines of engineering, ecology, urban design, architecture and art into one mega discipline and offer a single 'maximum specialization'.

Known for creating highly celebrated urban and natural spaces, when asked what he would do to make better cities of the future, Batlle's response is as unsurprising as it is challenging: 'Create cities that are liveable, natural, agricultural, urban, easy, interesting and beautiful.'

Favourite colour

'Green – of course.'

Favourite plants

1 Roses (*Rosa*)
2 Chinese wisteria (*Wisteria sinensis*)
3 Peppermint (*Mentha* x *piperita*)
4 Sweet basil (*Ocimum basilicum*)
5 Tomato (*Solanum lycopersicum*)

Favourite trees

1 Canary Island date palm
  (*Phoenix canariensis*)
2 Bitter orange
  (*Citrus* x *aurantium*)
3 Common olive (*Olea europaea*)
4 Loquat (*Eriobotrya japonica*)
5 Rosewood (*Tipuana tipu*)

Favourite contemporary artists

1 Richard Long
2 Jaume Plensa
3 Eduardo Chillida
4 Robert Smithson
5 Jacques Simon

Environmental Recovery of the Llobregat River, Barcelona, Spain (2011)

For the stretch of the Llobregat River between the towns of Sant Boi and El Prat de Llobregat, Batlle i Roig has devised a landscape that restores biotopes and redefines its riverfront edge for both social and leisure activities. The result is a new park that improves connectivity between the river's embankments and the towns along the river.

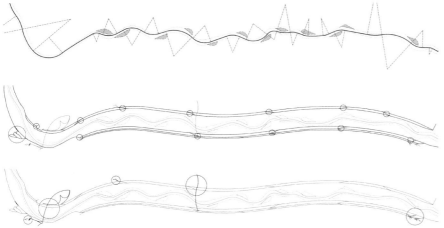

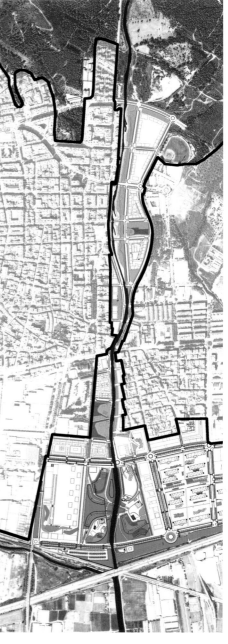

Marina Park, Viladecans, Spain (2008)

This project is the final part of Batlle i Roig's linear green park project, Riera de Sant Climent. In order to prevent flooding, large basins along the side of the park's watercourse are designed to accommodate high water levels. The park features amphitheatre seating areas, path networks and diverse planting to create a new park that forms a green link to the city and its surrounding area.

Atlantic Park, Santander, Spain (2008)

This park's location next to El Sardinero beach, together with its long and narrow riverbed topography, influenced this project's design. The project explores both botanical and biological concepts to create a diverse park framed by stepped embankments and featuring a central water body around which angular paths lead visitors through the park.

Garraf Waste Landfill, Begues, Spain (ongoing)

The overall aim of this restoration project was to reintegrate the formal landfill site into the Garraf Natural Park. The project enhances accessible open space, creates a new gateway into the park, connects a long-distance footpath, utilizes endemic vegetation and significantly ameliorates a previously polluted landscape.

Favourite plants and trees

'When choosing plants I value adaptation, scale relation to human proportion, growth rate, light/shade quality, dynamics through seasons and other criteria.'

Favourite materials

1 Light
2 Shade
3 Bedrock
4 Earth
5 Wind

Favourite natural landscapes

'I enjoy unveiling the peculiarities in all of them.'
1 Mediterranean dry terraced landscapes
2 Deciduous forests
3 Coral reefs
4 Deserts
5 Rainforests
6 Rice terraces
7 Industrial harbours

Martí Franch trained as a landscape architect at the University of Greenwich, London, and studied horticulture at Escola Superior d'Agricultura de Barcelona before working in Amsterdam and Berlin. In 1999 he set up his interdisciplinary practice, EMF landscape architects, which includes professionals from both urban and environmental design. Based in Girona, Spain, Franch has received numerous awards, including an Honor Award from the American Society of Landscape Architects and the Rosa Barba Landscape Prize in 2012, for projects that explore hybrid connections between ecological and cultural systems.

Taking an almost theatrical approach to the way he creates his award-winning projects, Franch begins with an attempt to 'ground the design project to the site'. Working with something like a 'taxonomist's view', he and his team engage with plans of various scales, collaborate with specialists to 'comprehend the landform and to learn how to harness processes inherent to the site'. And, similar to a director putting his own interpretation on a production that already has the set in place, Franch 'distills the site's idiosyncratic "ingredients" and mechanisms' to 'land the brief on site' and allow a concept for the project to emerge. This concept is then tried and tested through sections, models and further site walks in order to 'compose the project's choreography ... both in suggesting movement through the space and also in celebrating and highlighting process through time'. Franch's design process then evolves from conception to construction, and even after completion when he returns to sites to learn from 'errors and successes'.

One such project is Franch's Tudela-Culip (Club Med) restoration project. Located in northeastern Spain, on the Cap de Creus peninsula, the project measures 90 hectares (222 acres) and is one of the biggest restoration projects in the Mediterranean basin. 'BIG, wild, ever-changing, harsh and desolated', Franch describes the project as 'one of those places where one can experience solitude and confront smallness and insignificance.' A former Club Med resort, it became a national park in 1998 and this reclamation project saw the removal of buildings, elimination of invasive plants, restoration of its natural drainage and introduction of unconventional signage and grading, allowing it to be open to the public. Franch believes it is 'a place that carries a message. It subliminally whispers that un-doing or deconstructing is also project-making and that the results of these processes can be powerful, meaningful and replicable.'

EMF's experientially choreographed projects immerse visitors in a 'journey through landscape, cycles and seasons', which Franch believes is 'as important as the design of space and form'. Franch feels that his landscapes are 'earthy, real and occur at an intimate human scale', and participation in the journey offers a renewed relationship with the natural environment that reconnects users with the land.

Often designing rehabilitated landscapes, Franch believes that today's most pressing global issue is the consequence of climate change. His work, ranging from large- to small-scale projects, deals with and tests these issues consistently. As Franch explains: 'We use run-off farming and infiltration as ways to trigger ecological processes, generate landscape diversity and mitigate irrigation. Human comfort and the physical corporeal experience of the environment is a central concern of our practice. We take care to maximize the quality of light and shade, to provide thermal comfort, to deliberately regulate microclimate [and] to protect against radiation ... There is a symbiosis, therefore, between our mode of practice and sustainable design without it being core to our narrative.'

With MónNatura Delta de l'Ebre Eco Museum, Amposta, Spain, Franch converted the relics of an old fish farm into an 'eco museum' and a nature reserve celebrating the natural and cultural wonders of a delta landscape. The project's programme has been overlaid on a series of islands, exploring the concept of the 'liquid landscape' while promoting eco-tourism.

Choreographing connections to the landscape is not just project specific. Creating a landscape 'infrastructure' that connects a city's smaller spaces to the surrounding landscape is something that Franch believes would make better cities of the future. 'Big is beautiful,' Franch states, 'I would make a transition from the dominant "archipelago" system of open spaces to an interconnected "network" system.' He hopes that landscape architecture of the future would be interpreted as 'meta-infrastructure', a hybridized system whereby 'other' infrastructures symbiotically function better socially, economically and environmentally. At urban scale these changes would perhaps create an environment where walking and cycling are more convenient than driving, and Franch believes that the field of landscape architecture could take the lead on such 'holistic changes' to space-making.

When asked about his approach to designing landscapes that must retain existing buildings, Franch reiterates his design process, responding with an appropriately theatrical vocabulary: 'I look for a dialogue in terms of spatial relations, porosity and materiality. Depending on the site and the detail of the programme, this dialogue or relationship may be "filtered" as in Can Framis, "staged" as in Les Echasses, "choreographed" as in La Tancada Salt Fields or "somatic" as in Begles Eco-Quarter.'

Franch's affinity for creating projects that out perform their current existence is something that he challenges future generations to do by inviting them 'to (re-)search for affordable ways of project making that distill site/time-specifics and contribute to the construction of landscape infrastructures.'

Martí Franch,
EMF landscape architects
Girona, Spain

'The confluence of culture and nature: Martí Franch's projects take advantage of the opportunities that each place offers, with minimal interventions, creating dynamic landscapes that are full of value, beauty and identity.' Enric Batlle on Martí Franch

Martí Franch, EMF landscape architects

MónNatura Delta de l'Ebre Eco Museum, Amposta, Spain (2011)

This project saw the restoration of pools and buildings from an old fish farm converted into an eco museum devoted to the natural and cultural wonders of the delta landscape, featuring a 'salt garden'. Exploring the concept of a liquid landscape, the museum's activities and programme have been organized over an excavated archipelago.

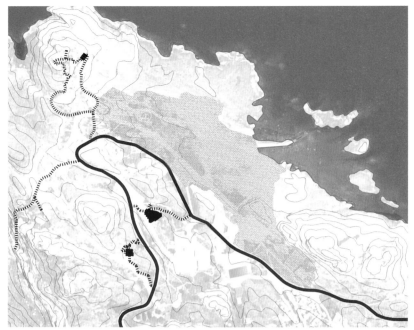

Martí Franch, EMF landscape architects

<u>Tudela-Culip (Club Med) restoration project</u>, Cadaqués, Spain (2010)

A former Club Med resort, this 90-hectare (222-acre) reclamation project saw the selected removal of buildings, the elimination of invasive plant species, restoration of its natural drainage and grading which allowed the project to be opened for public use. This also included the introduction of playful signage to identify rocks, further enhancing the visitor's experience.

Andrea Cochran,
Andrea Cochran Landscape Architecture
San Francisco, CA, USA

Andrea Cochran's work is defined by an emphasis on detail, a restricted palette of materials and a sympathetic response to site conditions. Her award-winning projects are imbued with narratives that enhance their sensorial appeal, bringing them to the attention of an international audience. Based in San Francisco, her studio has tackled a range of projects that include affordable housing, wineries, residential homes, institutions and public parks. Known for seamlessly interweaving sustainable landscapes, art and architecture, Cochran's designs highlight the experiential qualities of the built environment.

Reflecting on her recent projects, Cochran would select Stone Edge Farm, located in Sonoma, California, to spend the day in, stating 'this 1-hectare (3.5-acre) site has a number of elements that make it interesting over the course of the day'. Located on an alluvial plain, marked by California bay trees, oaks and buckeyes and bordered by a seasonal stream, the landscape has been designed 'to express the passage of time'. Cochran explains: 'The stone pyramid acts like a sundial, with the shadow of the ancient bay tree passing over its canted surface. The sun also makes the meadow glow in the warm light of early morning and late afternoon, creating a golden mass that vibrates in the breeze. The reflecting pools change from inky black voids at dawn and dusk that draw you in, to shiny mirrored surfaces that reflect the sky and landscape at midday. It is meditative and mesmerizing.'

A raised pool links the new structures – an observatory and viewing lounge – together, while rows of ancient olive trees reinforce relationships on a larger scale. The entire composition floats within meadows of drought-tolerant grasses, connecting the garden to the larger Sonoma Valley landscape.

Cochran's subtle, yet effective work is inspired by minimalist artists such as Robert Irwin and Donald Judd and works such as *The Lightning Fields* by Walter De Maria. 'I am interested in the intersections between art, architecture and landscape and how these elements can blend together seamlessly so it's not clear where one ends and the other begins,' Cochran explains. With the aim of enabling people to 'comprehend or connect to their environment on both an intimate level and on a larger scale', Cochran's designs provide visitors with a sensuous experience of nature and its evolutions over time.

Describing herself as an intuitive person, Cochran concedes that while some ideas appear 'in a flash', most often 'it's a slow grind', an iterative process where ideas are tested and made better. 'The devil is often in the details,' she explains; it is about refining the idea, rather than revisiting the concept, and she believes that, 'the success of our work is not creative brilliance but the relentless pursuit of working it until it's great'.

Her firm's competition-winning design for Buhl Community Park, sponsored by the Children's Museum of Pittsburgh, Pennsylvania, transformed an underused 1960s concrete plaza adjacent to the museum into a vibrant civic space. Incorporating significant community input based on a series of public meetings, the design for the new park provides flexible spaces that accommodate a wide variety of activities. A native planting palette and storm water bioswale – the process of using vegetation to filter run-off water – educates visitors about sustainability, while an eye-catching interactive mist sculpture by artist Ned Kahn attracts visitors inside. In line with her design ambitions, this project highlights Cochran's flawless integration of landscape architecture with art.

'I love collaborations,' Cochran enthuses, 'I work best when brainstorming with others, sitting around a table sketching and talking about ideas. It's free-flowing and exciting – much more fun than sitting alone in front of a blank piece of paper.' Talking gets her 'imagination flowing', but integral to the collaborative process is the client, whom Cochran credits with planting 'the seeds from which the design grows ... by layers around the initial concept, getting richer and richer as it develops'.

Landscape architects are uniquely placed to deal with what Cochran believes are today's most pressing global issues: water resources and population growth. In her work, Cochran makes use of porous landscapes that can 'detain storm water runoff, minimizing pollution to streams and rivers and recharging the aquifers' as well as incorporating drought-tolerant plants and efficient irrigation techniques. In terms of the degradation of the environment due to population growth, Cochran feels that landscape architects are 'well-equipped as generalists to lead teams of experts required to provide solutions to complex environmental issues'. A bold, new entry plaza and courtyard for the Smith Cardiovascular Research Building in San Francisco, illustrates Cochran's sustainable strategies. Here, the LEED (Leadership in Energy and Environmental Design) Gold-certified project evokes the site's historic salt marsh ecology, with the courtyard's design utilizing bands of grasses to filter and absorb storm water runoff and define recreation and meeting areas. The design for the campus gateway features a translucent screen of corrugated aluminium enclosing a bamboo hedge, an *allée* of palm trees and a limestone pillar welcoming visitors.

When asked about how she would like to influence future generations, Cochran responds: 'I would like to show by example that good design can be sustainable. A well-designed landscape can be beautiful while also heightening people's awareness of ecological issues, helping them to become better stewards of the environment.'

Favourite plants

1 Christmas rose
  (*Helleborus argutifolius*)
2 Spoon flower
  (*Dasylirion wheeleri*)
3 Boston ivy
  (*Parthenocissus tricuspidata*)
4 Mediterranean spurge
  (*Euphorbia characias* subsp.
  wulfenii)
5 Slender veldt grass
  (*Pennisetum spathiolatum*)

Favourite trees

1 Coast live oak (*Quercus agrifolia*)
2 California buckeye
  (*Aesculus californica*)
3 Japanese persimmon
  (*Diospyros kaki*)
4 Japanese maple (*Acer palmatum*)
5 Saucer magnolia
  (*Magnolia* x *soulangeana*)

Favourite materials

1 Cor-Ten steel
2 Gravel
3 Water
4 Basalt
5 Decomposed granite

Stone Edge Farm, Sonoma, CA, USA (2007)
This site is bordered by a seasonal stream and features several ancient California bay trees, oaks and buckeyes. A raised pool is the link between the new structures, while rows of ancient olive trees reinforce relationships at a larger scale. Built from the native alluvial stones unearthed during construction, a pyramidal sculpture defines the eastern perimeter. The design is set within drought-tolerant grasses.

This lively civic space incorporated significant community input, based on a series of public meetings, to create the design for this new park. Providing flexible spaces that accommodate a wide variety of activities, the park's design features a native planting palette and a storm water bioswale while the interactive mist sculpture by artist Ned Kahn entices participation.

This new entry plaza and a 0.7-hectare (1.75-acre) courtyard aim to foster inter-action among researchers and forge strong connections with the rest of campus. The courtyard's design features bands of grasses to filter and absorb storm water runoff and defines outdoor meeting areas. The campus gateway features a translucent screen of corrugated aluminium enclosing a bamboo hedge.

After receiving a degree in architecture from the University of Southern California and landscape architecture from Harvard Graduate School of Design, followed by a professional career working with Peter Walker, Martha Schwartz and George Hargreaves, James A Lord founded Surfacedesign in 2006. Established together with Roderick Wyllie and Geoff di Girolamo, the firm has a reputation for creating award-winning urban design and sustainable landscape architecture projects that aim to 'create poetic spaces and experiences' while 'balancing culture, ecology and design vision with fiscal realities'. Since its establishment the firm has won numerous awards, including the Architectural League of New York's Emerging Voices Award in 2014.

'I take inspiration from listening to the stories – geological, cultural, ecological and historical – of a place.' Although fundamentally Lord believes he is a 'problem-solver', resolving space and functionality issues on site, his projects also aim to combine the site's landscape 'poetry' with its 'cultural history narratives'. In doing this, Lord creates designs that relate to their context while orchestrating new experiences for users. In one such example of this, with the IBM Victoria Ward Tower Courtyard in Honolulu, Hawaii, Lord went beyond 'rooting the design in the historical and visual context of the existing building' to using the landscape as a medium to celebrate Hawaii's creation myth. 'After meeting with Native Hawaiian descendants,' he says, 'we worked to articulate physical expressions of this sacred oral history.' The creation story's mysticism, relating to people who descend from Earth Mother and Sky Father, is told through the use of patterned water reflecting light (Sky Father) through to the base of the water feature (Earth Mother), which has been planted with the native crop, taro (their earthly son – Taro).

In addition to expressing the Hawaiian creation story, the landscape design provides an elevated, 37-metre (120-foot) long linear water feature that 'creates a linkage to the ocean's horizon line and reflects the play and ephemerality of light throughout the day'. The project's minimal, although dynamic, palette of materials includes the use of a volcanic stone, evoking Hawaii's geology, with three different surface treatments, each responding to Hawaii's charismatic light: a reflective honed surface; a flamed textured surface that shimmers when viewed from above; and a split-faced finish that exposes the courtyard's rugged depth'.

As one might imagine, Lord begins each project with a site visit whereby 'listening to a site and imagining all of its potential' is part of his design process. Working with the community enables Lord to understand how he might be able to 'capture a story – a moment' and make it relate both physically and spatially to the landscape. 'Ultimately, I dream – I dream of what a place can be, and how to design a landscape that is a poetic gesture that evokes curiosity in people who engage with that place.' This process evolves through sketches, iterations and modelling (both physical and digital) and team collaborations to 'distil the essence of my original ideas and dreams to create meaningful places that are fun and engaging for all users'. Beyond internal team collaborations, his projects take on board a wide range of specialists from on-site grading teams to native communities and artisan stone layers. In his words, 'Who don't we collaborate with? Maybe dentists.' Lord appreciates that each collaborator brings a unique perspective and level of ability to each design, helping to create projects that 'have resonance on many levels'. This can be seen in Surfacedesign's collaboration with Claudia Harari on Horno 3 – Museum of Steel in Monterrey, NL, Mexico (see page 280).

In his latest project, Golden Gate Bridge 75th Anniversary Plaza/Fort Point Overlook, in San Francisco, Lord created a new public space and visitor centre that honour the bridge while explaining its creation. Formerly part of the bridge's tollbooth infrastructure, the site has been brought to life through the creation of an arrival space, destination point and a viewing platform from which to take in sights of, and from, this iconic place. Here, visitors can experience San Francisco's weather phenomena as the light, fog, and cables collide to provide panoramic views.

Places such as the Golden Gate Bridge's tollbooth infrastructure that, once a necessity of urban growth, now finds itself obsolete, are just one of the areas Lord believes landscape architects play a future role in developing. 'It is the job of landscape architects to embed these remnant spaces with new uses and new meaning', he enthuses. When space is at a premium, landscape 'becomes a calming and stimulating antidote to the cacophony of distractions that result from the new digital paradigm of urban living'. With global warming influencing the 'resource availability', landscape architects need to 'create beautiful and productive systems that serve multiple functions'.

When asked about today's most pressing global issues, Lord feels that 'homogenization of the built environment' is one of them. As cities are developing and needs are changing, safety requirements are becoming 'overly conservative', Lord believes, creating overly complicated engineering solutions that take away from smart design solutions. Lord's projects challenge him to employ 'holistic thinking', using multiple design threads to weave use, meaning and ecological systems together in an attempt to resolve design issues, and in the process tell the story of the place, while creating a landscape which creates 'new and whimsical interpretations of these stories, and integrates ecological functions seamlessly to create a new paradigm for development'.

James A Lord, Surfacedesign San Francisco, CA, USA

'I admire the work of James and his firm Surfacedesign for its strong architectural structure contrasted with a sophisticated planting palette. The work is bold and sculptural; it is rooted in the craft of building yet displays an artistic sensibility with a passion for exploring materiality.'

Andrea Cochran on James A Lord

James A Lord, Surfacedesign

Golden Gate Bridge 75th Anniversary Plaza/Fort Point Overlook, San Francisco, CA, USA (2014)

Nestled on the San Francisco side of the Golden Gate Bridge, this plaza honours the bridge and bears its name. This site has been transformed into a place of arrival, a destination for meeting and a frame for a new spectrum of views. Here, the dramatic collision of fog, light and bridge filter through the bridge cables, creating a dramatic setting for visitors to experience this phenomenon.

James A Lord, Surfacedesign

IBM Victoria Ward Tower Courtyard, Honolulu, HI, USA (2014)

This courtyard showcases a landscape expression of modern Hawaiian architectural motifs and powerful cultural history. The elevated water feature is a visual and experiential connection to the site's context and an expression of the surrounding sea and island sky. The minimalist palette of plants and stone expresses a distillation of the materiality and plantings of the Hawaiian landscape.

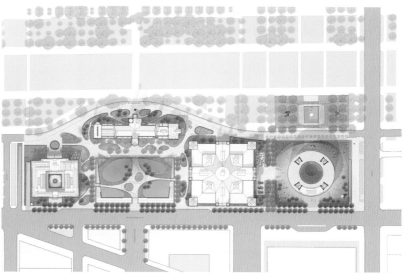

Smithsonian Masterplan, Washington DC, USA (2033)

As part of the masterplan team, Surfacedesign has reimagined the landscape of the South Mall as a cohesive campus that integrates the gardens with the visionary architectural design of Bjarke Ingels Group (BIG). New garden spaces reflect their architectural adjacencies and extend indoor programmes into the landscape. Rich horticultural plantings frame new views and create multiple-scaled spaces for individuals, groups and large events.

Sacha Coles,
ASPECT Studios
Sydney, NSW, Australia

Sacha Coles is director of ASPECT Studios and the founder of the Sydney studio. ASPECT Studios, an Australian-owned landscape architecture company with six studios across Australia and China, specializes in the design of places where people want to be. Coles' focus is to ensure that the studios are recognized as rigorous design offices, consistently producing high-quality work across both public and private sectors. Designing landscapes both nationally and internationally, his works have been enthusiastically received and have won numerous design awards. Widely published, Coles is passionate about promoting and advancing the field of landscape architecture, giving talks worldwide, lecturing at several Australian universities and critiquing graduate design studios.

'I am a huge advocate of social equity and environmental sustainability,' Coles explains, 'which sit side by side with a desire to create more beauty and joy in the everyday life of the city. This is my interest and design motivation.' Coles' selection of individuals who have influenced his work highlights his own design interests and strengths, and he credits environmentalist David Suzuki as keeping 'a sustainable core to [his] practice', as well as Clover More, 'an incorruptible politician who has delivered design excellence' and 'city observer and flâneur', Michael Sorkin.

His diverse projects range from landscape installations to large-scale developments, such as the revitalization of the 15,000-square metre (161,458-square foot) Darling Quarter, Sydney, which Coles describes as 'the best people-watching project; it is a project with a human-centred core'. Its design saw the rejuvenation of Darling Harbour through the upgrading of all public elements, including a new, eccentric play space forming a central part of the urban environment. Not being fenced off, the play space is clearly open for all and tempts people from all ages and backgrounds to participate. 'The design incentivizes socialization as people have to work together to get the most out of the water play,' Coles points out. He believes the project successfully combines various layers to provide 'complexity of experiences within a designed environment – retail, play, workspace, sport, strolling'. Indeed, the site's interactive water play facilities have become a regional attraction for Sydney.

According to Coles, his design process 'always starts with a reading of the site'. He states that, 'Where there is a rich site history or discernible landscape morphology, it is about amplifying those qualities.' His design concepts are developed through diagrams and sketches. 'I talk with people through drawings,' he explains. And in this way Coles sets the framework for the design; it is from these initial sketches and conversations that the design is developed by his team members. In his words: 'I find it rewarding to put a design out to others to add to, contribute and develop. If the initial concept is strong, it more often than not benefits from layering.' As one might imagine, collaboration is crucial to his design process, whether it's with internal team members, Kate Luckraft, his studio partner, his studio's senior designers or external architects and artists.

Part architectural sculpture, part social experiment, The Meeting Place was a temporary installation that transformed a Sydney laneway in 2010. The installation encouraged participation, play and interaction, while heightening the experience of moving through the urban surrounds. Tensioned fabric created an architectural space not unlike a sculpture, a place that narrows to a point of compression and that echoes and amplifies the virtues of the popular peak-time thoroughfare. Enhancing a neglected space, the fabric's opacity allowed glimpsed shadows and blurred silhouettes to create a sense of intrigue and a desire to engage – a spirit Coles imparts to most projects.

Working in highly populated areas, Coles is all too aware of the impact population growth and subsequent rapid urbanization have on cities, citing it as one of today's most pressing global issues. He responds by 'advocating for equity of access to public space and wherever possible, striving for a higher percentage of green space in our cities', and he believes that landscape architects are well placed for guiding cities to becoming more sustainable. In order to make this possible, and make better future cities, Coles would like to see 'landscape architects take up leadership in city-making projects – from policy to place ... a landscape-led urbanism is fundamental to a thriving city'.

Determined to create socially stimulating, ecologically rich and aesthetically pleasing designs, ASPECT Studios' latest project, The Goods Line in Sydney, is conceived of as being a new kind of civic space and 'public campus'. The project blurs the boundaries of land ownership along its length while also facilitating strong community connections beyond its site boundary. Not only will this redesigned, elevated civic space transform an industrial relic into an innovative example of urban green space, it will also have a transformative social and environmental role in the precinct through the creation of gardens, playscapes, communal tables, study pods, exercise areas and platforms for performance and display.

When asked how he'd like to influence future generations of landscape architects, Coles' response underscores the ideals behind his projects to date: 'I would like to know that I have influenced emerging landscape architects by making a more joyous and playful, resilient and thoughtful city through design [and] to encourage others to collaborate widely and lead through participatory design processes.'

Favourite plants

1 Timor black bamboo (*Bambusa lako*)
2 Fiddle-leaf fig (*Ficus lyrata*)
3 Flannel flower (*Actinotus helianthi*)
4 Fragrant olive (*Osmanthus fragrans*)
5 Blue chalksticks (*Senecio serpens*)

Favourite trees

1 Smooth-barked apple (*Angophora costata*)
2 Frangipani (*Plumeria*)
3 Baobab (*Adansonia*)
4 Chinese banyan (*Ficus microcarpa*)
5 A fully laden mango (*Mangifera*)

Favourite materials

1 Timber
2 Concrete
3 Glazed bricks
4 Perforated steel
5 Stone

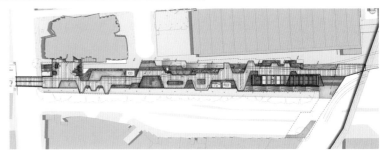

Revitalizing Darling Harbour's included upgrading all public domain elements, such as ground plane materials, sustainable lighting, planting and bespoke public furniture. While a range of new place-making facilities has been introduced, including an enlarged park with an innovative playground, moveable public seating, custom-made table-tennis tables and rugs. The park's urban playground includes a highly popular interactive water-play facility.

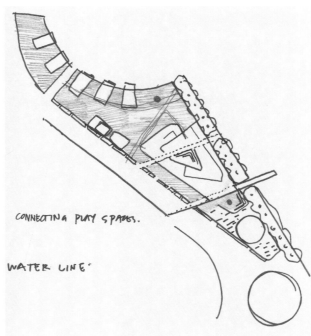

This urban park delivers unique, waterside community facilities, bespoke furniture and innovative sustainable components, including solar energy and storm water initiatives. The park is organized around a shared-use pedestrian and bicycle path, anchoring it to a series of park rooms and new path networks. The waterfront promenade is the backbone to the park and forms an important link in a network of harbour-side open spaces.

The Meeting Place, Little Hunter Street, Sydney, NSW, Australia (2010)

Transforming a Sydney laneway, The Meeting Place was a temporary installation that, part architectural sculpture, part social experiment, encouraged participation, play and interaction. Tensioned fabric created an architectural space between two 4-metre (13-feet) walls, requiring pedestrians to negotiate with those moving in the opposite direction, as well as with the taut and yielding fabric of the space.

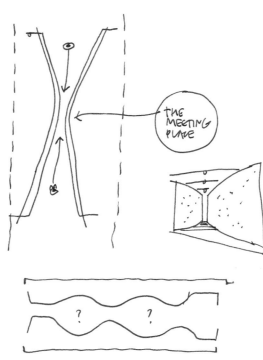

Favourite plants

1 Poor knights lily
(*Xeronema callistemon*)
2 Oioi (*Apodasmia similis*)
3 Horokaka (*Disphyma australe*)
4 New Zealand flax
(*Phormium tenax*)

Favourite trees

1 Pohutukawa
(*Metrosideros excelsa*)
2 Kowhai (*Sophora*)
3 Cabbage palm
(*Cordyline australis*)
4 Cherry (*Prunus*)
5 Nikau palm (*Rhopalostylis sapida*)

Favourite materials

1 Natural stone (like local basalt)
2 Timber
3 Concrete (without added colour
or decorative aggregates)
4 Cor-Ten steel
5 Brass

Favourite natural landscape

Auckland's volcanic field

The founder of the firm LandLAB, Henry Crothers has been involved in some of the most significant urban renewal and public realm transformation projects in New Zealand, including the Auckland City streetscapes and 'shared space' programme, the masterplanning and delivery of projects for Waterfront Auckland and recent projects that form a part of the rebuilding of Christchurch following the earthquake in 2011. It is significant then that the New Zealand-based designer has strong views on the industry's current status: 'I'd like to see landscape architects and urban designers [become] more visible and influential in the design community. In architecture you can do a pretty bathroom and get widely published. In contrast, we deliver projects which can influence the way a whole city is perceived and operates, yet no one wants to know.'

Previously working for Architectus Auckland as a landscape architect, urban designer and associate director, his work has been acknowledged for its strategic and conceptual clarity and sensitivity to time, place and process. His built projects demonstrate the integration of green infrastructure, low impact design, sustainability and innovation as well as creative collaborations with other design disciplines. His firm's philosophy (and practice name) integrates a site-specific approach – Land – with a creative and rigorous design process – LAB.

After initially wanting to be an architect as he admired 'their rigour and confidence', and briefly working in town planning, Crothers became involved in landscape architecture, finding that 'its diversity and potential made sense'. He enjoys the range of scales landscape architecture allows for, from furniture to urban territories, and finds inspiration in the 'idea of "landscape" or "ecological" urbanism, which combines the temporal aspects of ecologies and systems with the intellectual and strategic capacity of design'. With a good number of public realm projects under his belt and experience of different professions, it is no surprise that he gains further inspiration from 'cities, great places and many other design disciplines'.

As the lead designer at Architectus, Crothers designed Karanga Plaza in Auckland, a project that re-establishes a previously severed waterfront connection via a new pedestrian bascule bridge. As his choice of one of his own works in which he would happily spend a day, the plaza provides a 'hardstand' – a functional and flexible space – and an urban beach, referencing the waterfront's former industrial activities. The plaza incorporates modular furniture in the form of timber platforms on railway tracks. If Crothers were to spend a day here he'd recommend a swim from the plaza's 'sculptural' tidal stairs, followed by a 'dry-off' on the timber loungers, with food and drink from the café while enjoying the waterfront view. The plaza's gardens incorporate native coastal plants with relocated trees and enable a low-impact design strategy. A pavilion, housing an information kiosk made from recycled shipping containers, animates the plaza and greets visitors.

Crothers believes that 'fundamentally projects are about improving a situation … immediately and in the long term'. As demonstrated in Karanga Plaza, water is a vital commodity and accordingly Crothers' designs function with the principles of low-impact design. Crothers chooses a holistic approach to delivering sustainable design solutions, not just the 'end or built project'. Considering natural and urban systems as integrated and interrelated, Crothers believes the ability to create successful spaces requires 'creative leadership, strategic communication, tactical intervention and determination'.

His own determination can be seen in his creative process, which involves a 'pencil, black pens (only black), paper, cardboard models and then a computer,' and over the years, 'a few sketch books'. For Crothers, 'a project's logic, and visual collateral, is typically choreographed by organizing drawings and images on a wall'. In his creative process the designs that freely emerge are then refined through 'research, observation and analysis'. His work on Daldy Street Linear Park, Auckland, also commencing while he was lead designer at Architectus, demonstrates a finely tuned urban landscape that establishes a new connection between former and existing water edges. From his choreographed sketches, Crothers' rhythmic direction led to an enhanced spatial sequencing that enables storm water, walking, cycling and public transport infrastructure to interact seamlessly. Referencing the site's marine and industrial activity, the design uses materials and language to express its past, while found objects and recycled materials (such as a series of tank elements) combine to create opportunities for play and environmental features used on site.

When asked if good design can save the world, Crothers doesn't believe alone it will, but that brilliant ideas 'come from a process of immersion, collaboration and interrogation through which potentials emerge and are developed'. He believes that a focus on design thinking, in which both design and process are given prominence, provides great potential. Unlike the more common problem-solving approaches, design thinking 'utilizes intuition, imagination and systemic reasoning in order to resolve design challenges'. This approach, Crothers believes, 'requires flexibility and openness to potentials, not problems'. As a visual person himself, Crothers explains that the ability landscape architects have 'to think in terms of open systems and time are uniquely suited to this way of working,' and that they have 'a cross-disciplinary sensibility suited to navigating and negotiating through complex projects'. Perhaps as the importance of these unique abilities becomes more widely understood, landscape architects will begin to see the recognition they deserve.

Henry Crothers, LandLAB
Auckland, New Zealand

'Henry is a critical and conceptual thinker with the ability to communicate with a wide group of audiences. He has an open willingness to engage and learn through collaborations, all of which are core traits of a great designer.' Sacha Coles on Henry Crothers

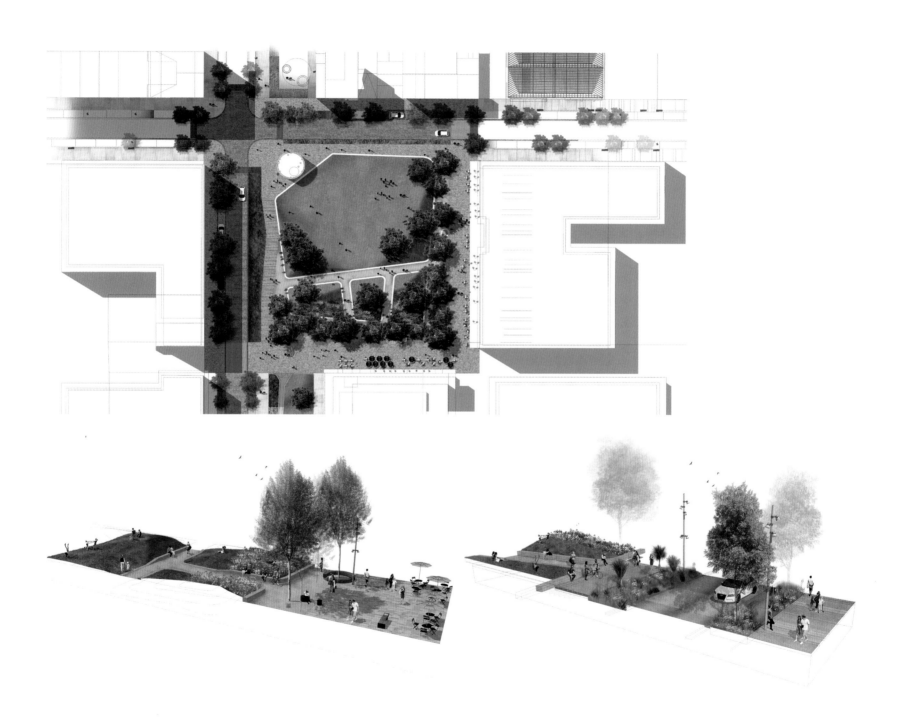

Henry Crothers, LandLAB

Wynyard Commons, Auckland, New Zealand (2016)

This project is envisaged as a focal point for the development of a new community in Auckland's Wynyard Quarter. The design unifies the street and park via a connecting ground plane (basalt), defining a shared-use space for both pedestrians and vehicles on the park's edges. Sculptural lawn edges designate recreational and garden areas while a rare native garden zone provides biological and ecological diversity.

Henry Crothers, LandLAB

Daldy Street Linear Park, Wynyard Quarter, Auckland, New Zealand (2013)

This park establishes a new strategic city connection, between previous and existing water edges, with materiality and design language informed by the former marine and industrial activity. Curving seating forms, in concrete and steel, reference the tanks that previously occupied the site. Found objects and recycled materials have been retained and appropriated into park features; phase two will be completed in 2017.

Karanga Plaza, Wynyard Quarter, Auckland, New Zealand (2011)

The plaza re-establishes a previously severed waterfront connection via a new pedestrian bascule bridge. The space incorporates a movable landscape and low-impact design strategies, in the form of a family of timber platforms on rail tracks and rain gardens featuring native coastal plants and relocated trees. A pavilion structure, formed of recycled shipping containers, provides an information kiosk for visitors and a dramatic focus for the site.

Claude Cormier,
Claude Cormier et Associés
Montreal, Québec, Canada

Since establishing his eponymous landscape architecture firm in 1995, in Montreal, Québec, Claude Cormier's internationally celebrated works have been noted for their highly graphic, colourful and innovative style. Questioning the mundane aspects of the everyday, he creates spaces that render visible the invisible, awakening a sense of fun, curiosity and pleasure for visitors. Cormier himself explains that his designs draw on strong concepts which 'demand authenticity', while often applying the mantra 'artificial, but not fake'. In 2009, Cormier received the highest distinction given in Québec, Knight of the Ordre national du Québec, an honour bestowed on individuals who have contributed significantly to the development and leadership of Québec.

Creating seemingly familiar spaces that have been modernized and adapted to provoke a childhood-like sense of discovery, Cormier attributes his projects' success to having an 'apparent simplicity that is complex, but not complicated', and Toronto, Canada's Sugar Beach exemplifies this approach. Sugar Beach is the second urban beach proposed for Toronto's downtown waterfront, and the latest addition to the amber necklace of Toronto's lakefront beachscape. Wafting in on waves of 'sugar spray' carried on westerly breezes from the neighbouring Redpath Sugar Factory, the beach is formed of a series of 'hard rock candies' with coloured stripes and dozens of pink umbrellas scattered across a sandy wedge of beach along the Jarvis Slip in Toronto. In fact, if Roald Dahl had included a beach in his 1964 novel *Charlie and the Chocolate Factory* it would arguably have been Cormier's Sugar Beach. Edibly delicious from above, at ground level the project hints at the city's 'industrial mood' while playfully accommodating beaches, trees, seating areas, plazas and water play at the doorstep of Toronto's urban horizon.

Describing the 'visual arts field' as instrumental to the studio's creative process, Cormier believes that 'a particular art piece holds within itself an attitude as well as a material quality that triggers an experience – and that's just what a successful landscape should achieve. There is a natural transposition that occurs between a piece's narrative and the evocative quality of a landscape.' For Sugar Beach it was Georges Seurat's painting *A Sunday Afternoon on the Island of La Grande Jatte*, which informed the 'attitude of the first urban beach on the Toronto waterfront', Cormier explains. This was before any design work had been done. Later, the representation of a 'leisurely afternoon against an industrial backdrop' in Seurat's *Bathers at Asnières* helped to define 'the spirit' of Sugar Beach 'and inscribed it as an embryo on the city's emerging waterfront culture'. Acknowledging that having a 'core concept' helps give aesthetic direction to his projects, Cormier explains that 'where conceptualism tends to be self-referential, the goal is to unfold the concept through a narrative that will encompass every aspect of the love triangle formed by the landscape, its users and the context in which it sits'. A seductive narrative helps to create 'genuine design responses'. Loathing conformity, Cormier strives for bold designs that he believes, 'makes for honest diplomacy'.

True to his design philosophy, Cormier's projects retaliate against something he feels is one of today's most pressing design issues: 'standardization' – the feeling that in a highly accessible and diverse world 'the palette in which our society is painted seems to get flatter and duller'. As Cormier sees it, 'being clear, expressive, peculiar and subversive has never been so important. Codes are what we are working with, but ultimately, diversity is what we are working for.'

With Four Seasons Hotel and Residences in Toronto, Cormier resolves the eclectic mixture of nineteenth-century Victorian architecture and twenty-first century skyscrapers, and the addition of a world-class hotel, with an ornate urban landscape. By incorporating accentuated common landscape features, Cormier explains that 'the style of the former era is amplified to the habits and perceptions of the present'. The public space includes familiar urban elements, only amplified to exaggerate their features: a four-storey, cast-aluminium fountain, an 'urban carpet' which features a paved knot density of 100 cobbles per square metre (1,076 per square foot) and a 'rose-less' rose garden – the paths and planting beds of which reference the flowing petal pattern of an open rose. Far from dull, this design offers visitors a dynamic landscape experience both when viewed from above and at ground level.

Cormier believes landscape architecture is a 'hard discipline to crack – it flirts with art and nods at engineering, it is essentially social yet inherently naturalistic'. In future he'd like to see 'strong and competent leaders with loud voices'. Describing landscape architecture as 'a craft ... made by humans for humans', Cormier would like to show future generations that 'vulnerability' and 'grandeur' are complementary to their work, explaining that the balance of these two attributes entails being 'close to your sensible, generous side' while at the same time 'making things happen the way you envisioned them'. It is through this, together with hard work and patience, that one gains the knowledge necessary to be able to make something that 'fosters hope and pleasure, something that awakens and challenges the people it touches'.

Favourite plants

1 Peonies (*Paeonia*)
2 Lilacs (*Syringa*)
3 Climbing roses (*Rosa*)
4 Wisteria

Favourite trees

'Generally, I like noble, majestic trees that have distinctive personalities and qualities.'
1 Eastern redbud (*Cercis canadensis*)
2 Tulip (*Liriodendron tulipifera*)
3 Black locust (*Robinia pseudoacacia*)
4 Magnolia
5 White oak (*Quercus alba*)
6 Eastern white pine (*Pinus strobus*)

Favourite materials

1 Limestone
2 White marble
3 White oak planks
4 Polished stainless steel
5 Artificial things

The contradiction between this neighbourhood's traditional Victorian dwellings and the new metropolitan-scale skyscraper and world-class hotel is reconciled in this urban landscape. Here, the taste and style of the former era is amplified through the habits and perceptions of the present: a grand, cast-aluminium fountain, an urban carpet with a knot density of 100 cobbles per square metre (1,076 per square foot), and a 'rose-less' rose garden.

Pink Balls, Montreal, Québec, Canada (2011–14)
170,000 pink plastic balls, in three different sizes and five subtle shades of pink, are strung together with bracing wire, crisscrossing the street and stretching through tree branches at varying heights. The result is a range of spirited motifs, some dense, others open and airy, transforming a Montreal street into a pedestrian mall during summer months.

Positioned along this urban beach are a series of 'hard rock candies' with colourful stripes, mounded greenery, glistening sand and dozens of pink umbrellas. Integrating the future Waterfront Promenade, along with a plaza for events, the design playfully adopts some of the most enduring elements from Toronto's emerging landscape identity – beaches, bedrock, trees and water – as well as the urban horizon and a trace of the city's industrial past.

Marc Ryan is principal and co-founder of PUBLIC WORK office for urban design and landscape architecture, a design studio engaged in building the contemporary city. In partnership with Adam Nicklin, the practice of PUBLIC WORK looks to make innovative additions to a city's public realm by readdressing the connection between landscape architecture, architecture, civic infrastructure, the site context and the visitor experience. Prior to co-founding PUBLIC WORK, Ryan was project leader at West 8 Rotterdam and studio director of West 8 Toronto, and his background in both landscape architecture and urbanism informs his unique ability to translate a city's infrastructure needs into an exciting public realm.

When asked what the 'tipping point' was that led him to establish his firm, Ryan responds that he had always wanted to have his own practice, but knew that the complexity demanded from the urban projects he wanted to work on would require a partner with the same ambitions to 'transform the quality and experience of public life in the city'. After working together on the Toronto Central Waterfront (while with West 8 and DTAH), and seeing creative offices, such as Claude Cormier's, 'delivering courageous and refreshing projects', Nicklin and Ryan decided to establish their own studio in Toronto, Ryan's hometown. Since founding PUBLIC WORK, the duo has focused their design on 'anticipating and cultivating new urban dynamics – human movement, social interaction, interplay of materials and light, weather, etc.', and enjoy seeing how their 'projects activate and are activated by the "live" city'.

Waterloo Park, in Waterloo, Ontario, Canada, exemplifies the dynamic qualities PUBLIC WORK instils in urban settings. The park builds upon the site's existing assets and spatial qualities to create a functional public space that incorporates a series of Green Rooms. These rooms form a collection of dynamic landscape settings containing a series of new park programmes created for the community. The park's design plays with the attributes of light and dark, sun and shadow, smooth and rough, giving the project a strong identity while providing a place for relaxation, play and gatherings. As with Waterloo Park, the development of clear spatial ideas is a recurrent feature throughout their work, enhancing the overall organization of a project. Inspired by 'the site and the city', Ryan explains that their work is 'extremely context-driven', and their projects 'try to enhance the often hidden qualities of a site to produce a transformed experience of even the most familiar spaces'.

Their designs are also inspired by art, specifically Surrealism, as seen with their movable timber platform in Jubilee Plaza, located in Regional Municipality of Wood Buffalo, Canada, which seemingly drapes across the plaza, blanketing it with its sinuous form. Jubilee Plaza is a catalyst project for the Municipality's ambitious City Centre Revitalization Initiative; the 'main challenge here was to create a thriving venue for public life in a previously transient community,' Ryan explains. In this case, the timber platform can be moved to allow the plaza to be adapted for multiple uses; the podium itself is a space to inhabit and a platform for events. Its organic form is offset by a rectilinear 'weather catcher' that takes the form of a sculptural tower from which water drips, and in cold months freezes, providing a glimmering 'natural' chandelier.

PUBLIC WORK's projects attempt to establish a connection between past and future 'using the site's design to activate a new future from an existing context'. Ryan outlines the studio's creative process as beginning with a series of questions in regards to the site's role, how it fits into the larger context and its contribution to the community. 'We look for overlapping capacities and ambitions,' Ryan explains, 'between the brief, the site's characteristics and the adjacent city context that can form the starting points for a common narrative.' The process then evolves through collaborations and interactions with consultants, the public, the client and so on. 'We love to collaborate with architects who are civic minded, with engineers who challenge conventions and with artists who help us see the world differently,' he states. But their most rewarding collaborations come from experts who 'are so confident in their specialized fields' that they're willing to use their skills to go outside their comfort zone to 'produce new effects'.

One of today's most pressing design issues, Ryan believes, is 'the role of landscape and the public realm in shaping the quality of the contemporary city'. PUBLIC WORK's new Creek Park, located in Toronto, to be completed in 2017, occupies a unique position within Toronto's history and within its downtown core, and is set to be an exemplary, high-quality park. Straddling the threshold of the city's past and future, the park is simultaneously part of the Fort York National Historic Site and a densifying downtown neighbourhood. To serve both of these important roles, Creek Park is designed as a public space for both the Fort and the city. Aptly applying their design ambitions, this park activates the collective memory of the past and the evolving, expanding needs of the community. The design strategically uses the site's sloping terrain to reshape a promontory landform – a feature of Toronto's original shoreline – for multipurpose activities. In their design, the site's terrain is manipulated to create three distinct landscapes, each supporting different visitor experiences, programming and vegetative communities. 'As designers,' Ryan states, 'we see the future not as a distant possibility, but as a subject of design that we can begin to establish today, which is really exciting.'

Marc Ryan,
PUBLIC WORK
Toronto, Ontario, Canada

'PUBLIC WORK have so much talent and so much resilience in their attitude ... and yet they always behave like gentlemen.' Claude Cormier on Marc Ryan

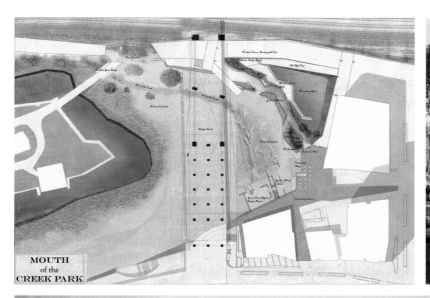

Creek Park, Toronto, Ontario, Canada (2017)

This park is part of both the Fort York National Historic Site and a densifying downtown neighbourhood. Created as a public space for both, the design strategically uses the site's sloping terrain to reshape a promontory landform for various activities. Manipulation of the site's terrain creates three distinct landscapes, each supporting visitor experiences, activities and plant communities.

Marc Ryan, PUBLIC WORK

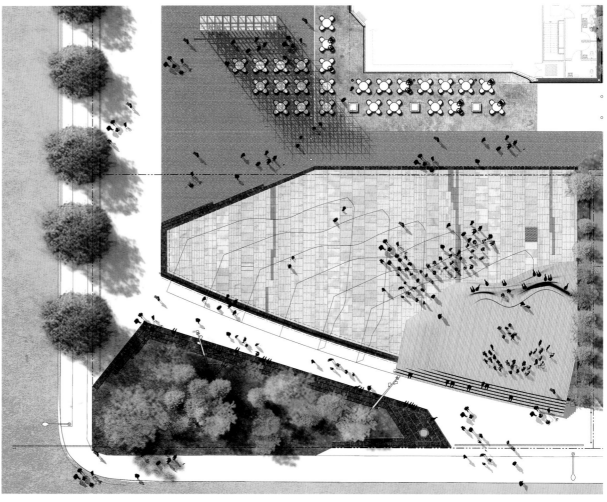

Marc Ryan, PUBLIC WORK

Jubilee Plaza, Regional Municipality of Wood Buffalo, Canada (2015)

This flexible public plaza both engages with the community and relates to its context. Here, a moveable timber platform allows the plaza to be adapted for multiple uses. The podium itself is both an inhabitable space and a platform for events, while a tall, linear 'weather catcher' takes the form of a sculptural tower from which icicles hang in winter to create a natural chandelier.

Waterloo Park, Waterloo, Ontario, Canada (2014)

This project saw the revision of part of the 122-year-old Waterloo Park's masterplan to include a highly programmed Festival Area. The design builds upon the existing spatial qualities to provide a functional public space serving the needs of the community. The frontage features a series of Green Rooms – a collection of distinct landscape settings containing a host of new park programmes and functions.

James Corner,
James Corner Field Operations
New York, NY, USA

A leading landscape architect of international renown, James Corner has created widely celebrated designs in some of today's most populated cities: New York City, London, Seattle, Chicago and Qianhai – a new city for two million people in Shenzhen, China. However, according to Corner, it is cities that provide the most pressing issue that landscape architects face today. He highlights that in order for cities to be attractive during a time when they are faced with increased population growth and diminished resources, they 'not only need buildings, streets and institutions but also robust open space structures that provide a rich variety of public spaces for recreation, health, fitness, pleasure, civic identity and social novelty'. Consequently, these spaces will provide essential 'ecological and sustainability functions'. Corner believes that landscape architects 'will need to be more adept at understanding the full panoply of attributes that undergird urbanism more broadly and that inform often complex and multifunctional forms of urban space, urban ecology and public life. This requires both sides of the brain at once: a highly analytical, organizational and broad-scope reach on the one side, and a freshly creative, imaginative and magical approach on the other.'

Based in New York City, Corner's work is acclaimed for its strong contemporary design across a variety of project types and scales. His work illustrates commitment to the design of a vibrant and dynamic public realm, informed by the ecology of both people and nature. Corner is also Professor of Landscape Architecture and Urbanism at the University of Pennsylvania School of Design and an author of several books. One of his studio's most celebrated designs is the High Line in New York City. Corner himself chooses it as one of his most recent works in which to spend the day, explaining, 'It is so varied every time I visit – different people doing different things, different plants in bloom or in transition, changing views, light and adjacencies. It continues to delight as a great urban promenade, bisecting Manhattan.' A collaboration between Corner's studio (as project lead), architects Diller Scofidio + Renfro and the garden designer Piet Oudolf, located in Manhattan's West Side, this project saw the conversion of an elevated railway twenty-three blocks long into a dynamic public space. An orchestrated choreography of movement, with lush plantings, dynamic lighting and multiple seating types, the High Line is an enormously successful project that sets the precedence for revitalizing public spaces in the city.

Corner's inspiration is initially taken from 'an interesting collusion of subjects: geography and the land; biology and evolutionary processes; art and the visual imagination; and urbanism and the life of cities. Taken together, these continue to provide orientation and inspiration for a practice that is ultimately synthetic, time-based and lived through everyday experience.' From here, Corner follows a fairly pragmatic creative process, starting with analysing the site, the programme (brief) and any other site-specific issues. 'Once understood,' he explains, 'a variety of more creative and experimental issues ensue', such as organizational diagrams, spatial and programming studies, mood and qualitative images, models (physical and digital), narrative structures 'and any other mechanisms to spawn alternative trial-and-error speculations'. Finally, this process of distillation arrives at 'the best result with the most interesting set of possibilities ... [eventually] the design acquires its own life and momentum, offering a large range of imaginative and suggestive potentials, both pragmatic and aesthetic.' The creative aspect then evolves through imaging and modelling studies, in Corner's words, 'pushing it to new horizons and (hopefully) resulting in an elegant and novel synthesis'.

With Field Operations' recent project, Tongva Park, in Santa Monica, California, Corner's team transformed a former parking lot into a rolling landscape of lush topography, meadows and gardens and destination point. Inspired by the Southern California arroyo landscape, where topographic washes and ravines once formed a part of the site, the community's involvement in the park's design helped create a valuable community park. Since being built, the project has received numerous national design awards.

When asked how he'd like to influence future generations of landscape architects, Corner responds 'I would like to think I have contributed to raising the bar for landscape architects, raising the profile and visibility of the field ... challenging us all to work harder, think deeper, push boundaries and produce exceptional works.' Corner believes 'a more inclusive mindset' is key, 'avoiding the easy ... specialization of ecology, art, city and countryside ... and seeing all ingredients more synthetically, as all integrated and part of our larger milieu'.

In defining what would make better cities of the future, Corner responds: 'Both scope and scalability are critical. Scope means looking beyond the typical concerns of the landscape architect (topography, planting, circulation, etc.) to include urbanistic considerations of streets, blocks, buildings, infrastructures, mobility, sustainability and programming. Scalability means broaching all scales at the same time – working with large-scale organization systems and formats alongside mid- and small-scale interventions. The best cities in the world comprise incredibly complex interwoven systems that are broad and diverse in both scope and scale. We need tools, techniques and imaginations capable of working in this way.'

Favourite plants

1 Winterberry (*Ilex verticillata*)
2 Switchgrass (*Panicum virgatum*)
3 Coneflower (*Echinacea*)

Favourite trees

1 Beech (*Fagus*)
2 Oak (*Quercus*)
3 Dogwood (*Cornus*)
4 Magnolia
5 Eastern redbud
 (*Cercis canadensis*)

Favourite contemporary artists

1 Olafur Eliasson
2 Anish Kapoor
3 Jaume Plensa
4 Antony Gormley
5 Rachel Whiteread

Favourite natural landscape

Scottish Highlands

Favourite sound

Birdsong

Knight Plaza connects the Pérez Art Museum Miami by Herzog & de Meuron and the Frost Museum of Science by Grimshaw Architects. The plaza features bespoke planters, featuring subtropical plants, with sinuous edges that undulate outwards to form seating edges. Situated on the Biscayne Bay, this plaza creates a tropical paradise between the two museums.

Already an icon of design innovation, this elevated public space spans twenty-three city blocks. This design coordinates multiple perspectives, offering bifurcating pathways and dynamic paving and lighting, while seating and luscious planting provide social spaces and platforms to enjoy unique city views.

A former parking lot, this design transforms what was once asphalt and parked cars to a verdant landscape of lush topography, meadows and gardens. This site is now a highly celebrated community park. Inspired by the arroyo landscape, this design was shaped by a comprehensive community process and includes sculptural viewing platforms which offer views of the Pacific Ocean.

As shown in the early concept rendering below, this park is situated among the ArcelorMittal Orbit by Anish Kapoor, the park's stadium and Zaha Hadid's Aquatics Centre. A promenade area provides an *allée* of trees, forming the park's central spine, while the 'play room' includes planting and interactive play features, such as a timber climbing forest, rolling hills and slides.

Favourite plants

1 Russian sage
   (*Perovskia atriplicifolia*)
2 Bayberry (*Myrica*)
3 Red switch grass (*Panicum*)
4 Pyracantha
5 White hydrangea

Favourite trees

1 London plane
   (*Platanus x hispanica*)
2 Birch (*Betula*)
3 Stone pine (*Pinus pinea*)
4 Maidenhair (*Ginkgo biloba*)
5 Magnolia

Favourite materials

1 Cor-Ten steel
2 Black locust wood
3 Poured rubber
4 Stainless steel
5 Precast concrete

Favourite natural landscape

'Iceland – the most fantastic,
alien, varied landscape ever.'

Christopher Marcinkoski is an Assistant Professor of Landscape Architecture and Urban Design at the University of Pennsylvania and received both a bachelor and master's degree in architecture from Pennsylvania State University and Yale University respectively. Prior to setting up the firm, PORT, together with fellow architect Andrew Moddrell, Marcinkoski worked with James Corner Field Operations in New York City as a senior associate. Established in 2010, PORT's work specializes in the 'analysis, visioning, design and implementation of new forms of collective urban space'. Based in Chicago, Illinois, PORT draws on its expertise as a multidisciplinary firm, including ecology, urban design and landscape architecture to 'provide the hybrid model of design services necessary to negotiate today's increasingly complex public realm challenges'. Their innovative designs create dynamic and exciting public realm proposals.

One such example is their Re-Cultivating the Forest City project located in Cleveland, Ohio, a city in the Cuyahoga River Valley that, some forty years ago, appeared as the iconic burning river image on the cover of *Time* magazine. Today, Cleveland is 'again ascendant', however its Valley remains forgotten. PORT's proposals aim to create a 're-cultivated valley', signifying its recovery and in turn demonstrating 'a revised definition of a twenty-first century "working" landscape'. The reclamation project aims to 'reimagine' the lower river valley so as to create a landscape that upgrades social opportunities, augments and extends the ecological value of the area 'while simultaneously serving to reorient the economy and urban form of the City of Cleveland'.

The inspiration for PORT's designs comes from the places in which they work. Rather than superimposing 'an authorial design idea', they actively search to augment what they find, 'searching for both solutions and potentials in what is already present'. PORT aims to create designs that sympathetically and pragmatically respond to the site while also being 'hyperbolic, surprising and dramatic', but without being artificially complex. PORT's competition-winning design for a new intergenerational play landscape at the centre of the City Park in Denver, Colorado, highlights the success of such a design process. The design, and title of the project, is the City Loop, which acts as a mobility loop connecting users to the 5.7-hectare (14-acre) parcel within the larger 133.5-hectare (330-acre) park. Activating the space, the loop is complemented by a 'kinetic tube' that provides 'abstract activity pods' as it bends, twists and folds.

When asked how PORT deals with large-scale, multifaceted projects, Marcinkoski acknowledges that, although they have not yet 'realized a project of this measure and complication', they believe urban design must coexist 'on two very different levels. On one hand there is the requisite open-ended nature of the big vision – what we refer to as the "empty vessel" of possibilities', whereby the project's 'intentional lack of comprehensive specificity' allows for all affiliated parties to state what they want to get out of it – building support without prematurely committing to an outcome. At the same time there is the necessity for 'the definition and elaboration of easily implementable elements – physical and event-based interventions that can quickly build momentum and excitement without alienating early supporters'. This allows for 'open-ended possibilities' of the vision that seem 'attainable', while also encouraging enthusiasm. These types of highly complex projects 'are as much about design resolution as they are implementation strategy … [and] require a political savvy that goes beyond the traditional domains of urban design into a more agile and aware form of design intelligence'.

In creating successful multifaceted projects, PORT likes to collaborate 'with really, really smart people – creative thinkers, strategic operators, thoughtful inquirers, etc.'. Their choice of collaboration is not defined by a specific discipline's expertise; they're as excited to work with environmental scientists as children's play specialists. But in 'engaging the inherent complexity' in their projects they attempt to break the intricacy down into 'essential aspects', and then select collaborators based on 'whomever best contributes to such an endeavour'.

PORT believes today's most pressing design issue is 'the radical instrumentalization of urbanization activities (expansion of infrastructure and settlement) for emphatically political and economic purposes', the idea that 'speculative building' treats urban design as a collation of 'easily deployable products', regardless of the social or environmental repercussions. Thus, 'while landscape architecture has achieved a newfound cultural status in helping to recuperate formerly industrial landscapes … it must shift its attention towards endeavouring to projectively manage and navigate what has become the ultimate twenty-first century industry – speculative city building.' In order for this to happen, PORT believes that landscape architecture must expand beyond its 'singular infatuation' with environmental ecology, particularly with urban spaces. 'There are other equally critical operative elements at play when considering the physical manipulation of an anthropogenic territory – politics, economics, cultural demands, etc.'. In focusing on just one area of their expertise, PORT believes, landscape architects are limiting their 'efficacy and appeal'.

When asked what one thing they would do to improve future cities, PORT would rather they not be thought of in terms of 'single, preferred outcomes', but to 'approach urban design and planning as the elaboration of dynamic systems of operation capable of being recalibrated and amended throughout the processes of implementation and occupation. This is not indeterminacy, but rather continual modulation, correction and adjustment over time.'

Christopher Marcinkoski, PORT
Chicago, IL, USA

'Through his firm, PORT, Christopher Marcinkoski develops innovative designs to resolve large-scale, multifaceted challenges in the urban landscape; and in doing so unleashes their potential, harnessing sustainability and providing a new identity for the public realm.' James Corner on Christopher Marcinkoski

Christopher Marcinkoski, PORT

Re-Cultivating the Forest City, Cleveland, OH, USA (2013)

This speculative proposal looks to reclaim and reimagine the entirety of the lower Cuyahoga River Valley. The design approach utilizes a strategy of productive recolonization, combining economic, ecological and social initiatives to transform the lower Cuyahoga River Valley into a new river landscape infrastructure that enhances the river corridor's ecological value.

Christopher Marcinkoski, PORT

<u>City Loop at City Park</u>, Denver, CO, USA (2016)

City Loop creates a fully accessible recreation circuit that activates the entire parcel, as well as its surrounding context. The project is defined by a mobility loop (ideal for walking, running, rolling, riding) that is paralleled by a kinetic tube that bends, folds, inflates and twists into a variety of abstract activity pods.

Herbert Dreiseitl, Rambøll/Atelier Dreiseitl
Überlingen, Germany/Singapore

Known for his innovative, contemporary projects in the fields of urban design, urban hydrology, water art, storm water management, planning and landscape architecture, Herbert Dreiseitl is an internationally respected expert in creating liveable cities around the world. As the director of the Liveable Cities Lab, the new think tank at the Rambøll Group International, and as founder of Atelier Dreiseitl, a globally integrated, highly regarded design studio, Dreiseitl incorporates these organizations' strategic design and planning efforts within a portfolio of site-responsive interventions in urban planning, hydrology and environmental engineering. He is currently exploring the potential for Liveable Cities in the future, evaluating ways to create a culture of inspiration and social value, involving considerate policy-making and good governance and the proficient implementation of urban infrastructures.

One of Dreiseitl's latest projects, the Kallang River and Bishan-Ang Mo Kio Park, forms part of the Active, Beautiful, Clean Waters (ABC Waters) Program, a long-term proposal to transform Singapore's water bodies beyond their current functions of drainage and water supply, into lively, new spaces for community bonding and recreation. Dreiseitl has uncovered what was once a river entrapped in a drainage channel, to form a dynamic river system that adjusts to fluctuating water levels while providing maximum benefit for users, reminding us that water 'is not a hidden design element, it is a phenomenon that is happening in the park, taking space and time, and the park is designed to accommodate this'. The park not only provides a resilient landscape able to cope with heavy rainfall, but it provides users with an experience of nature to inspire the imagination – particularly important for Dreiseitl, who believes 'we have become so isolated within our own cities [that we are] losing all connection to our natural environment'. As his choice of a recent project in which he would happily spend the day, Dreiseitl explains that the park 'is all about reconnecting the individual, and their imagination, with the environment'. To enable this, Dreiseitl has created platforms for people to take in often unconsidered minutiae of natural life, such as 'where water comes from and where it goes [and] how dragonflies are created'. Today, Bishan-Ang Mo Kio Park is one of the most popular parks in the heartlands of Singapore and a significant representation of his work.

Much of Dreiseitl's own inspiration comes from writers and philosophers such as Nietzsche, Steiner and Goethe, all of whom 'had strong ideas about making the link between the spiritual and physical world', together with artists like Joseph Beuys (whom Dreiseitl met as a young man) and Wassily Kandinsky. 'I believe art is one of mankind's most important discoveries,' he explains, 'allowing the freedom of creation without the necessity to fix a problem.' Naming other inspirations, such as his professor Theodor Schwenk – with his thoughts on the phenomena of water – and John Wilkes's studies on water's metamorphic qualities, Dreiseitl clarifies that 'it is not so much the people who inspire me, but their explanation of the processes of change and the fact that diversity and polarity are driving forces for life's processes'.

In the initial design stages, Dreiseitl often works without any graphics, creating the landscape in his head followed by pencil and paper and sometimes clay. He enjoys the 'absence of ideas' in a project's infancy, insisting 'the computer comes later in my work, always'. Careful not to become too attached to the first idea, he aims 'to create something like a "vacuum" where everything is possible and nothing is fixed: it is a sensitive chaos'. From here the idea is created, tested, sketched and often set aside until the next day to review if the idea is 'any good, or not'.

Without a doubt, his Tanner Springs Park in Portland, Oregon, established itself as 'a good idea'. A former wetland, this post-industrial site was peeled back to reveal the urban skin of a downtown block, creating a new city park. Storm water runoff from the park block is fed into the park's central water feature with a spring and natural cleansing system. Undulating in and out, an Art Wall recycles historic rail tracks and features inlaid pieces of glass which Dreiseitl hand-painted. The park provides areas for wildlife, such as diving ospreys, as well as performances, children's play and quiet refuge.

Regarding the issue of climate change, Dreiseitl believes that 'the most important problem is space and time'. However, along with the increasing tightening of space and accelerating disappearance of available land, he is concerned that 'people don't understand the process of change'. A landscape itself takes time, 'it is a process with seasons, with natural characteristics'. Unlike the creations of most other design professions, a finished landscape is not fully developed for five to ten years, and as it evolves and changes it needs maintenance. Consequently, Dreiseitl feels that landscape architecture should 'be completely reinvented', explaining: 'It is not about greenery, nice flowers and trees in cities. It is much more fundamental. The future of landscape architecture has to influence politics and decision makers. Landscape architecture, and by this I mean urban landscape architecture, has an enormous job to fulfil – not just for biodiversity in our urban fabric, but the enormous challenge of "liveability".'

Liveability, he believes, incorporates tangible factors like money and health, and more importantly, intangible factors like satisfaction and happiness. 'All these things have a lot to do with our relationship to the external environment ... [and] this is what is important for a healthy society; this is the future of landscape architecture.'

Favourite plants

1 Siberian iris (*Iris sibirica*)
2 Canna down (*Eriophorum vaginatum*)
3 Flowering rush (*Butomus umbellatus*)
4 Columbine (*Aquilegia ottonis*)
5 Martagon lily (*Lilium martagon*)

Favourite trees

1 Pin oak (*Quercus palustris*)
2 Bald cypress (*Taxodium distichum*)
3 Swiss stone pine (*Pinus cembra*)
4 European larch (*Larix decidua*)
5 Tulip (*Liriodendron tulipifera*)

Favourite natural landscapes

1 High-altitude landscapes found in the Alps, Europe
2 The erosive landscapes of a mountain stream – with very little vegetation
3 A fragile, yet powerful mountain valley landscape

Tanner Springs Park, Portland, OR, USA (2010)

Stripping back this industrial site to reveal its former glory as a wetland has created a green oasis for all: diving ospreys, passive visitors and exploring children. The park's central water feature is fed by a natural spring and storm water runoff from the park, while the park's Art Wall comprises recycled railway tracks inlaid with fused glass pieces hand-painted with images of nature.

Bishan-Ang Mo Kio Park, Singapore (2012)

At Bishan-Ang Mo Kio Park, a long, straight concrete drainage channel has been restored into a sinuous, natural river that meanders through the park. The redesign accommodates the river system's dynamic process, including fluctuating water levels, while providing amenity spaces for all. The new park includes playgrounds, restaurants, a new look-out point and plenty of open green spaces.

Sentral Parken, Fornebu, Oslo, Norway (2008)

After the relocation of Oslo's main airport, the surrounding city districts of Fornebu immediately saw the potential for an attractive housing and business development close to Oslo city centre. This project saw the creation of a park and lake system. The lake is not just a great place to splash and play, but is an ecological infrastructure ready to receive the development's storm water runoff.

Sungei Buloh, Singapore (2015)

The masterplan for the Sungei Buloh Wetlands Reserve aims to anchor its position in international nature conservation while still meeting the local recreational needs. The design defines a spatial strategy, which protects an inner core, with a sustainably designed activities loop featuring interactive and educational stations.

Favourite trees

1 Stone pine (*Pinus pinea*)
2 Dogwood (*Cornus*
3 Maple (*Acer*)
4 Crape myrtle
  (*Lagerstroemia indica*)
5 Cypress

Favourite materials

1 Wood
2 Steel
3 Concrete
4 Stone
5 Plastic

Favourite contemporary artists

1 Martin Puryear
2 Brice Marden
3 Carrie Mae Weems
4 Jeff Koons
5 Carl Andre

Favourite sounds

1 Ocean lapping on the shore
2 Children playing outside in
  the streets
3 Distant trains and boats

Walter Hood is a California-based artist, designer and educator. Through his practice, Hood Design Studio, he engages in landscape, architectural, urban design and art installation projects. The projects range in type and scale from smaller sites such as Baisley Park, 50 Cent Garden in Queens, New York, funded by American rapper 50 Cent's G-Unity Foundation, to larger projects – as seen with the landscape surrounding the de Young Museum in San Francisco, California, designed by Herzog & de Meuron. His works are regarded as transformative designs within the field of landscape architecture and perform on many levels, especially in cultivating relationships with the surrounding community and addressing ecological concerns.

Baisley Park, 50 Cent Garden exemplifies Hood's work with communities. Influenced by the Kitchen Gardens of Château de Villandry, France, this 1,405-square metre (15,120-square foot) space has been reinvigorated to create a modern community garden. Central to the design are ten funnel-shaped rain catchment devices that channel rainwater into in an underground cistern from where it is used for irrigation. With local residents aiding in its planting, the garden features a learning garden, vegetable plots and a patio area; together the design elements create a dynamic space which is brought to life by community participation. In this design, Hood provided the community with the framework for a neighbourhood garden, but it is the community who have taken ownership of the park and who reap the culinary and aesthetic benefits.

When asked how he designs parks to encourage the client and users to take ownership of its living systems, Hood's response is clear: 'if we get clients and users to see, experience and be articulate about the landscape then they have a better understanding of what to expect and what to nurture'. To Hood, it is 'preposterous' that landscapes should be 'codified' and 'standardized' in such a way that doesn't allow for the community to evolve, or are too complex to manage. Hood's designs aim to have the flexibility to allow for fluctuations in community needs and programming while still retaining an overall aesthetic.

The creative process in his studio is quite rational. Beginning with questions about the site itself, they then take a theoretical position. This might mean 'reinforcing' the clients programme or challenging 'assumptions', Hood explains, but 'whatever the programme or project type, we view the entire work through the lens of the landscape'. Examining the site through its flora, fauna, hydrology, geology, microclimate and so on, the studio creates different improvisational concepts to be explored further and refined. His projects sometimes work in collaboration with architects, engineers and artists. 'We love to work with engineering firms that are multidisciplinary,' Hood establishes, but 'we like to collaborate with firms and people that know how to collaborate! Not everyone knows how.'

The landscape Hood created for the Herzog & de Meuron's de Young Museum in 2005 highlights the successful integration of different disciplines within the realm of landscape architecture. Blurring the boundary between all three, the landscape provides both a platform from which to view and a backdrop against which to set the art and architecture. Located in Golden Gate Park, this design re-made a sand dune and created a landscape that wraps around the new museum. In this case, Hood restored 2 hectares (5 acres), retaining some existing features, but creating distinct landscape spaces with varying landforms, plants and materials selected so as to best set the stage for the artworks that inhabit the landscape and the architecture it surrounds. The museum's entrance landscapes combines linear strips of limestone paving slabs, palms and lawn to set the stage for the arriving visitors.

In an equally distinctive way, the *Coastlines* Wilmington Trail artwork reinterprets the historic water's edge for the city of Wilmington, California. A 800-metre (0.5-mile) stretch of eight sandstone towers rise in reference to the coastal bluffs of the community of San Pedro and its industrial condition, including numerous smoke stacks and large cranes, found just north of the site. Sandblasted historic waterlines along the sidewalks trace the water's historic edge.

The flexibility of Hood's designs highlights one of his concerns for the future of landscape architecture. Believing that 'we (people) control everything in the environment ... we have to learn to let some things go and ... be willing to change', Hood advises creating malleable landscapes. The diversity of his work and discipline illustrates his own ability to evolve in scale, design field and context, while the dynamics of communities and nature, which he prioritizes in his designs, can be found in an eclectic list of his favourite sounds which includes 'the ocean lapping on the shore, children outside playing in the streets and distant trains and boats'.

Hood's work is dynamic and varying but always respects the sociological and ecological values of the area in which it is created. In discussing one thing he would do to make better cities for the future, on reflection, Hood explains that as 'our cities occupy diverse landscapes ... wouldn't it be great if our cities emerged from the culture of place?'

Walter Hood, Hood Design Studio Oakland, CA, USA

'Walter Hood always surprises me in a very positive way; he offers fresh and authentic responses to the challenges and topics of today's society and cities. His creative, artistic work gives honest hope to people and the environment – a quality we need today and even more so in the future.'

Herbert Dreiseitl on Walter Hood

Walter Hood, Hood Design Studio

Baisley Park, 50 Cent Garden, Queens, NY, USA (2008)

Funded by 50 Cent's G-Unity Foundation, this project takes inspiration from the Kitchen Gardens of Château de Villandry in France. Planted by the residents of Jamaica, Queens, the garden offers an educational, multifunctional park for the community. A funnel-shaped rain catchment system adds a playful element to the space, recycling rainwater to an underground cistern that is later used for irrigation.

Walter Hood, Hood Design Studio

de Young Museum, San Francisco, CA, USA (2005)

This design is an integration of the urban and the constructed natural landscape. The landscape extends its arms to encompass the new building, creating spaces that are an interaction between art and park. The extent of the works saw 2 hectares (5 acres) of the park restored, retaining existing landscape features while creating spaces to explore and enjoy the artwork in a natural setting.

Coastlines Wilmington Trail, Wilmington, CA, USA (2013)

Reinterpreting Wilmington's historic water edge, the *Coastlines* Wilmington Trail artwork presents a series of stacked towers. Laid out over an 800-metre (0.5-mile) stretch, the sandstone towers reference the coastal bluffs of San Pedro, to the north of the site, while along the sidewalk sandblasted waterlines trace the historic water's edge.

Andrew Grant,
Grant Associates
Bath, England, UK

Exploring the emerging frontiers of landscape architecture within sustainable development, Grant is known for a creative approach to ecologically sustainable landscape design and the integration of landscape with engineering and architecture to create distinctive contemporary places with a strong ecological character. In 2012, the Royal Society of Arts awarded Grant the title of Royal Designer for Industry (RDI) in recognition of his pioneering global work in landscape architecture.

'I would like to "rewild" landscape architecture and landscape architects,' Andrew Grant reveals when asked how he would like to influence future generations of professionals. Grant believes 'our future role is to create distinctive real world landscape experiences to counter the sanitized global aesthetic. In the world of inclusive design, super high definition film and TV ... we need to reconnect people with the tooth and claw aspects of the natural world, even at the heart of cities.' He explains that this can be done by 'injecting more primal responses into our landscape designs, rather than yet more signature paving and planting concepts'. Comparing this to a 'contemporary rerun' of the eighteenth-century picturesque and sublime debates, today, Grant explains, 'it is much more than an aesthetic diversion, it goes to the heart of our future relationship with the natural world'.

Most recently Grant and his team have developed the Gardens by the Bay project at Bay South in Singapore, a 54-hectare (133-acre) park that explores the technical boundaries of landscape and horticulture, winning the World Building of the Year Award at the 2012 World Architecture Festival. Considering the project's innovative design and impressive scale, it's not surprising that Grant has chosen it as one of his recently built projects in which to spend the day. 'Gardens by the Bay took up the best part of seven years of my life so whenever I am in Singapore I make a point of visiting the Gardens in an attempt to get some of this time back,' he explains.

Bay South is the first, and largest, of the project's three gardens, which blend flora and fauna, state of the art technology, environmental management and creativity to make a world-class park focusing on tropical horticulture, giving Singapore an outstanding destination park. It includes eighteen 'Supertrees', measuring 25–50 metres (82–164 feet) high, to act as vertical gardens with a seemingly floating walkway and a treetop bar with panoramic views of the city and park. Discussing this project, Grant reveals that 'tropical landscapes are alive day and night', which is why he would 'love to spend a whole twenty-four hours in the Gardens reflecting on the delight and fear and patterns of people, rain, birds, shadows and sky'. The Gardens include Cooled Conservatories, Heritage Gardens, World of Plants Gardens, Dragonfly Lake and Dragonfly Bridge, as well as numerous sculptures and architectural features. 'The best thing though,' he explains, 'is watching people from all parts of the planet and of all ages taking something positive from being in the Gardens.'

Grant's inspiration comes from, in his words, 'the physiology, structure, forms and behaviour of animate things (humans, water, trees, octopi, tigers, orchids, clouds, birds and fish) and from the "hero's journey" narrative structure of books and films. The natural references provide a physical structure to the ideas, the "hero's journey" gives an emotional structure to the experience.' With Gardens by the Bay, Grant explains he was inspired by the 'physiology and form of the orchid and by the narrative of the film *Princess Mononoke* by Hayao Miyazaki'.

Grant believes that every 'place and moment in the global landscape is unique', and accordingly has its own specific design solution. 'I find this emerges through dreaming, intuitive research, exploration of the site's natural and cultural DNA and through interrogation of the project brief. Most times the seed of an idea eventually takes root, typically discovered within a million sketches that leap between crude doodles expressing a thought and scaled, accurate plans and sections testing the reality.' Each project evolves through a team effort, shaped and guided by input through collaborations both within the office and outside of it; in Grant's experience 'collaboration leads to richer, more intelligent and sustainable solutions'.

During a time when 'everywhere is becoming like everywhere else, especially in the context of contemporary urbanism', Grant feels that the 'notion of landscape's "genius of place" and the biogeographical uniqueness of each site' is being challenged by the 'development of generic international-style cities together with the consequent destruction of wild landscapes'. He expresses concern that if we add to this the serious issues of 'climate change, biodiversity loss, food and water insecurity and social unrest then you have the greatest ever challenge for sustaining the cultural and natural richness of our planet'. Grant believes 'we have a duty to shout out about these threats and the consequent opportunities', and he does just this when asked about the future of landscape architecture: 'The next fifty years HAS to be the greatest ever era of landscape architecture. It is in this period that the world could lose the battle with climate change and be altered forever, or a time in which we rediscover an equilibrium with nature. As landscape architect Geoffrey Jellicoe anticipated [in his 1964 book *The Landscape of Man*], this is our time to deliver "a landscape art on a scale never conceived of in history".'

Favourite colour combinations

1 Black and black
2 Mangosteen (purple/black), white, raspberry red and lime green
3 Bone, lead and burnt sienna
4 Banana-leaf green, aquamarine and white
5 Tiger orange, black and white

Favourite plants

1 Common reed (*Phragmites australis*)
2 Soft tree fern (*Dicksonia antarctica*)
3 Lavender (*Lavandula*)
4 Rose Iceberg (*Rosa* 'Iceberg')
5 Wild strawberry (*Fragaria vesca*)

Favourite trees

1 English oak (*Quercus robur*)
2 Holm oak (*Quercus ilex*)
3 Black poplar (*Populus nigra*)
4 Scots pine (*Pinus sylvestris*)
5 Silver lime (*Tilia tomentosa*)

The Hive, Worcester, England, UK (2012)

The Hive is Europe's first joint university and public library – a unique academic, educational and learning centre for the city of Worcester and its University. The design's landscape and public realm strategy defines a path around the building and a series of terraces and garden rooms based on a strong narrative and geometry inspired by the surrounding natural landscape: the River Severn and the Malvern Hills.

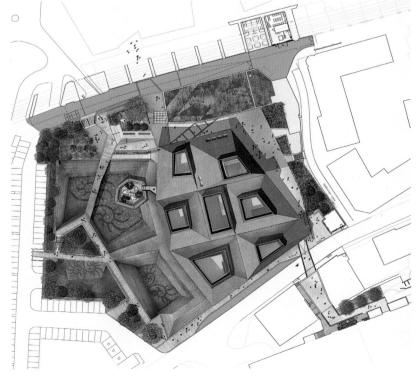

Accordia, Cambridge, England, UK (2004)

Guiding this housing scheme's masterplan, Grant Associates created a hierarchy of spaces across the site, including large open spaces, play areas and differently themed gardens, all linked by a network of paths and clearly defined by walls, hedges and boundaries. Circulation through the scheme is via a series of mews streets, for shared use by pedestrians, cyclists and vehicles.

British Pavillion Garden at Japan Expo, Aichi, Japan (2005)

Together with the Natural History Museum, Ten Alps and Land Design Studio, Grant Associates created the British Pavilion Garden at Japan Expo 2005. Based on the concept 'Nature's Wisdom', an internal exhibition celebrated scientific innovation while the external exhibition examined the human effect on the natural world, featuring lime trees with an understorey of native British species.

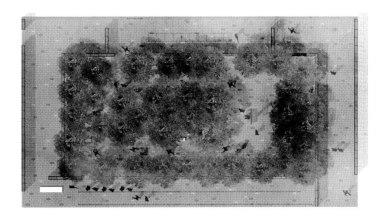

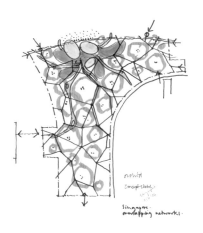

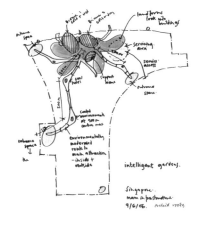

Bay South is the first of three gardens at Singapore's Gardens by the Bay. Designed as a twenty-first century focus for tropical horticulture and a unique destination experience, it incorporates planted vertical gardens standing sixteen storeys high. These iconic 'Supertrees' provide viewing platforms for surveying the site's World of Plants Gardens, Heritage Gardens, Dragonfly Lake and Dragonfly Bridge.

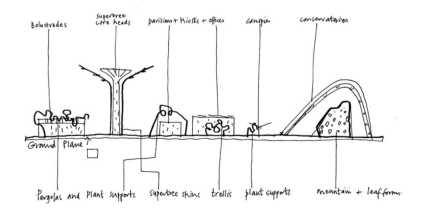

Favourite plants

1 Century plant (*Agave americana*)
2 Hollyhock (*Alcea rosea*)
3 Argentinian vervain
   (*Verbena bonariensis*)
4 Japanese anemone 'Honorine
   Jobert' (*Anemone* x *hybrida*
   'Honorine Jobert')
5 Indian fig (*Opuntia ficus-indica*)

Favourite trees

1 Black locust
   (*Robinia pseudoacacia*)
2 Canary Island date palm
   (*Phoenix canariensis*)
3 Saucer magnolia
   (*Magnolia* x *soulangeana*)
4 Stone pine (*Pinus pinea*)
5 Apple (*Malus domestica*)

Favourite materials

1 Wool
2 Bronze
3 Paper
4 Linen
5 Soil
6 Plaster

Anouk Vogel's internationally acclaimed work focuses on the complex interface between landscape, art, design and architecture. Born in Geneva, Switzerland, Vogel studied landscape architecture at Metropolitan University of Manchester in the United Kingdom, graduating in 2001. In 2007 she established her firm in Amsterdam and has since created various award-winning designs. She was one of the winners of the prestigious Professional Prix de Rome Architecture in 2010. Recently, Vogel was commissioned to design new furniture for Vondelpark, a 47-hectare (116-acre) park in the centre of Amsterdam listed as a Dutch national heritage site.

When asked if there is a place for 'wildness and non-designed landscape' in her work, Vogel asserts, 'One of the ways I understand landscape architecture is as a simultaneously precise and raw discipline. The intentions and the drawings are precise, the materials often natural and informal.' Vogel explores this wildness in her project Courtesy of Nature, an installation created with architect Johan Selbing in Grand-Métis, Québec, Canada. The installation allows for multiple interpretations while inviting the visitor to explore their relationship with nature. In this design Vogel created an exhibition space around the 'existing element' by producing a 'container' for nature. In this way, instead of designing its content, she provided a frame within which to view it. Intrigued by the apparently 'antagonistic and symbiotic' relationship between the wild and the designed, in the future Vogel would like to explore this idea further by 'physically defining a wildness' that would be described as an untamed piece of land completely devoid of human activity.

'Inspiration is always lurking around the corner for me,' Vogel reveals. Observing the minute details of everyday life, especially those which are so familiar they're hardly noticed, her work seeks to illuminate these elements, creating designs which 'render their quality perceptible'. She references a passage from Karl Ove Knausgård's book *A Death in the Family* which describes Knausgård's obsession with clouds, where he wants everyone to stop and appreciate their beauty but realizes that their permanent presence renders them mundane. Vogel herself wants to explore this relationship between reinterpreting these common, everyday details and representing them in such a way that both excites people and implores reflection: 'I am interested in the making of identifiable objects that distinguish themselves from their context, but are yet informed by it.'

This can be seen with her project Cacticity, located in Bilbao, Spain, where 1,000 cacti, ranging in height from 10 centimetres (4 inches) to 1 metre (3 feet, 3 inches), create a unique section of landscape in the square adjoining the Bilbao Museum of Fine Arts. True to Vogel's inspiration, this project takes a common cactus, planted en masse, to create an ordered landscape that, as she describes, compels 'recognition as a tactile space to be explored visually. This allows for an open interpretation of the garden-urban dialectic by appropriating the classical language of the garden in an unorthodox way.'

Vogel states that 'autonomy and freedom' are important elements of her design process, and her studio has been kept intentionally small in order to control the types of projects she is commissioned to do. This also allows her to create her own schedule aligning a project's needs with those of her own. As Vogel explains, if she doesn't feel like going to her studio one morning, 'I take the freedom to go to a museum instead, which tends to be more fruitful than to follow a routine for the sake of it. When my agenda allows it I spend half a day reading, half a day writing, and half a day drawing freely per week, next to working on my projects.' Apart from visiting the site, her creative process begins with an open mind as she lets 'the luggage of accumulated impressions unfold itself'. The excitement of the design process's open-ended journey instils enthusiasm and motivates her design; the only sure thing in this process's result is 'the emotion that I'm pursuing'. Once this is achieved, she begins an analysis where the idea is justified historically, geographically and culturally.

Vogel defines her way of working as 'introvert and personal', and although she does occasionally collaborate with 'like-minded' designers, appreciating the value they can add. However, she believes that 'in many ways I remain a soloist'. She is inspired, though, by 'professional craftsmen ... the ones that still have an enormous knowledge and passion for the materials and techniques they deal with, like foundries, forgeries, specialized nurseries and so on.'

Vogel's Paper Garden project constructed in Nagasaki, Japan involved such a collaboration. The project brief called for a 24-square metre (258-square foot) garden to be displayed for ten days. And instead of temporarily installing plants and discarding them afterwards, all of the plants were folded out of white paper. 600 flower heads, 600 stems and 1,800 leaves were crafted in fifteen days with the help of fifteen local people. The resulting instillation was a delicate and impermanent landscape with a lifespan matching the exhibition's duration period. Vogel reflects that 'the true meaning of this garden could [possibly] be understood in the tension created by the intensity of the labour in relation to the extremely ephemeral nature of the resulting work.'

Anouk Vogel,
Anouk Vogel landscape architecture
Amsterdam, The Netherlands

'Anouk Vogel's work belongs to a future time where art and design have effortlessly fused with biology and nature. Crossing between gardens, installations, interiors and furniture she brings a sense of nature to the smallest detail whilst revealing the wider magic of landscape.'

Andrew Grant on Anouk Vogel

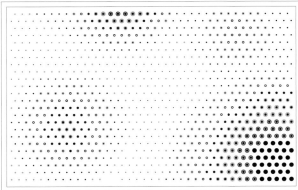

Anouk Vogel, Anouk Vogel landscape architecture

Cacticity, Bilbao, Spain (2009)

Located on a square adjacent to the Bilbao Museum of Fine Arts, this installation comprises 1,000 cacti ranging in height from 1 metre (3 feet 3 inches) to 10 centimetres (4 inches). Planted together in a graphically intriguing way, the common cactus creates a tactile composition that is to be explored visually.

Anouk Vogel, Anouk Vogel landscape architecture

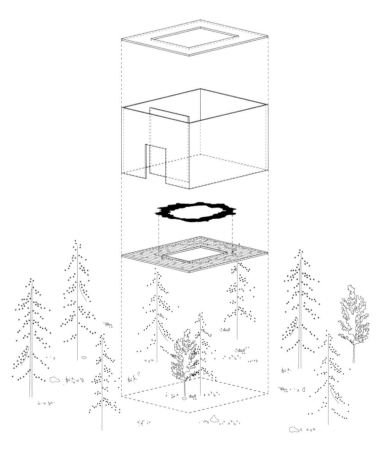

<u>Courtesy of Nature</u>, Grand-Métis, Québec, Canada (2013)

This contextual installation invites the visitor to reflect upon their relationship with nature. Instead of creating a piece to be displayed in an exhibition, this design creates an exhibition space around an existing element – nature. By creating a container in which to celebrate the installation, this project explores the concept of making something seemingly banal appear extraordinary.

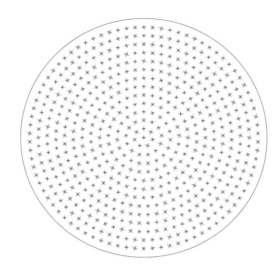

Paper Garden, Nagasaki, Japan (2011)

Designed as a solution for a garden exhibition that lasted for just ten days, as its name reveals, this garden was made entirely from paper. Distributed over a circular 24 metre-square (258 foot-square) space, the garden was constructed of 600 flower heads, 600 stems and 1,800 leaves by local the Japanese community over fifteen days.

Juan Grimm,
Studio Juan Grimm
Santiago, Chile

Juan Grimm has landscaped more than 2,600 hectares (6,424 acres) of land in Chile, Argentina, Peru and Uruguay, ranging from private gardens to parks to commercial projects. Originally trained as an architect, he has devoted the last thirty years to the profession of landscape architecture. His practice creates harmonious landscapes that draw inspiration from the organic forms found in nature. Beyond his studio work, Grimm has given numerous lectures worldwide and is a Professor of Landscape Architecture in several Chilean universities.

For decades, through his own work and conveyed through lectures, Grimm has demonstrated that 'the [most] important thing [in landscape architecture] is found in nature'. He believes that 'more than knowledge, nature gives us wisdom and understanding to act properly when we need to intervene in her presence'. He advocates that landscape architects should observe and listen to nature rather than inventing and discussing, and, through humble eyes, work with the natural landscape instead of challenging it. His Transoceánica Garden in Santiago, Chile, represents his commitment to using nature as his inspiration. Despite its proximity to the city, Grimm describes it as a quiet place to hear the birds, and chooses it as one of his most recent works in which to spend a day. The garden, designed around a commercial building – the first Chilean building to receive LEED (Leadership in Energy and Environmental Design) Gold-certification, is nestled in the foothills of the Andes Mountains. Consequently, the site's naturalistic setting creates areas for one to relax and absorb nature.

One of Grimm's major concerns, and one that helps define his creation process, is how a new landscape is situated in its existing natural setting. 'To intervene in a certain place,' Grimm explains, 'first of all I recognize the order of the surroundings, so that the overall design will be inserted in harmony with the existing landscape.' This process helps to interlock the natural and the proposed landscape and also helps to highlight nature, or hide unwanted views. From here he defines zones of activities, and with the 'movement of soil and plants' he gives these areas their 'own character'. To give structure he defines an area he calls the 'plot of vegetation' – the plants and trees – and a second area called 'the plot of circulation'. These plots need to respond to one another and are combined to define the site's structure. The order and prominence of these plots, and their relationship to nature, depend on the landscape and the architecture. With the Transoceánica Garden, the 'great curving staircase' was created so as to absorb the slope of the land and as a way to 'strengthen the presence'

Favourite plants

1 Lucumo silvestre
   (*Pouteria splendens*)
2 Japanese pittosporum
   (*Pittosporum tobira*)
3 Indian hawthorn
   (*Raphiolepis indica*)
4 Cherry laurel 'Otto Luyken'
   (*Prunus laurocerasus* 'Otto Luyken')
5 Japanese snowball
   (*Viburnum plicatum*)

Favourite trees

1 Roble beech (*Nothofagus oblique*)
2 Coigue (*Nothofagus dombeyi*)
3 Peumo (*Cryptocarya alba*)
4 Japanese maple (*Acer palmatum*)
5 Bull bay (*Magnolia grandiflora*)

Inspiration

1 Landscape architect Óscar Prager
2 Landscape architect Roberto Burle Marx
3 Architect Luis Barragán
4 Artist/landscape architect Isamu Noguchi

of the surrounding hills. A high percentage of native plants was established so as to have a direct relationship to surrounding terrain: with larger species planted along the perimeter, shrubs planted along the slopes (as they would be found in the hills), and a pond featuring aquatic grasses.

'From an early age I felt a great attraction to nature, especially the landscapes of Chile and South America due to the richness and identity I find in them,' Grimm explains. It is through his intense study of these landscapes that he has created a mental library of 'readings and patterns ... which have been the true inspiration for my designs'. Careful observations of the landscape allow him to learn the 'characteristics of vegetation and how different species are associated, or how they grow and spread on the slopes [as opposed to level terrain], or what is the difference between the water channels in certain situations, or the effects of wind and rain on the hills and rocks.' While manmade interventions like Machu Picchu and Roman aqueducts have also influenced his work, it is these natural events that constitute much of his designs.

Working with the architect Siamak Hariri (Hariri Pontarini Architects) for the last eight years has provided Grimm with an opportunity to create the gardens for South America's first, and only, Bahá'í Temple, located in Santiago. An outstanding landscape set to the stunning backdrop of the Andes Mountains, Grimm's design upholds his sustainable design values, through a landscape that sympathetically responds to its sloping location while providing native planting that reduces the need for artificial irrigation. To be completed in 2016, the temple and the surrounding landscape will provide visitors with areas to meditate, pray and reflect, and connect to the surrounding, serene natural setting. Accordingly, Grimm has carefully considered plant species, routes and view corridors so that, as he explains, 'contemplation and prayer can be given in fullness'.

Grimm believes landscape architects need to create seductive designs in order to combat issues such as loss of ecology and lack of sustainability. In doing so, he explains, '[we generate] awareness of the natural values that we have and how we have lost them in such an accelerated way'. Concerned for the damage to the Earth caused through large-scale manmade transformations, Grimm believes that 'sometimes small gestures in a design solve big problems, if they are well thought [through] to harmonize in every way with the nature of that place.' In this way, Grimm hopes that through a certain design '... we can teach [about] our [beautiful landscapes so that] eventually we will love them and in addition look after them'.

Errazuriz Winery Garden, Panquehue, Valparaiso Region, Chile (2009)

Located in one of Chile's oldest vineyards, this garden is organized around a central water feature and surrounded by boxwood hedges planted in an irregular geometric pattern. The project culminates at the new wine cellar, designed by the architect Samuel Claro, where an access staircase designed with waterfalls and plants unites the garden and building together.

Transoceánica Garden, Vitacura district, Santiago, Chile (2010)
Inspired by the surrounding Andes Mountains, this corporate garden's planting strategy locates taller, native trees around the site's perimeter, supported internally by shrubs. This, together with the use of native plants, creates continuity between the garden and the distant landscape. Around the building, garden lagoons add aesthetic and sustainable value, retaining rain and groundwater for irrigation.

Montevideo, Montevideo, Uruguay (2014)

Formerly a landfill site, the poor soil permeability saw its masterplan feature three lagoons. The site's design includes the installation of large stone pieces, endemic palms and plants and exotic specimens, such as bald cypresses, camphor trees, willows and oaks. Earmarked for future low-density housing, this site is now home to a myriad of birds, providing further ecological enrichment.

Gardens of Bahá'í Temple, Peñalolén, Santiago, Chile (2016)

Surrounding architect Siamak Hariri's new Bahá'í Temple in the Andes Mountains, these gardens connect with the building's unique architecture and Bahá'í faith symbol – the nine-pointed star. Nine paths, corresponding to nine gateways and water features, are orientated around the building's main square; formalistic planting areas around the building contrast with naturalistic perimeter planting.

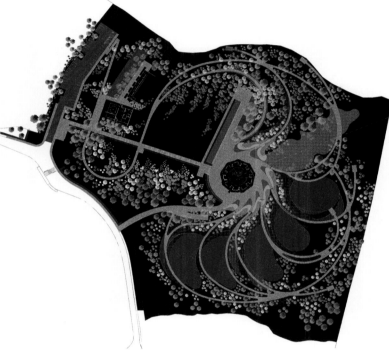

Based in Santiago Chile, Karin Oetjen and her company KO Paisajismo specialize in creating works that are well organized and offer a 'deep sense of space' and balanced proportions. Oetjen's style is characterized as 'primarily modern' and, using a minimal colour and materials palette, she aims to build landscapes that celebrate the 'beauty of simplicity'. Aspiring to achieve a 'seamless integration' between the landscape and architecture, Oetjen creates 'an atmosphere of contemplation and spiritual revitalization' in her projects.

The gardens completed for the Awad residence located on a hillside overlooking Santiago and the surrounding Andes Mountains, are an example of one of Oetjen's most atmospheric spaces. The project's limited selection of materials, including wood, stone and plants, are organized over different levels in order create well-proportioned spaces. At the heart of this landscape is a walled garden room; measuring 58 square metres (624 square feet), the cube-shaped space establishes a quiet area for meditation. Here, large planks of marble, orientated over different levels, strengthen the character of this tranquil space.

Although Oetjen does not have one 'fixed inspiration', her work is always founded in the concept of 'pure and clean architecture' and is always grounded in its natural setting. Regarding 'beauty and elegance', her motto 'less is always more' forms much of how she develops her projects. Oetjen's designs always start by interpreting the site location, architecture and the client's ambitions – the design then evolves through a quick 'base design' through which the design's structure and form are outlined. A surprise element, such as the addition of an exclusive colour, texture or vegetation, is always included in order to give a unique character to each one of her designs.

Oetjen's landmark project Mirador Santa Anita, built in the hills surrounding Santiago, comprises seven apartment buildings organized around a central park. Completed in 2014, the project's rustic-looking stone combined with existing and native vegetation anchors the landscape into its scenic location. Each building benefits from its own garden and pedestrian connections to the central park. The landscape's minimal yet formal planting palette, together with small streams and pools, offers endless possibilities for users to enjoy its tranquil setting.

Although water is a part of Oetjen's designs, she recognizes the need for landscape architects to address issues of water scarcity and the use of chemical substances in their work. Her designs aim to minimize the use of grass so as to decrease the amount of irrigation needed. This is also the case with her plant choices and required maintenance regimes, which are selected so as to avoid the use of chemical substances. Although her own works always instil both ecological and sustainable processes, she believes that important consideration for animals and wildlife as well as a respect for 'cultural custom', all of which 'deliver [a] richer and complementary view', are too often overlooked. Understanding that 'every landscape work is just an artificial creation', beyond using sustainable irrigation methods and plant choices, Oetjen aims to 'never lose sight of [the] people who [will] experience my work'.

When asked about the one thing she would do to create better cities for the future, Oetjen feels that all landscape architects need to work together to create a 'unitary urban plan' whereby green zones are defined but are in keeping with clearly delineated 'city sectors'. To ensure this, Oetjen insists that 'all decision-makers in a city landscape design must be conscious that a generous urbanism [needs to be] rich in green areas and with a sense of respect to the native trees'. She compares this to New York City's Central Park, where one forgets one is surrounded by skyscrapers, explaining that these 'green surfaces are the only way of oxygenating a life of concrete'.

On discussing her favourite landscape project, Oetjen does not have a preference. Instead, 'each one of my artworks has a part of me. They are like sons, with a single and unique spirit that responds to my vision of the landscape of a particular project.' Her vision for the Arrigoni residence, located in Santiago and completed in 2011, saw the creation of a residential garden situated over several platforms connected by large paving stones. As Oetjen explains, 'the main challenge of this project was to achieve a proper balance and interaction between [the] different areas of the house's exterior'. Oetjen states that this project – like all her projects – has been 'limited to what is deemed basic and essential. I love the simplicity and the profound refinement that it generates'.

Oetjen designs her landscapes with the aim of creating 'beauty' for her end users. At the completion of her projects, she believes them to be successful if users feel 'immersed in the landscape, perceiving the beauty, the order in nature and the harmony in the lines' that she has created. She acknowledges, however, that landscape architecture, like anything human, is not flawless; and that her design efforts are not complete until visitors become part of the landscape, 'observing the same unity and peace that nature brings'. In regards to her own future aspirations, Oetjen would like to create a large public space or park which provides people respite from the stresses of the city and their 'urban concrete' setting.

Karin Oetjen,
KO Paisajismo
Santiago, Chile

'Her designs are very well organized and characterized by a good sense of space, composition and proportions. Her style is eminently contemporary, minimalist and clean, with delimited use of colour both in vegetation and materials.' Juan Grimm on Karin Oetjen

Karin Oetjen, KO Paisajismo

Arrigoni Residence, Lo Barnechea, Santiago, Chile (2011)

This design creates a cohesive garden through a series of well-proportioned spaces organized over a series of levels. Through the layering of materials and spaces, the design defines different zones around the house's exterior, and connects them together through large paving stones. The garden's planting species include maidenhair tree, red oak, full moon maple and the lily of the valley tree.

Karin Oetjen, KO Paisajismo

<u>Mirador Santa Anita</u>, Lo Barnechea, Santiago, Chile (2014)

Situated on a hill with views of the Andes Mountains, this landscape anchors seven apartment buildings to their native surroundings. Organized around a 19,000-square metre (204,514-square foot) central park, each building has garden access and pedestrian links to the park. The design's rustic materials, native vegetation and pools create a lush backdrop for this housing complex's residents.

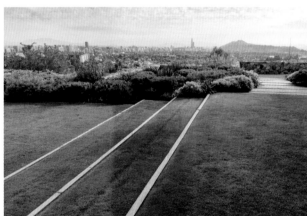

<u>Awad Residence</u>, Vitacura, Santiago, Chile (2004)

Located on the hills overlooking Santiago, this garden has been designed with a contemporary formal landscape aesthetic. Contained by a stone wall, this project's design uses a limited palette of materials to define grass-planted stairs, a pool and garden spaces. The project's centrepiece is a walled-garden room, a cube-shaped space with marble planks organized over different levels, offering a space for quiet meditation.

George Hargreaves,
Hargreaves Associates
San Francisco, CA, USA

Based in Sonoma County, California, George Hargreaves practises in collaboration with fellow senior principals Mary Margaret Jones and Gavin McMillan at Hargreaves Associates, a professional consulting firm comprised of landscape architects and planners with offices in San Francisco, Cambridge, Massachusetts and New York City. Among numerous award-winning projects, the Queen Elizabeth Olympic Park for the London 2012 Olympic Games, preceded by the masterplan design for the Sydney 2000 Olympic Games, brought his highly acclaimed works to the attention of billions. Hargreaves has taught at the Harvard Graduate School of Design, serving as chairman of the Department of Landscape Architecture, and recently cultivated his own vineyards in Sonoma County.

That Hargreaves counts 'birds in the morning' among his favourite sounds is perhaps fittingly symbolic for a landscape architect who has built a career creating designs that breathe new life into unwanted, polluted locations around the world. His inspirational flair for transforming a site's post-industrial doom and gloom can clearly be seen at the Queen Elizabeth Olympic Park in London, England, created in collaboration with LDA Design, Nigel Dunnett and James Hitchmough, University of Sheffield, Landscape Department and Sarah Price Landscapes. The project saw the conversion of a brownfield site into a twenty-first century park centred on a restored stretch of the River Lea. Chosen as a recent project in which he'd spend a day, Hargreaves acknowledges that 'in many ways the Olympic Park is an extension of all the projects we have done ... highlighting our earthwork and reclamation strategies as well as the most diverse planting we've ever been involved with '. In his design process, Hargreaves reflects that he likes 'to visit [his] projects and learn from them, to find out which things work and which don't', explaining that with the Olympic Park he's 'still in the discovery phase'.

Hargreaves' design process evolves simultaneously in 2D and 3D. He states a preference for using pencil, paper and clay, as he feels that 'with computers you have to set the design before you can input the data and what I like about pencil and clay is that you can go back and forth between the mediums to create a 3D design'. Using an iterative design process, Hargreaves's team seeks 'to understand the grain of the site and how the programme has been envisioned for it and then step back and do something very creative'. Working between scales, he explains that 'looking at the detailed moments informs the larger picture and the bigger picture informs the details, otherwise known as the hermeneutic circle'. This design methodology helped create a unified, large-scale project with Haihe Riverfront, Ribbon Island Park project, a waterfront park for a mixed-use development district located on the Haihe River in Tanggu District, Tianjin Municipality, China. Produced in collaboration with Bohai Urban Planning & Design, the park offers a variety of active and passive spaces connecting by paths that weave in and out of lushly planted landscape areas. The park's configuration establishes strong links between future urban land developments, while sustainable design principles underpin the park's design.

This layered approach to design stems from Hargreaves's inspiration: environmental art, history and rigorous design principles. Classically trained, his discovery of environmental art, where artists were 'working with natural processes in shape and form' was, Hargreaves acknowledges, 'a real jumping-off point'. This influence is clear in early projects such as Candlestick Point State Recreation Area, San Francisco, California, where, he explains, 'I was working in a way that embraces the site's natural processes – not attempting to make it "look like nature", but highlighting the elements that isolate "nature" within the park.' Harnessing natural phenomena is an essential layer of all Hargreaves's designs. However, it's through the historical layer that Hargreaves tries to understand 'what was there before, what economic structure was in place when the project was created, how it lasted and has been maintained'. He explains that through an interest in history he 'began to appreciate what makes a landscape survive, become an icon, a place that people cherish and spend money to maintain'. The third layer in Hargreaves's work evolves through working with architects, and he expresses appreciation for 'the rigour with which they approach problems ... They have identifiable goals they are working towards and they evaluate the project as they move forward to achieve these goals.' This layering of design principles helps create projects rich in sociological, environmental and artistic values that function on numerous programmatic levels – particularly important in the United States where publicly funded parks are rare and privately funded parks are often designed with a 'fairground approach', filled with capital-creating programming.

Regarding the future of landscape architecture, Hargreaves feels the need for 'a great degree of consistency in terms of the integrity with which we approach each project'. He expresses concern that too much contemporary work 'tends to be very plan-orientated, graphic-orientated and does not delve into the meat of the site'. Encouragingly though, he believes 'The future of landscape architecture is bright, but can become brighter with better education in critical thinking and three-dimensional imagination.'

Favourite materials

1 Water
2 Soil
3 Stone
4 Wood
5 Glass

Favourite landscapes

1 The sandy pine plant communities of southeast America where my first awareness of ecology occurred thanks to my uncle Leon Hargreaves, PhD.
2 A healthy and productive vineyard
3 Great Britain and Ireland's linksland, understood best when played strategically.
4 The highway earthworks of cuts and ramps, thank you author John McPhee.
5 A forgotten *allée* of trees in Hyde Park

Favourite sounds

Birds in the morning

This arrival plaza for the office tower designed by architects Kohn Pedersen Fox Associates efficiently uses the compact space to form an enchanting pedestrian passage. The plaza features works by sculptors Ugo Rondinone and Jonathan Borofsky, with atmospheric lighting, seating areas, trees offering dappled shade and a lush green wall, together creating an escape from the surrounding urban context.

Queen Elizabeth Olympic Park, London, England, UK (2012)
Combining a twenty-first century park aesthetic with cutting-edge sustainability techniques, this project sees the transformation of a post-industrial brownfield site to an expansive park centred on a restored section of the River Lea. The North Park converts the channelized canal into a naturalized river corridor with sweeping lawns and sculpted banks. The South Park terraces the riverbanks and includes themed botanical gardens. Together they create the largest park built in London over the last hundred years.

This waterfront park serves a mixed-use development district located on the
Haihe River in Tianjin. The 30-hectare (74-acre) park offers amenities such as
riverfront boardwalks, plazas, promenades, natural forests, riparian wetlands and
botanical gardens. The park's sustainable strategies assist in revitalizing the
natural ecological systems, while its overall organization establishes strong connections with the adjacent area, city and river.

117

Discovery Green, Houston, TX, USA (2008)
Located at the centre of downtown, this urban park has become a key open space for the surrounding offices, residences and hotel development. The park has become a stimulus for downtown growth and activity and can accommodate a large number of outdoor activities, including events and recreation. The design's highlights include an interactive fountain, water and botanical gardens, an amphitheatre and a custom-designed playground.

Favourite plants

'Plants like hawthorn and devil's walking stick (*Aralia spinosa*) that have not been denuded of their thorns, I love the texture and the sense of danger.'

1 Bamboo
2 Ferns
3 Palms
4 Bougainvillea

Favourite trees

1 Maidenhair (*Ginkgo biloba*)
2 Buttonwood (*Platanus occidentalis*)
3 Bald cypress (*Taxodium distichum*)
4 Black willow (*Salix nigra*)
5 Foxglove (*Paulownia tomentosa*)

Favourite materials

1 Fog
2 Heat
3 Synthetics
4 Biologically derived products

Participating in competitions and installations on three continents, Chris Reed's forward-thinking approach to the public realm has been widely praised. The founding principal of Stoss Landscape Urbanism, Reed cites his research interests as including 'the impact of ecological sciences on design thinking and city-making strategies informed by landscape systems and dynamics'. After receiving a Bachelor of Arts in Urban Studies from Harvard College, Reed went on to obtain a Master in Landscape Architecture from the University of Pennsylvania. He is currently the Associate Professor in the Practice of Landscape Architecture at Harvard University Graduate School of Design.

The Plaza at Harvard University in Cambridge, Massachusetts, built in 2013, 'is a constantly changing array of humanity and urban life', explains Reed, choosing it as one of his most recent projects in which to spend the day. Designed to become the university's new social hub, Reed believes 'it's a place for everyone, for people simply to do the things that people do'. Placed on top of a vehicular tunnel, adjacent to Harvard's historic Yard, the 'design articulates the space as a new kind of public infrastructure, an active threshold between the Yard and the North Campus'. Incorporating recycled materials and storm water infiltration, in line with the university's sustainable mission, the plaza features a 'distinct paver field' that is intermittently interrupted by clusters of sculptural benches. Constructed as a flexible space, the benches respond accordingly by providing various types of seating configurations, adjusting for performances, movies, skating rinks and art installations.

When asked where he takes his inspiration from and how it has informed his work, Reed's four-part response provides some insight into his hybridized approach to design. Reed believes that infrastructure extends across large scales and functions as a 'set of parts that are deployed according to operational parameters, and it can adjust to conditions on the ground', while ecology – adaptive and dynamic – works across various scales at the same time: 'ecosystems have the ability to shift states, to change outward appearances without ever losing their identity'. His final two 'inspirations' are the landscape architect Frederick Law Olmsted and American sociologist William Whyte. Reed considers the park systems of the former as 'far more than simple pleasure grounds, they were city-making projects that included transportation and hydrological infrastructures, habitat-making strategies and new recreational opportunities'. These spaces, Reed reiterates, 'framed out new urban districts, gave physical form and economic value to entirely new neighbourhoods'. Whyte, a

'recorder of human behaviour', is described by Reed as giving 'value to the simple desires of people in public space and how their curiosities and intuitive actions could inform design tuned to both the human body and collective use'.

The Erie Street Plaza in Milwaukee, Wisconsin, highlights the synthesis of Reed's design inspiration. This new waterfront plaza is a catalyst for public access along the Milwaukee Riverwalk. One in a series of public spaces to be created, this plaza is designed to be a flexible landscape which supports social and environmental life. Adhering to sustainable principles, the site recycles storm water runoff for use in the site's wetland and irrigates plants with river water. The plaza itself can adapt to variously scaled events, from large-scale celebrations, such as festivals and winter carnivals, to smaller functions including fishing and sunbathing.

In creating his designs, Reed gathers a group of specialists 'for each project, for each challenge'. Reed explains that 'It's important for us to find the very best folks working in their particular discipline, and to allow their expertise and insight to be put on the table right up front.' In developing their creative process, Reed and his team conduct extensive research, including site analytics and programme testing. In addition to using collaborators 'to get at critical issues', Stoss also 'look for opportunities, wastes and excess resources that might be redirected to more productive ends'. The key to their process is repetitive testing and refinement, enabling them to find connections between 'desires, needs and technical parameters'.

One such product of this process is Stoss's Trinity Riverfront in Dallas, Texas. It is a masterplan project that incorporates a series of lush and active landscapes that Reed describes as 'a kind of twenty-first century public garden, one that is as much about infrastructure and ecology as it is about creating incredibly sensuous spaces for people'. The proposal extends the natural systems of the Trinity River towards Dallas's downtown, providing new open space and habitats. The plan will shape new urban neighbourhoods while also creating a series of landscapes that sustainably transform a disconnected flood basin into a beautiful chain of parks and water gardens. These include water gardens with lush islands and floating cafés, water amphitheatres, playgrounds and wet forests, floodable sports courts and new wetland habitats.

Looking to the future, Reed would like landscape architects to take more of a 'proactive' role in the creation of projects, instead of simply 'responding' to briefs created by others. This 'curatorial' role would see landscape architects expanding their current remit of 'document delivery and contract administration' to include 'ongoing roles in the cultivation, maintenance, operations and evolution of projects'. Rather than simply acting as service providers, Reed believes 'we should be provocateurs, generators of ideas about the city and active participants in the unfolding lives of our projects and the people, plants and animals that interact in them'.

Chris Reed,
Stoss Landscape Urbanism
Boston, MA, USA

'Chris Reed has an astute analytical mind. Beyond the rhetoric, he is becoming an assured form giver and problem solver. He is poised to become one of the leaders of his generation.' George Hargreaves on Chris Reed

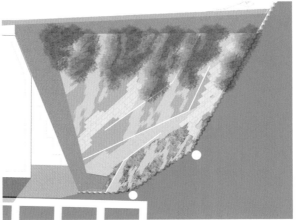

Chris Reed, Stoss Landscape Urbanism

Erie Street Plaza, Milwaukee, WI, USA (2010)

Located on the Milwaukee Riverwalk, this waterfront plaza creates a flexible social space that can accommodate large gatherings and daily activities. Built on sustainable design principles, the plaza utilizes storm water by collecting runoff to support a reconstituted marsh wetland, recharges the groundwater tables and uses river water for irrigation. Sculptural fibreglass pieces act both as seats and lighting elements.

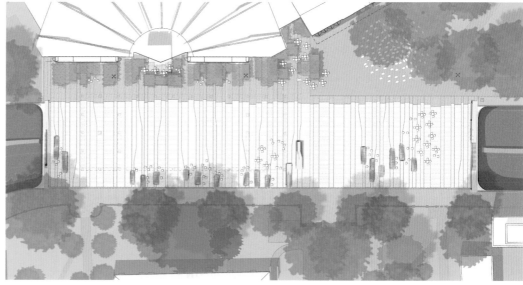

Chris Reed, Stoss Landscape Urbanism

<u>The Plaza at Harvard University</u>, Cambridge, MA, USA (2013)

Designed to become a new social hub and a meeting place, this plaza sits atop a vehicular tunnel, adjacent to Harvard's historic Yard. A distinct paving pattern extends across the tunnel cap, intermittently interrupted by clusters of sculptural benches. These benches accommodate people's bodies in various ways, and aggregate differently, creating a flexible space for a range of gathering situations.

Trinity Riverfront, Dallas, TX, USA (2018)

This masterplan proposes a new green infrastructure of water woven into urban grids, transportation corridors and highway infrastructure. Revitalized through a series of sustainable transformations, the central Old River is transformed from a disconnected flood basin into a series of parks and water gardens. New public amenities will offer opportunities to experience the river in a new way.

Mikyoung Kim,
Mikyoung Kim Design
Boston, MA, USA

Over the last twenty years, Mikyoung Kim and her firm have developed an exceptional collection of projects spanning across a wide range of landscape typologies around the world. Prior to studying landscape architecture at Harvard Graduate School of Design, Kim received her Bachelor of Arts from Oberlin College and Conservatory (where she also trained as a concert pianist), majoring in sculpture and art history. Drawing from her diverse background, Kim has developed an animated design aesthetic that merges her interests in art, landscape and performance. Since 1994, Kim's work has been focused on creating sustainably driven, family-orientated spaces that engage hydrologic elements in thought-provoking ways. Her culturally significant designs have become well known for their ability to both improve well-being and invigorate the public realm.

Armed with the knowledge that 'the natural world regulates the systems of our bodies, including electrical circuitry, brain function and blood flow', Kim explains that 'the natural world engages us on a multisensory level and can return balance to our inner psychological well-being'. As we experience her landscapes through touch, hearing, sight and smell, her works stimulate natural responses and inner healing. Kim's Downtown Plaza at 140 West – *Exhale* in Chapel Hill, North Carolina achieves this through a sculptural fog-fountain centrepiece that both symbolizes, and playfully recreates, the hydrologic cycle through the evaporation and condensation of water. Colourfully lit at night, water vapour escapes through the sculpture's perforated surface, cooling the surrounding air and invigorating spectators with an enchanting demonstration of water's transitional nature.

Much of Kim's own inspiration comes from equally sensorial places in the 'everyday world', such as 'a dress designed by Isabel Toledo, hearing a new interpretation of the *Goldberg Variations* by Bach or seeing a Piero della Francesca painting'. Experiencing synaesthesia, a neurological phenomenon whereby one sensory experience causes the involuntary or automatic reaction of another sense, Kim sees colours when listening to the *Goldberg Variations*. However, she explains that 'innovation does not just come from a linear process of collecting facts and figures and solving a design problem, but also comes from inspirations that transform the design into something remarkable. Most importantly, inspiration comes from the community and the landscape itself.'
'We are always designing and evolving our work from the conceptual phase all the way through construction,' Kim explains. 'We are very lucky that we have clients who support this process by building full-scale mock-ups so that we can understand the

materials and scale most effectively.' With a background in sculpture it comes as no surprise that Kim works on her projects three-dimensionally, and she explains that making hand and computer-generated models helps her 'understand the experience of the space. We often start by 3D printing a concept and then developing the idea through manual hand models and drawings and then going back to the computer once the concept is clear.' In a world where technology allows for a multitude of ways to explore concepts, Kim finds 'strengths and weaknesses' in all of them; manual processes tend to be quicker while computer programs offer 'long-term flexibility'. Made up of an eclectic mix of design disciplines, Kim's office takes a collaborative approach, which, she explains, 'allows for us to continue to develop fresh ideas as we [blur] the boundaries between landscape, art and architecture'. These collaborations go outside the office to include the client, architects and consultants such as fabricators and light engineers. Kim explains 'we work closely with our project team in order to develop a cohesive and successful project'.

A healing garden covering the eleventh floor of a new hospital building, the Ann & Robert H. Lurie Children's Hospital of Chicago – Crown Sky Garden, is an example of a project that unites Kim's flare for creating sensuous spaces within a highly sculptural setting. Here, interactive light and sound elements are incorporated into resin walls, locally reclaimed wood provides tactile sculptures for children to explore and sounds of nature are triggered by the children's interaction with the space. Curvaceous beds planted with bamboo define more secluded areas for quiet reflection or to survey the spectacular views of the surrounding city. In Kim's words, 'Our design for the Crown Sky Garden reminds me as a landscape architect [that] the power of design includes its ability to transform the body physiologically and offer the public a place of regeneration.'

When asked about the future of landscape architecture, Kim states: 'As a discipline, I think it's about regeneration, finding solutions that heal the body and mind while restoring the environment.' Unsurprisingly for someone who lists 'fog' as one of her favourite materials, Kim believes 'the future of the profession relies on a complex understanding of ourselves as multisensory beings, while alloying environmental imperatives with restorative processes, bringing rejuvenation and whimsy to our daily experience'.

Kim's response when asked about the most pressing issues facing landscape architects today is indicative of her atmospheric projects and her design philosophy: 'I think there are so many global issues that face landscape architects, from environmental sustainability to the pressures of population growth and green house gases; for me it is how the human physiological experience is impacted by all of these changes. How can the work that we do allow for the body to exhale?'

Favourite plants

1 Cinnamon fern
 (*Osmundastrum cinnamomeum*)
2 Maidenhair fern (*Adiantum*)
3 Mosses (phylum)
4 Onion (*Allium*) flower
5 Snow pea plant (*Pisum sativum*)
6 Dill (*Anethum graveolens*)

Favourite trees

1 Quaking aspen
 (*Populus tremuloides*)
2 Maidenhair (*Ginkgo biloba*)
3 Eucalyptus
4 Sweet gum
 (*Liquidambar styraciflua*)
5 American sycamore
 (*Platanus occidentalis*)

Favourite materials

1 Cast resin at least 50 millimetres
 (2 inches) thick
2 Fog
3 Glass
4 Bronze
5 Slabs of hardwood – such as teak
 and ironwood

Situated within a native hardwood forest overlooking Farrar Pond, this design harmonizes contemporary materials and design elements with native planting and the site's natural topography. The rich tapestry of plants transforms over the seasons, weaving seamlessly through the existing forest, while the sculptural fence flows over various surfaces to both define and blur boundaries.

Farrar Pond Residence - FlexFENCE, Lincoln, MA, USA (2007)

This project offers a new paradigm for health-care design that integrates healing gardens as part of the health-care regime. The centre of the garden houses interactive elements of light and sound in resin walls and reclaimed wood play sculptures. Along the garden's perimeter, bamboo and marble fountains frame more contemplative spaces to view the surrounding city.

Downtown Plaza at 140 West – *Exhale*, Chapel Hill, NC, USA (2013)

This plaza's design represents the dispersion and evaporation of water, expressing the environment's hydrologic cycles. The plaza's central sculptural fog fountain transforms water into a fog-like state, emitting its vapour from its perforated sides. Both cooling the amenity space and creating an ephemeral backdrop, the sculpture transforms the plaza with movement, colour and luminosity, engaging the public day and night.

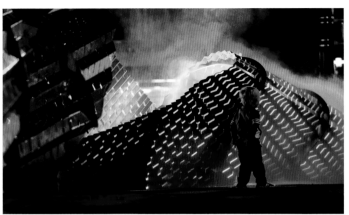

This arrival plaza for the adjacent Prudential retail and office tower features a series of stainless steel light columns. Wind vanes rotating on top of the light columns change colour in relation to the wind's intensity, highlighting the site's air currents. Wind turbines on top of the Prudential Tower power all of the plaza's lighting, demonstrating the sustainable nature of the project.

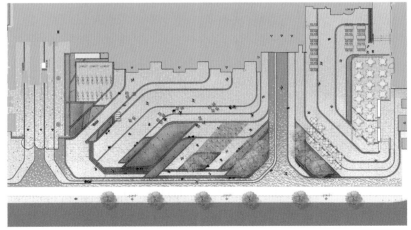

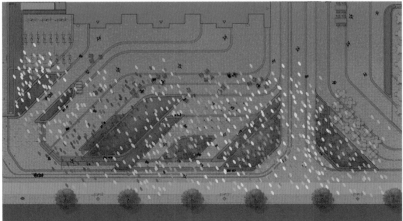

Graduating with distinction in both landscape architecture, from Harvard University, and architecture, from Southern California Institute of Architecture, Karen M'Closkey is well placed to create designs that focus on the potential of digital modelling, fabrication technologies and simulation in landscape. In 2004, she, together with her co-founder Keith VanDerSys established PEG office of landscape + architecture based in Philadelphia, Pennsylvania. Through new media and fabrication technologies, their work often utilizes pattern-finding and pattern-forming as a means to heighten the understanding and perception of temporal and ephemeral phenomena, winning numerous awards, including the 2010 Architectural League Prize for Young Architects and Designers. M'Closkey cites fashion designers and musicians among her favourite contemporary artists, and considering the rhythmical influence in these fields, it seems reasonable that much of the firm's inspiration comes from 'patterns found in nature'. For M'Closkey, 'patterns are both [the] expression and shaping influence of environmental processes and they can be an effective means for making such processes legible in our designed landscapes'. PEG's interest in 'artists and designers whose work deals with recursion, which involves precisely structured relationships to enable feedback between the design process and the resultant form' can clearly be seen in their highly visual designs.

Much of their work involves exploratory digital visualizations and installations. One such self-initiated project explores the customization of geotextile, a permeable material that can filter, separate and/or reinforce soil. Entitled Not Garden, a play on the traditional knot garden's pattern, the design realizes the potential of creating custom-made subsurface material to create cost-efficient, above-ground patterns. Here, the geotextile material was laser cut and laid to form patterns into which seeds were sown.

Although their more recent collaborations have been with architects, as their project focus changes to environmental modelling they will 'be collaborating more often with environmental and civil engineers in order to test the limits and presumptions of their models and ours'. Their design process involves both VanDerSys and M'Closkey discussing the project's objectives followed by gathering information and creating a project outline. 'We usually settle quickly on a direction so that the design has time to evolve through iterative analytic modelling, material testing, and organizational variations.' In the future they'd like to be able to take this process and, on smaller projects, collaborate with fashion designers or manufacturers for two reasons: 'one, because of the correlation between textiles and patterns; and the second is to rethink the use of common landscape materials that are woven (geotextiles, fences and so on)'.

Today's most pressing design issues, M'Closkey believes, are 'with resources, resource extraction and settlement patterns in response to resource availability'. The management of water and its uneven allocation is of primary concern. M'Closkey would like landscape architects to lead this 'conversation on urbanization and resilience', but insists that it should be led in a way not just 'simply to "solve" problems but to use our design imagination to provide multiple scenarios that provoke questions'. Commenting that landscape architects need to be familiar with 'the tools and measures used by other fields and interests', PEG's Edaphic Effects in Philadelphia 'explores customized substrates to develop alternatives to conventional on-site storm water collection'. With the use of parametric modelling and laser cutters, PEG developed a series of geocells, three-dimensional panels used for their reinforcement and protection properties. Currently limited because of their uniformity, PEG's bespoke geocells can be formed to various shapes and densities. 'This technique can be used to produce infiltration features that conjoin the functional requirement of water collection with an expressive surface that can add colour, pattern and texture to vacant sites.'

When asked about landscape architecture's future, M'Closkey sees the field as incredibly broad in the sense of scope and scale, 'so I do not think its future will be, or should be, single-focused'. However, M'Closkey feels that the one thing landscape architects should not lose the ability to do is 'to work relationally across scales'. Landscape architects need to simultaneously think about various types of information and create strategies 'that give spatial, formal and material resolution to such information'. M'Closkey believes one big change to how landscape architects will work will be due to the 'emergence of environmental and parametric modelling'. Moving beyond the traditional geographic information system (GIS) and 2D tools and 'into fluid and dynamic modelling and 3D topographic space' will allow for greater opportunities.

HB:BX Building Cultural Infrastructure, an ideas competition sponsored by Emerging New York Architects Committee, awarded PEG First Place for their design of the abandoned High Bridge aqueduct. Entitled Ripple Effect, their proposal redesigns the aqueduct's surroundings into a connected circuit of curving spaces. These 'infra-blooms' are collecting spaces for people, activities and water that intertwine art, recreation and environmental fluctuation. The infra-blooms gather and filter rainwater before it is eventually returned to the river via the aqueduct as an intermittent shower display. With a renewed purpose, the project effectively re-establishes the aqueduct's water-bearing identity. The project is in keeping with PEG's desire to apply the techniques they've developed to landscapes and materials. There is no doubt that their work reveals experimental, exploratory and imaginative proposals that address realistic problems in a very creative way.

Karen M'Closkey, PEG office of landscape + architecture Philadelphia, PA, USA

'I think Karen's work does what all firms should do: looking at ideas of environmental efficacy and sustainability through multiple lenses and scales. PEG's hybrid approach to design allows them to integrate landscape into architecture, infrastructure and geology in very interesting ways.'

Mikyoung Kim on Karen M'Closkey

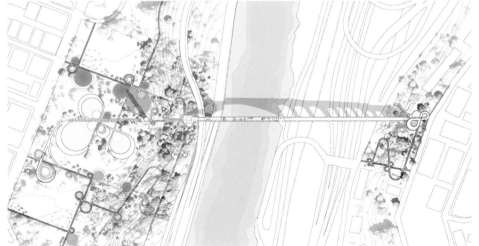

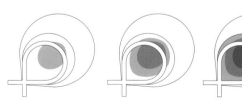

Karen M'Closkey, PEG office of landscape + architecture

Ripple Effect, New York, NY, USA (2010)

This competition-winning design transforms a historic aqueduct's surroundings into a sinuous circuit of infra-blooms that intertwine art, recreation and environmental fluctuation. In addition to defining spaces for people and activities, the infra-blooms collect and filter rainfall, channelling it through the aqueduct to the Harlem River, inverting the historic trend of creating isolated infrastructures that promote a disregard for local waterways.

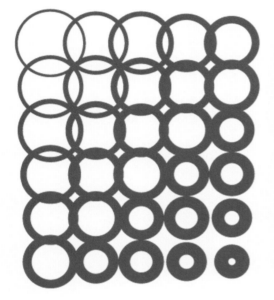

Karen M'Closkey, PEG office of landscape + architecture

Not Garden, Philadelphia, PA, USA (2009)

Installed on a vacant site in West Philadelphia, this project explores the potential for customizing materials below ground, which create planted surface patterns above ground. Inspired by the traditional knot garden's geometric pattern, laser cut geotextiles (weed control barriers) are placed on site and seeded. The technique illustrates the ability to create diverse compositions with minimal maintenance and installation costs.

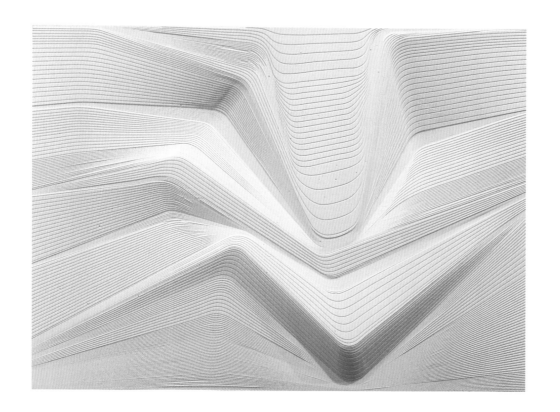

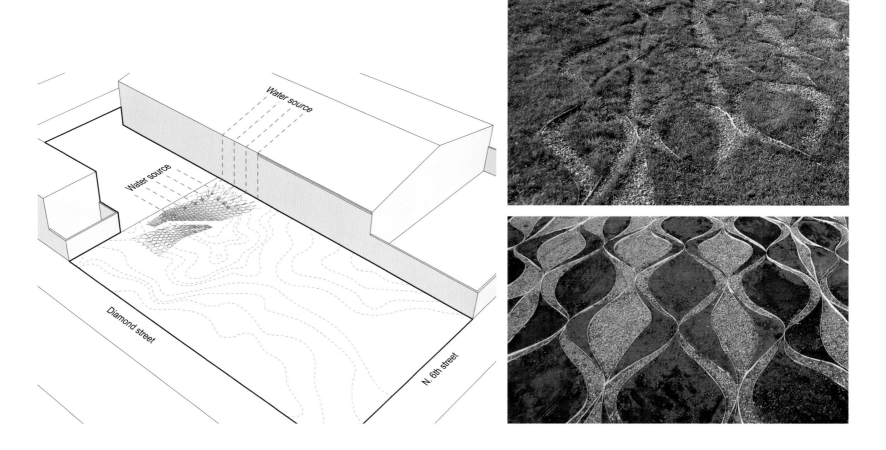

Edaphic Effects, Philadelphia, PA, USA (2011)

This project explores customized substrates to develop alternatives to conventional on-site storm water collection. By manipulating the form of geocells, a three-dimensional product used for reinforcement and protection, PEG created a system that offers a greater degree of variation in their cellular shape, density and profile. This allows for site-specific water collection and adds patterned surface texture.

Martin Knuijt, OKRA
Utrecht, The Netherlands

Since forming his studio, OKRA, Martin Knuijt has realized numerous successful projects and designs, including the competition-winning project Athens City Centre, expected to be completed in 2017. Central to his work is his belief that humankind understands and manipulates the landscape and that the landscape itself reacts to this intervention in fascinating and dynamic ways. The author of several publications, it is his experience with open spaces in inner cities and his understanding of the transformative qualities of both humans and nature that makes his works so successful.

Knuijt would like to see cities become more resilient, and at a time when more than half the world's population lives in city centres, he feels landscape architects should be 'providing good examples to transform cities into urban landscapes in harmony with natural resources, providing space for spiritual reflection. It starts from acknowledging the city's complexity and its relationship to the original landscape and from that point taking the step to true integrated design.' Believing that ideas of 'functionalism' have led to decades of monotonous building, Knuijt would like to see the creation of more meaningful spaces that are flexible enough to allow for future adaptations. In this way he prescribes that landscape architects should provide the framework in which designs can mature, evolve and accommodate change.

Interested in how, once manipulated by human intervention, 'The landscape reacts in a protracted process, revealing the force of vegetation, the wind or the sea', Knuijt explains that 'The tension between human intervention interacting with the dynamics and the force of nature stirs the imagination.' He cites Machu Picchu in Peru or the urban myths about the Hanging Gardens of Babylon as examples of how 'Things change, but something remains; they have vanished, but their impact is still there in our collective memory.' Design interventions also participate in the 'process of change', as designers 're-think the landscape or 're-invent the city'. For Knuijt, the city flows like a 'perpetual machine', but never in the same way. With this in mind, his designs 'fit into a scenography, suitable for daily, weekly and annual rhythm'.

The adaptability and vibrancy, both day and night, of OKRA's Storaa Stream Holstebro in Denmark illustrates Knuijt's passion to create experiential landscapes that meet the needs of many. This public realm project has made a major difference to the city of Holstebro, connecting the north and south sides of the city centre together by a unifying bridge that has been turned into a central focal point that ties the 'folded urban realm of both riverbanks together'. The topographically low position of the river has allowed its banks to be transformed into a sculptural multiuse space, made continuous through a series of 'foldings', at times revealed as paths, other times as areas to sit and immerse oneself in the landscape. Along the south bank, a theatre has been created with amphitheatre-style steps for seating, and a programme of dynamic lighting plays an important role in positively reinforcing the space's playful and theatrical public use.

Knuijt looks to 'cohabitation of green and blue' as a key to creating better cities of the future. He suggests 'we could think of the creation of an "urban water machine" by involving water in the public realm, or bringing it back where it has disappeared'. Indeed, reflecting on metropolitan growth in the past decades, Knuijt would like to see a coherent water system in urban landscapes. This entails the retention and redistribution of on-site water and thus regenerating the 'urban water machine', which he feels is 'key to a contemporary and healthy relationship between man and nature'. To address this, he advocates the creation of 'a basic sustainable spatial framework … upgrading and connecting larger green and water structures, and linking those blue-green structures within the city and within its neighbourhoods'. This link between the water system and the built environment would help to re-introduce clean water in 'normal doses' to rivers and eventually the sea. 'Innovation over the next decades is about improving connections between the city system and its surrounding landscape', Knuijt explains, believing that, 'The creation of sustainable cities today leads to interesting cities of tomorrow.' Connecting the natural with the urban, combined with efficient transportation systems, creates a framework for sustainable development.

His competition-winning project for the redesign of Athens city centre is destined to reinvent a city and regenerate the public realm. In this way he will create a safer and healthier environment, featuring three characteristic places: Omonia Square and Dikaiosynis Square, both of which will become green, urban squares with prominent water elements, and in the middle, Panepistimou Street, which will be transformed into the city's central green spine, providing shade and shelter. The resilient strategy includes specific attitudes towards reducing urban heat and improving thermal comfort. A 'greening' strategy for Athens is combined with a water strategy, as well-maintained plants will enhance overall heat reduction. The green framework will be treated as a coherent network of the public realm, linking together the adjacent neighbourhoods. Restoration of the nodes at street crossings will create continuity in the walking experience, while demarking the new tramline contributes to cohesion. This project aims to transform Athens into a resilient, accessible and vibrant city.

Favourite plants

1 Feather reed-grass 'Karl Foerster' (*Calamagrostis x acutiflora* 'Karl Foerster')
2 Blue fescue (*Festuca glauca*)
3 Burnet (*Sanguisorba officinalis* 'Red Thunder')
4 Baker's larkspur (*Delphinium bakeri*)
5 American blue vervain (*Verbena hastate*)

Favourite trees

1 Black locust (*Robinia pseudoacacia*)
2 Pagoda (*Sophora japonica*)
3 Honey locust (*Gleditsia triacanthos*)
4 Sweet gum (*Liquidambar styraciflua*)
5 English oak (*Quercus robur*)

Favourite natural landscape

Salar de Uyuni, Bolivia

Cutty Sark Gardens, London, England, UK (2009)

Designed to provide easy access over different levels, these gardens offer maximum flexibility to hold variously scaled events. Improving connection to the surrounding urban environment, the design allows people to experience a sequence of atmospheric landscapes, including a raised plaza and accompanying linear water feature, the square around the *Cutty Sark*, the gardens and the River Thames walkway.

Storaa Stream Holstebro, Holstebro, Denmark (2009)

This public realm project connects the north and south sides together through a new sculptural bridge. Taking advantage of the river's low-lying position, a series of multiuse spaces has been created along the riverbanks, including amphitheatre seating, paths and seating areas. Together with the bridge, these elements fold inwards and outwards throughout the site, dramatically enhanced by night-time lighting.

As the first intervention into this square's transformation, this design demarcates a Roman fort (castellum) sitting 4 metres (13 feet) below ground, indicating the boundary of the future square. Marked with Cor-Ten steel elements at street level, the line sits directly above the original wall below and mirrors its width, while light and mist emanate from its void.

Athens City Centre, Athens, Greece (2017)

This design transforms Athens city centre into a coherent network of public realm spaces, featuring three characteristic places, two of which, Omonia Square and Dikaiosynis Square will become urban squares with prominent water features; the third, Panepistimou Street, will be transformed into the city's central green spine. A green network will improve links to adjacent neighbourhoods and strengthen intercity connections.

Favourite plant
Powerplant

Favourite material
Concrete

Favourite design tools
1 Pen and pencil
2 Knife
3 Cardboard
4 Clay
5 3D printing
6 Paint
7 Computer

Favourite sound
F–15E Strike Eagle

Inspiration
1 Film director David Lynch
2 Berlin nightclub Berghain
3 Industrial metal band Rammstein
4 Photographer Anton Corbijn
5 German electronic band Kraftwerk
6 Dutch footballer Johan Cruijff

A graduate in landscape architecture from the Academy of Architecture, Amsterdam, Ronald Rietveld went on to win the Prix de Rome Architecture in 2006. That same year Rietveld founded his firm, RAAAF [Rietveld Architecture-Art-Affordances], together with philosopher Erik Rietveld. Their respective backgrounds inform the creation of RAAAF's site-specific work, which has developed their unique design approach of 'strategy interventions'.

More recently, RAAAF was the curator of *Vacant NL* in the Dutch Pavilion for the 12th Venice Architecture Biennale in 2010. The installation demonstrated the potential of 10,000 governmentally owned vacant buildings, opening up discussions concerning innovative reuse. In 2013 RAAAF was elected Dutch Architect of the Year and has exhibited international installations in numerous exhibitions around the globe, including Museum Boijmans Van Beuningen in Rotterdam, The Netherlands, and at the São Paulo Biennial in Brazil.

His radical designs can perhaps best be summed up in his project entitled Bunker 599 which 'unorthodoxly questions' policies on cultural heritage. The project slices open a seemingly indestructible bunker of 'monumental status' to reveal its minuscule interior, normally completely out of sight. Running down the centre of the bunker and into the surrounding water, a long boardwalk slices through the gap between the two halves of the cleanly cut bunker giving people a view of their surroundings from a different perspective. Designed together with Atelier de Lyon, the project opens up secrets of the New Dutch Waterline – the bunker's interior and the fact that these were used as a military line of defence by means of intentional flooding.

Landscape architect Ronald and philosopher Erik, together with the architect Arna Mackic, form RAAAF's core team whose projects offer dramatic new perspectives from which to experience the every day. Naming film director David Lynch as a typical source of their inspiration, their work is complete with a theatrical tension set within an expressive landscape. Their design process comprises research compiled in collaboration with multidisciplinary teams, consisting of scientists and other specialists, which progresses to form concise concepts, evocative imagery and visualizations and thought-provoking schemes.

In talking about his design process, Ronald explains that it is a complex process of 'strategy intervention', as outlined in their book, *Vacancy Studies – Experiments and Strategic Interventions in Architecture*. A combination of 'intuition and narrative with analytics', their process very much starts with their 'own fascinations,' Ronald states, adding that while this may appear obvious, '... all too often, new designs are based on other people's fascinations or on existing architectural references, creating an obstacle to the development of genuinely new perspectives'. Their work tends to be site-specific and their 'fascinations and ambitions' inform their designs – in material ways, such as the 6-metre (19-foot 8-inch) thick wall of Bunker 599, or 'invisible phenomena', as seen in the Dutch Pavilion in Venice.

When asked for their predictions regarding the future of landscape architecture, RAAAF respond that 'We don't predict. We just try to build futures.' Their Fort Werk aan het Spoel project located in The Netherlands, in fact takes an historic 1794 national monument from the past and energetically transforms it into the future 'without historicizing it'. Completed in 2011, with Gent & Monk Architects for the Fort House and Atelier de Lyon, the project is formed as a large grass sculpture encapsulating new and historic features, including bunkers, bombproof buildings, old inundation locks, the new Fort House and an amphitheatre. The Fort's design includes stairs inset into terraced banks, expansive lawns, trees and movable furniture. The Fort hosts a multitude of local and regional activities and has become one of the major attractions in the New Dutch Waterline.

Winner of the Prix de Rome Architecture Prize in 2006, RAAAF's Generating Dune Scapes has been exhibited around the world and illustrates an ambitious, 'yet realistic', plan for a hot springs in the IJmuiden, a port city located 27.5 kilometres (17 miles) west of Amsterdam. This project aims to harness the opportunities offered by natural forces, urban development and Kennemerduinen (a national park) to make an incredible urban dune landscape. Setting the hot spring within the 'apocalyptic décor' of the steel industry and the Kennemerduinen, the existing mineral-rich dune water will be heated by re-using industrial heat. The 'landscape of paradoxes' will allow visitors to enjoy the dune scape from the confines of a hot spring within a steaming bunker while looking out at protected bird species set against a backdrop of supertankers and cruise ships. The new evocative landscape will command novel forms of urban planning and spectacular architectural design.

Working across numerous mediums (Ronald uses pens, pencils, knives, cardboard, clay, 3D printing, paint and computers to design) and disciplines, RAAAF's work is experimental within the fields of design, science and art, and aims to create hauntingly inspiring projects.

Ronald Rietveld, RAAAF [Rietveld Architecture-Art-Affordances] Amsterdam, The Netherlands

'Ronald is one of the most intriguing contemporary landscape architects today. He's a master in making statements that make us look at reality differently, changing our environment with interventions that blur landscape architecture, philosophy, architecture and art seamlessly together.' Martin Knuijt on Ronald Rietveld

Bunker 599, Diefdijk 5 – Highway A2, The Netherlands (2010)

The project exposes two secrets of the New Dutch Waterline: a military line of defence in use from 1815 until 1940, protecting cities by means of intentional flooding, and the insides of one of 700 bunkers. Sliced in half to reveal its minuscule interior, normally completely concealed, the bunker's linear line is extended into the water via a long boardwalk.

Ronald Rietveld, RAAAF [Rietveld Architecture-Art-Affordances]

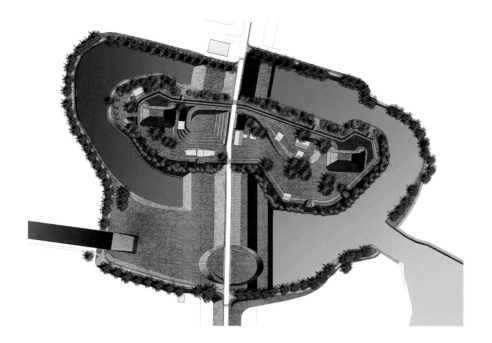

Ronald Rietveld, RAAAF [Rietveld Architecture-Art-Affordances]

Fort Werk aan het Spoel, Lek dike, Culemborg, The Netherlands (2011)

This new fort can be understood as an enormous grass sculpture integrating both new and historical elements such as the bunkers, bombproof buildings, old inundation locks, the new Fort House and an amphitheatre. The design takes its inspiration from the fort's past and creates a landscape for a wide variety of local and regional activities.

Generating Dune Scapes, IJmuiden, The Netherlands (2030)

This project plans to make the most of the opportunities offered by its location next to Kennemerduinen (a national park) and its urban setting. Hot springs, made from existing mineral-rich dune water and heated re-using industrial heat, will be set within the décor of the Hoogovens (steel industry). Visitors will have the paradoxical view of protected bird species and passing ships.

Tilman Latz,
Latz+Partner
Kranzberg, Germany

An architect, landscape architect and urban planner, Tilman Latz is the head of the firm Latz+Partner, originally founded by his parents Peter and Anneliese Latz in 1968. The firm is internationally recognized for their projects involving the conversion of post-industrial landscapes, including the celebrated Park Duisburg Nord in the Ruhr region of Germany. A guest lecturer and critic at universities worldwide, in his own work Latz maintains ecological urban redevelopment as a focus. His interest in the continued history of a site, both culturally and physically informs much of his practice, together with the socio-political potential of combined planning strategies.

'Inspiration comes mostly from being curious enough to really detect the many phenomena of a given site,' Latz explains, 'sometimes it is just a colour of some material or the odour of a certain moment, a tone or the movement of people, which can lead our thoughts and inform our approaches.' With Place Flagey, a large city plaza in Belgium completed in 2009, structure and colour informed its overall design and symbolically referenced the plaza's history. 'It is a thrilling experience to transform the traditions of a place, often called characteristics or history, into the structural basis of a project,' Latz states. However, this doesn't stop at the completion of construction – his projects are designed to evolve. As he explains, 'we love dealing with the weathering of materials and the ageing of a site (and its inhabitants) over time and to introduce that as a vital part of a project'. At Place Flagey his design integrated existing infrastructure, like the tram and underground entrances, and established links with the neighbouring park and adjacent public services. A new water feature, blue granite stone paving, lighting and informally planted trees establish the plaza's character and programme, while sinuous benches offer a reprieve from busy urban lives.

Through Latz's design process, once a site's phenomena have been identified, this information is then evaluated with regard to the potential for enriching a project's 'future characteristics'. A spatial matrix, based on a specific, or sometimes speculative programme, is then overlaid on the site. From here, he reveals, 'forms evolve intuitively'. This process is a team effort, as ideas are shared, discarded, strengthened and integrated. Regarding collaborations, Latz states that they 'collaborate with people we are interested in, whether their office is big or small, famous or relatively unknown, what counts is that we like and respect each other's work and personalities, have a really fruitful working relationship and have a bit of fun together since we only live once'.

With Parco Dora in Turin, northwest Italy, Latz+Partner created a stunning park that sympathetically responds to the site's industrial remains. In this case, the park has been divided into five separate areas with different functional uses and aesthetic qualities based on the quality of the industrial relics. Bridges, stairs and ramps connect the different parts of the park to each other and with the surrounding quarters. Parco Dora is an idiosyncratic example of Latz+Partner's compelling work, and when asked how he'd like to influence future generations of landscape architects, Latz responds: 'We live in a manmade environment, a complex topography of differences. Everything within that landscape represents narratives of common and individual cultural development, creation and destruction. I believe strongly that trying to understand the complexities of our cultural landscapes and societies, its technologies, its deeper sense and meanings, enables us landscape architects to really interact in a sustainable and successful way.'

Explaining that we inhabit a 'fragmented landscape full of mono-functional inhuman infrastructure and meaningless [short lived] spaces', something he sees as an unfortunate part of modern life, Latz states that his designs very much aim to 'humanize' infrastructures, re-fragment and make use of all those 'unused and neglected spaces', creating landscapes that are resilient and universally accessible. It is within this remit that, Latz believes, landscape architects are responsible for making relevant contributions to society. Moreover, if landscape architects 'extend their fields of operation beyond the classic boundaries of [their] profession, if we integrate all landscapes into our perspective, whether they are urban, green, industrial, natural and artificial or any other ... our profession will become more diverse, covering a multitude of different fields of action'. Latz sees the future of landscape architecture as providing 'an interface somewhere between architecture, infrastructure, nature (and its forces) and the people we're working for', a situation that should enhance landscape architects' ability to creatively design and manage complex urban landscapes.

Latz+Partner's Park Ariel Sharon in Tel Aviv, will convert a former landfill site and surrounding Ayalon floodplain into a 550-hectare (1,359-acre) park destined to make a significant impact. Partially built on a 60-metre (197-foot) high mountain of garbage, the park has overcome all negative aspects of its 'site' to create a dynamic landscape which will offer stunning recreational areas and panoramic views of Tel Aviv. The park will include an extensive path network, recreational areas, terraces, kiosks and a lake. According to Latz, 'After the Park Duisburg Nord, [this] might become our next major contribution for the international debate on our modern world and the history of landscape architecture.'

Favourite colour combination

'All shades of grey with one other colour, like red, yellow, blue, green or black.'

Favourite trees

1 Pine (*Pinus*)
2 Maple (*Acer*)
3 Oak (*Quercus*)
4 Aspen (*Populus*)
5 Plane (*Platanus*)

Favourite materials

1 Oak wood
2 Lava
3 Steel
4 Limestone
5 Concrete

Inspiration

1 Author Italo Calvino
2 Landscape architect Gustav Lange
3 Artist Ian Hamilton Finlay
4 Architect Françoise Hélène Jourda
5 Architect Peter Zumthor
6 Landscape architect Roberto Burle Marx

Place Flagey, Brussels, Belgium (2009)
Located above an underground garage, this city plaza's redesign includes fountains, trees, benches and blue granite paving. The design integrates traffic routes surrounding the plaza and forms connections to the adjacent spaces and parks. The use of one material provides consistency and enlarges the plaza's dimensions, while lighting and bespoke furniture frame the plaza as an area for special events.

From Turin's largest intra-urban industrial wasteland emerges a park characterized by its industrial past and spatially defined by the river Dora, main traffic arteries and residential quarters. The park has five separate areas, each with different functions and aesthetics based on the quality of the industrial remains. Bridges, stairs and ramps connect the five areas and surrounding quarters together.

This restructuring of the historic harbour area between the Weser River and the city centre reconnects the town with the waterfront landscape. With this upgrade, the Weser Dyke has become one of the city's most frequented and enjoyed spaces, necessary engineering features, like the pictured wave breakers, incorporate benches facing the midday sun and river.

Constructed on a former agricultural land, including a 60-metre (197-foot) high mountain of garbage, this park design transforms the Ayalon floodplain into a new public park. At the centre of the parkland The Wide Wild Wadi will serve as a large retention basin. A 'ring' infrastructure, incorporating promenades, kiosks, seating, planted terraces and lighting, will define The Human Corridor.

Favourite plants and trees

'Twisted trees, neglected species and weeds.'

1 Sangregado (*Croton funckianus*)
2 Arrayán sabanero (*Myrcianthes leucoxyla*)
3 Cecropia (*Cecropia telenitida*)
4 Encenillo (*Weinmannia tomentosa*)
5 Naranjillo (*Styloceras laurifolium*)
6 Angel's trumpet (*Brugmansia sanguinea*)
7 Rodamontes (*Escallonia myrtilloides*)

Favourite materials

'Materials that age with beauty.'

Favourite contemporary artists

1 Willem de Kooning
2 Alejandro Obregón
3 Juan Gris
4 Santiago Cardenas
5 Antoni Tàpies
6 Jean-Michel Basquiat

Practising landscape architecture in Bogotá, Colombia, Diana Wiesner's work seeks to integrate culturally based place-making with community participation in order to advance the health and well-being of both humans and ecosystems at local, regional and global scales. Her projects, working across the theme of urban ecology within public spaces, have won numerous awards and distinctions, including the World Landscape Art Exposition Prize in Jinzhou, Liaoning Province, China, in 2013.

At Julio Mario Santo Domingo Cultural Center, Wiesner's personal selection of one of her parks in which she would choose to spend the day, Wiesner designed a space that breaks away from the traditional rules and guidelines required for the public realm in Bogotá. This includes proposing permeable recycled paving, which allows rainwater runoff to be absorbed back into the land. These paving materials include crushed brick, providing texture and colour to the park, and permeable blocks in which plants can grow. The park uses a colourful planting palette that, together with the park's unique paving, forms a distinctive pattern that creates spaces for individuals to reflect and areas for larger groups to gather. The landscape continues up the slope over the roof of the Cultural Centre Bogotá's most important concert hall, creating a dynamic arrival space. The plant material on the roof helps insulate the building from sound pollution as well as reducing heat loss and gain, allowing the interior to function without the need for air conditioning. The park's striking patterned paving and planting arrangement, together with the vibrantly coloured crushed red brick are offset by a backdrop of luscious planting, giving this park a strong aesthetic, one which celebrates this Cultural Center's dynamic purpose.

When asked about her inspiration, Wiesner reiterates her design principles of 'urban ecology' and, more importantly, cultural needs. She explains that inspiration is not the focus, but rather 'careful work to understand the location and needs of the people involved', and these principles are clearly present in her work on the Cultural Center. Her creative process begins with the 'place and people' in which the site is set. By listening to both the community's needs and the 'poetry of the place', Wiesner builds a concept that evolves through collaborations with others to create solutions that meet the site's 'functional and technical requirements' while still representing her poetic and ecological design aims.

These collaborations, with professionals from various disciplines including ecologists, planners, biologists, hydrologists and environmentalists, are undertaken in order to generate comprehensive designs with an articulate and sensitive social and ecological solution that suits the needs of each project. The collaborations are coupled with research into the relationships between the site's society, geography and natural environment.

Located in Jinzhou, Liaoning Province, China, Droplet Park highlights this exploration of a poetic landscape that offers one and all the chance to explore the 'state of childhood' while experiencing a diverse and experiential park. The project is a competition-winning design that saw the creation of a landscape representing, and inspired by, the topography of a droplet of water in the form of the diverse valleys and peaks of the Colombian and Andean landscapes. The labyrinthine landscape harnesses the 'rhythmic, silent and harmonious movement' of a mountain landscape that evolves as you walk through the park, offering an element of surprise throughout. Wood, rope, metal and stone come together to create an active structure in which the planting selection, which includes species that are native to China but have connections to Colombian landscapes, accentuate the topographical nature of the designed forms. Elsewhere, playful climbing walls, curving steps and a web of rope create an exploratory setting for adventure and play.

Wiesner sees the future of landscape architecture as 'one of the most relevant professions to focus sustainable proposals [which] are sensitive [to] people and nature', and her work in Colombia very much represents Wiesner's mission to promote responsible development. As a director of the non-profit foundation Cerros de Bogotá, she hopes to work together with the community to sustainably develop the area in the hills to the east of Bogotá. The foundation's role is to work together with the community to create initiatives that will restore the foothills in a socially and ecologically responsible manner.

Wiesner's own project, Corredor Ecológico y Recreativo de los Cerros Orientales, situated over 415 hectares (1,025 acres) in the foothills and the city, is set to create a sustainable development that will restore the ecology of the landscape while allowing the community to explore, relax and enjoy the surrounding foothills. Wiesner believes that future landscape architects should remember that they are 'part of a group' and that they can 'change things proactively, poetically and [in a] socially sensitive manner'. However, she also insists that this is a shared responsibility, explaining that better and more resilient cities of the future will rely on all citizens applying 'good ethics with each other, and with the land'.

Diana Wiesner,
Diana Wiesner Arquitectura y Paisaje
Bogotá, Colombia

'Diana's wide range of highly interesting projects, covering all aspects of landscape architecture, and her outstanding ability to dive into South America's varying geographical, social and economic contexts, makes her one of the most interesting personalities in the design world.' Tilman Latz on Diana Wiesner

Diana Wiesner, Diana Wiesner Arquitectura y Paisaje

Droplet Park, Jinzhou, Liaoning Province, China (2013)

This park's design is represented, and inspired, by the topography of a droplet of water in the form of the diverse valleys and peaks of the Colombian and Andean landscapes. The design evokes mountain treks as visitors travel through the varied terrain. Planted terraced landscapes, defined by wood, rope and metal, accentuate the site's topographical nature.

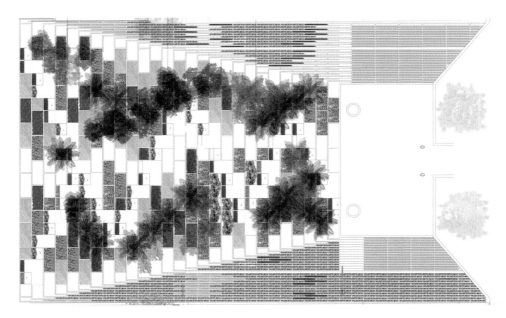

Diana Wiesner, Diana Wiesner Arquitectura y Paisaje

Julio Mario Santo Domingo Cultural Center, Bogotá, Colombia (2010)

This plaza breaks away from Bogotá's traditional planning regulations and uses permeable paving materials, such as crushed red brick and porous pavers, to add texture and colour. The sustainable selection of materials and plants creates diverse meeting areas, while the Center's concert hall features planted roof terraces, providing a unique backdrop to the gardens.

Perry Lethlean, Taylor Cullity Lethlean Melbourne, VIC, Australia

'To be part of the discipline of landscape architecture is in some ways a gift,' Perry Lethlean believes, adding that working with 'inspiring collaborators' to create new urban spaces, waterfronts and gardens 'is a great privilege'. A highly recognized urban and landscape designer, Lethlean has been widely published and his celebrated works include the Australian Garden in Cranbourne, VIC and the National Arboretum in Canberra, ACT, both winning the World Architecture Festival's Landscape of the Year award in 2013 and 2014, and the Auckland Waterfront redevelopment in New Zealand, which was awarded the prestigious Rosa Barba Landscape Prize in 2014. His skills in urban design, at both the large masterplanning and detailed design scales, makes him a valuable asset on any projects he develops. Lethlean is widely respected as a lecturer, critic and as a juror for professional practice awards and advisory design bodies.

Completed in 2012, Taylor Cullity Lethlean's Australian Garden created a major new contribution for the Royal Botanic Gardens at Cranbourne on the southeastern outskirts of Melbourne, VIC. The garden takes visitors on a metaphorical journey through the Australian landscape and offers a modern approach to addressing environmental and cultural issues. The new garden experience aims to focus visitors' attention on the unique qualities of Australian plants and stimulate further cultural interest. A common theme throughout the garden's design is the Australian people's ongoing relationship with the landscape. However, while the garden illustrates the tension that exists between the natural landscape and the desire to manipulate it, this tension is presented as the necessary driving force for creativity. Here, Taylor Cullity Lethlean uses water as the physical and symbolic mediating element between the natural and manipulated gardens.

Lethlean's influences are 'a constant companion' to his design process, he explains. 'They are many and varied, including the large coal mine in the Latrobe valley,' where his father worked, 'which, to my young naive eyes, manipulated the landscape on an impressively grand scale ... later the more compositionally inspired work of Le Nôtre similarly demonstrated the audacity of human imagination.' Added to the 'many and varied' inspirations is his time spent in Kyoto where he enjoyed the 'artistry of the small scale' and appreciated the ability to convey 'vast distances and an evocative narrative in diminutive spaces'. But for Lethlean, design is 'both a personal and collaborative act', and believing that collaborations with talented creatives enable a project to really come to life, he commends 'the late [urban designer] Kevin

Taylor for his holistic understanding of site and its culture, [landscape architect] Kate Cullity for her detailed artistry, [plant specialist] Paul Thompson for his creative use of Australian flora and artists like Robert Owen who bring a surprising and lateral viewpoint on many a creative issue'.

In fact, Lethlean feels that collaboration is 'one of the most enjoyable components of practice'. Within his own studio he has categorized collaborations in four ways: lateral thinking – where he tries to open up the space in between practice, skills and disciplines, thus fostering lateral thinking and unexpected outcomes; blurred disciplines – 'where a creative from an adjacent design discipline takes our landscape architecture world [in an unexpected direction]'; same but different – where collaboration with another landscape architect offers insight into a design that is different to your own; and transformation – where other people from outside the landscape world, such as artisan builders, 'transform an idea beyond our expectations'.

Reflecting on today's most pressing design issues, Lethlean explains that 'Our humble and collective ambition is to foster ... a window into our humanity, simply by reminding us all that we are not all there is to life.' Lethlean embeds issues of water scarcity, sustainability and plant vulnerability within his design process in order to, in his words, 'reveal, educate and inspire many in the beauty of our natural forms and landscapes'. Developed following the devastating fires in 2003, his firm's outstanding work on Canberra National Arboretum and its accompanying Pod Playground illustrates the results of such a design process. The project's vision aims to create a public destination over the next century. Its masterplan is centred on the creation of 100 forests highlighting the world's most endangered tree species. According to Lethlean, this project is 'grown out of the very real issues of sustainability, biodiversity and public environmental concern, the 100 Forests project not only offers a unique experience of being enveloped in a majestic forest of one tree species, but also provides seed banks for the future'. Included in the project is the Pod Playground – created for children and families, this dynamic landscape takes inspiration from the forest's early beginnings to create a fantasy world of enlarged acorns, seeds and cones.

When asked about landscape architecture's future, Lethlean sees a profession with 'design leadership, choreographing diverse disciplines to create truly integrated outcomes encompassing architecture, ecology, infrastructure and artistic practice'. But most importantly, Lethlean believes, 'We must find a means to permeate our world with a sense of hope and humanity. Creating spaces and environments that are sustainably driven is admirable. Capturing the hearts and emotions of those that inhabit them will be the more tangible measure of success.'

Favourite plants

1 Grey cottonheads
   (*Conostylis candicans*)
2 One-sided bottlebrush
   (*Calothamnus quadrifidus*)
3 Granite claw flower
   (*Calothamnus graniticus*)
4 Hairpin banksia
   (*Banksia spinulosa*)
5 Silky eremophila
   (*Eremophila nivea*)

Favourite trees

1 Pink iron bark
   (*Eucalyptus sideroxylon*)
2 Lemon-scented eucalyptus
   (*Eucalyptus citriodora*)
3 Small bull oak
   (*Allocasuarina striata*)
4 Hoop pine
   (*Araucaria cunninghamii*)
5 Morton Bay fig
   (*Ficus macrophylla*)

Favourite sound

Cicadas

Canberra National Arboretum and Pod Playground, Canberra, ACT, Australia (2013)

Developed in collaboration with Tonkin Zulaikha Greer Architects following the 2003 Canberra bushfires, this project addresses issues of sustainability, biodiversity and environmental concern. The masterplan creates 100 forests using the world's most endangered tree species, providing visitors with an incredible forest experience. Situated within the project, the Pod Playground allows families to explore cones, acorns and seeds of giant proportions.

Auckland Waterfront: North Wharf Promenade and Silo Park, Auckland,
New Zealand (2011)

Created in collaboration with Wraight+Associates, this project transforms a
former industrial and maritime district into a mixed-use precinct. By interpreting
the site's distinct archaeology of patterns and materiality, the design retains and
enhances the former maritime industries to create new public experiences. Silo
Park is a layered public space that facilitates a range of uses, from recreational
to event areas.

This botanic garden, designed in collaboration with Paul Thompson, sets the stage for visitors to explore Australian flora while inspiring them to learn more about their relationship with the Australian landscape. Rather than eliminating the tension between the natural landscape and our impulse to change it, this project uses it as a driving creative impulse for the discovery, expression and perception of the land and its endemic plant species.

Favourite plants

'Plants that are local to the site, as they always tell a very unique and compelling story about the place and the ecology.'

Favourite trees

'Australian trees that have evolved into unique and characterful species that grow in the shape that best suits them in spite of the poor, nutrient-deficient soils.'

Favourite materials

'Materials that activate the senses and have a warmth and tactility when touched, including timber, stone and vegetation.'

Inspiration

'All the people who inhabit public space in such deliriously exciting, wonderfully interesting and continuously unexpected ways.'

Christopher Sawyer forms one half of the firm Site Office. Since establishing the company, Sawyer, together with co-founder Susie Kumar, have developed projects that offer innovative designs, creating highly functional and exploratory urban spaces. Their particular interest is in how people use the spaces they design, explaining that 'the beauty of public space is its multiplicity and complexity; as such, we explore design strategies that avoid simplification and reduction and seek to draw out the inherent richness and diversity of the site and its inhabitants'. The landscapes Site Office produce create intriguing spaces that ignite a sense of curiosity and exploration. Recognizing that we live in an era that tends to focus on the individual rather than the community, Sawyer and Kumar explain that their projects 'seek to engender a strong sense of community ownership and pride in the site, to ensure the ongoing success of the design well after the designers have left'. In fact, when they've completed a project they view it as no longer being theirs, preferring 'to live vicariously through watching and hearing other people enjoy our landscapes'. The duo's focus is on creating spaces that allow for open-ended, spontaneous and often unpredictable explorations of public space. Drawing on its multiplicity and complexity, their design strategies for public space 'avoid simplification and reduction and seek to draw out the inherent richness and diversity of the site and its inhabitants'.

Their inspiration is 'present in the everyday'. Whether it comes from a conversation, an image, thoughtful exploration or careful observation, they believe, 'It is simultaneously hard research, unexpected moment and opportunistic creative spark.' The key 'is about maintaining an open mind, being receptive to ideas, asking lots of questions and having a good set of eyes'. Their creative process evolves through a journey, but with a map that leads you somewhere different than you initially thought. Landscape architecture relies on one's ability to 'transmute what you find along the way into something valuable,' they explain. 'In this sense, it is less about what we bring with us, and more about what we find along the way that is important.'

Site Offices's St Kilda Foreshore Promenade located in Melbourne, brings to fruition the result of just such an open-ended journey. Their design provides the groundwork for the 'unknown and unexpected' to occur, and it is this quality that gives the promenade its allure. According to Site Office, 'It is a space that remains gloriously un-programmed and free of functional constraints, where the primary function is left up to the creativity of those who use it.' In providing the clean-lined framework, Site Office has set the stage for a choreographed sequence of walking, meandering or promenading or opportunities to become a spectator, flâneur or participant. Site Office believes that promenades are one of the few typologies where 'the unexpected should be celebrated; where the act of appropriation is the very precursor to its success'.

Their work quite often looks at 'enabling collaborations' rather than emphasizing 'creative collaborations'. By enabling, they mean collecting groups of people together who might not stem from a 'typical creatives' list, people like 'clients prepared to take a risk in search of innovation, community members with a passion, knowledge and energy for a site, advocates pushing for a better project outcome or fabricators and artisans with a more effective way to build something'. It is these collaborations which give their design 'a critical edge'. Ideally, they elaborate, 'we would like to see collaboration at higher levels of governance, whereby broader issues can be dealt with more effectively and the reach of landscape architecture can be expanded'.

Working in Australia has no doubt informed the types of landscapes they create. Taking on board the importance of the role indigenous land management practices had in shaping Australia, they explain that their designs seek to incorporate better management techniques in order to 'create a sustainable and rich tapestry of people, plants and animals'. With this in mind, their subtle yet effective design for Keast Park aptly responds to the fragility of the surrounding dune landscape. In 2005, Site Office completed a comprehensive masterplan for Keast Park, a 2.5-hectare (6-acre) public park situated at the northern end of the Seaford foreshore on Port Phillip Bay, southeast of Melbourne. In 2011, the first stage of works arising from the masterplan was completed, including the construction of a new community building and the landscape connection to the foreshore and beach. Their design recognizes the constant fluctuations of water, light, air and season and unfolds in a series of sequential landscape spaces while respecting and reinstating the park's primary dune.

Reflecting on the role of our future cities in our ever-urbanizing world, Sawyer and Kumar question the strain the 'hinterland' is put under to 'support the voracious appetite and consumption of the people'. They believe a 'by-product of modern life is that the urban population is increasingly removed from the reality of these landscapes that support the city in which we live', and implore people to visit one of the many 'invisible landscapes' that 'support our bloated, unsustainable consumerist lifestyles'.

In their opinion, 'The future of landscape architecture will need to move beyond the singular focus on the "city" and urbanity as the (only) solution, and instead embrace the productive agricultural landscapes, natural systems and rural and "outback" geographies that make up the broader terrain of the country.'

Christopher Sawyer, Site Office
Brunswick East, VIC, Australia

'Chris Sawyer, founding director of Site Office, is one of Australia's most talented designers of public space. Chris places landscape architecture as sociology and is interested in how people use space, feel a sense of ownership over that space and appropriate it in a socially responsible way.'

Perry Lethlean on Christopher Sawyer

Christopher Sawyer, Site Office

Keast Park, Seaford Foreshore, Port Phillip Bay, VIC, Australia (2011)

The first stage of the 2.5-hectare (6-acre) public park masterplanned by Site Office includes the construction of a new community building, car parking and landscape connection to the foreshore and beach. Additionally, the protection and reinstatement of a primary dune was facilitated by the removal of existing structures and the addition of protective fencing.

Christopher Sawyer, Site Office

St Kilda Foreshore Promenade, St Kilda Beach, Melbourne, VIC, Australia (2009)

Through the widening and topographic articulation of the promenade edge, this design for the St Kilda Foreshore Promenade encourages greater adaptability for a broader range of uses. Un-programmed and free from functional constraints, the landscape's flexibility sets the stage for participants to create their own spectacle in the larger theatre of public life.

Xiaowei Ma,
AGER Group
Shanghai, China

Xiaowei Ma, founder and president of AGER Group, grew up in Beijing near the Imperial Garden. He studied landscape architecture at the Beijing Forestry University, frequently visiting the nearby Summer Palace and Yuanmingyuan gardens for inspiration. During his thirty years of practice, he spent twelve years studying and working in the United States before establishing his own firm in China. He has devoted himself to hundreds of projects, covering a wide range of scales in planning, architecture and landscape architecture. His experience has given him a valuable perspective on the challenges facing urbanization and environmental development in China. Ma's multicultural background, his interdisciplinary practice as an architect, planner and landscape designer and interest in academia empower him to play an active role in guiding the profession.

'My inspiration is the Theory of Borrowed Scenery by Professor Meng Zhaozhen,' Ma explains, 'a legend and the only academic of Landscape Architecture in the Chinese Academy of Engineering.' The term 'Borrowed Scenery' refers to an ancient Chinese tradition that involves the integration of a site's 'viewshed' or focal point – for example water, terrain or a visible natural element – within a design. According to Ma, 'The theory advocates site analysis that is both rational (topography, geomorphology, site conditions and orientation) and abstract (emotional connection and perception).' The 'emotional impact' comes from interpreting the site's evolution, both naturally and culturally, which, Ma believes, is the 'continuum of human living over the millennia. Understanding the site in such a way inspires design on the level of a spiritual connection to the material of landscape and place, which I think is very important.'

Evolving the design process, Ma applies a six-step process based on his education under Professor Meng, explaining, 'It is a methodology that moves from macro to micro, from concept development (macro), through site observation, to developing a metaphor for the poetic intention (theme setting), to form giving and general arrangement (macro), to detail design (micro) and back to idea development'. This constantly updated process, alternating between the macro and micro level, 'reflects the fact that across the continuum of time and space we live in constant flux and evolution, and we are all connected'. The design of Qiandao Lake Pearl Plaza employs this approach as it explores the regional culture and unique qualities of the site. Located 218 miles (350 kilometres) southwest of Shanghai, its design offers multiple access routes through terraced and floating planting beds and bodies of water. In addition to providing view corridors beyond the site's boundaries, the water itself acts like a mirror to reflect an almost painted image of the surrounding skyline, hills and terrain. Path networks are stitched across the terrain to create a lavish and seamlessly accessible public space while providing visitors with an emotional connection to the land itself.

Asked about the future of the profession, Ma reflects that 'from a macro perspective, human society has undergone several stages of development, from agricultural to industrial, to post-industrial, to the information age'. He states that, 'in a new era characterized by over-capacity, excessive consumption, serious ecological damage, rapid urban development, the threat of cultural negation and ignorance of human needs', landscape architecture will play an essential role in the 'reconciliation, recalibration and restoration' of the landscape. Reflecting on an excerpt taken from the famous Chinese poem by Du Fu 'Welcome Rain on a Spring Night', Ma compares the subtle and ubiquitous nature of landscape architecture to water, in that it 'moistens all things softly, without sound'. He believes the poem, which describes 'how rain benefits everything in nature, without making everyone realize it', provides an analogy for 'how our profession benefits society'.

This poetic inspiration not only reflects Ma's professional viewpoint, but also appears as a theme or inspiration in many of his designs. The landscape surrounding the Shanghai Cifi Century Square, which unites twelve buildings into an integrated, water-inspired landscape, provides one such example. The design uses an abstract water-flow pattern, linking the site to Shanghai's Suzhou Creek, to lead people through the site and between buildings. Its sinuous design accommodates indoor and outdoor spaces and reiterates the design theme 'innovative river' at ground level.

In China, Ma believes, there is currently a movement to put landscape forward as a priority in urban development projects. He explains: 'this trend places landscape architects in a leadership role, rather than a subordinate role. Chinese landscape history and art gives us some of the earliest examples of cultivating this mutually beneficial relationship between human ingenuity and nature and shows us the potential when a multidisciplinary approach is used to achieve this.' Ma believes that the future of landscape architecture requires the integration and collaboration of disciplines through which compelling results can be achieved through mutual respect and receptiveness. Ma takes on what he feels is today's biggest challenge facing global landscape architecture – ecology – by thinking of it in terms of a 'sustainable ecological cycle', that is 'taking full advantage of resources and allocating resources to maximize the advantage'. Ecology and culture follow a 'cyclical interdependent pattern' that is increasingly intensified, Ma suggests, and as landscape architects 'we need to balance cultural and ecological resources for the long term'.

Favourite trees

1 Cedar (*Cedrus*)
2 Camphor (*Cinnamomum camphora*)
3 Aspen (*Populus*)
4 Flowering peach (*Prunus persica*)
5 Maidenhair (*Ginkgo biloba*)

Favourite materials

1 Wood
2 Granite
3 Steel
4 Brick
5 Pebbles

Favourite contemporary artists

1 Andy Goldsworthy
2 Liu Xiaodong
3 Christo and Jeanne-Claude
4 Zhan Wang
5 René Portocarrero

Favourite sound

Piano

This project is a mixed-use development located in the Yangpu district in Shanghai. The design brings a cultural atmosphere to site by using a modern landscape approach combined with Shanghai style. The design combines classic garden elements and artisan pieces to make a dynamic landscape to be viewed from above and interacted with at ground level.

Qiandao Lake Pearl Plaza and Central Creek Landscape, Chun'An County, Zhejiang Province, China (2013)

The design of Qiandao Lake Pearl Plaza ingeniously solves this site's water level differences, while separating pedestrian and vehicular circulation and creating multiuse spaces. The design is animated by plaza space and arced planting beds that appear to float alongside bisecting access paths and sleek boardwalks, creating a landscape that both reflects and connects the hills and water together.

This project's landscape unifies twelve buildings through a series of winding shapes inspired by a flowing water pattern. Sinuous paths are dappled with texture, colour and form to create a lush human-scale landscape, diminishing the height of the surrounding towers. The design fully responds to its theme, 'innovative river', creating both intimate and open spaces.

Favourite plants

1 Bamboo
2 Hall crab apple
  (*Malus halliana*)
3 Water lilies (*Nymphaea*)
4 Swiss cheese plant
  (*Monstera deliciosa*)
5 Magnolia

Favourite trees

1 Bodhi (*Ficus religiosa*)
2 Horse chestnut
  (*Aesculus hippocastanum*)
3 Lime (*Tilia*)
4 Maidenhair (*Ginkgo biloba*)
5 Pine (*Pinus*)

Favourite contemporary artists

1 Robert Motherwell
2 Antoni Tàpies
3 Yves Klein
4 Joseph Beuys
5 Bill Viola

Inspiration

1 Philosopher / author Laozi
2 Philosopher / author Zhuang Zhou
3 Poet Wang Wei
4 Film director Sergei Eisenstein

As a Chinese-born landscape architect, Xiao Ying Xie grew up with the imprint of *shan shui*, the traditional Chinese art of painting natural landscapes, in her DNA. Xie, however, does not believe that it 'realistically' reflects the natural landscape, but rather is 'the mirrored reflection of the painter's abstract personality', which she describes as a type of 'psychological landscape'. Her own career began with a degree from the Landscape Architecture Department of Beijing Forestry University, followed by four years studying in The Netherlands where she researched regional planning, which included rebuilding the natural ecological landscape of agricultural land combined with modern tourism. This led to a period of working on projects in collaboration with the China Urban Construction Design and Research Institute (CUCD) before setting up her own practice, View Unlimited Landscape Architecture Studio CUCD, in 2004.

Discussing her inspiration, Xie reflects on today's world where commercially orientated design takes priority, inevitably influencing our thinking and choices. Yet Xie believes integrity will be maintained through our poetic instinct to keep eternity in mind. When beginning her projects, Xie visits the site with an open mind and observes its activity and inherited characteristics while searching for any 'psychological feelings' that exist and the explanations behind them. As a director would do with a movie montage, Xie collates the site's complex factors, and their relationships to each other, and reveals various story lines. She then reorganizes this information to provide a positive contribution to the landscape's evolving narrative. The design's propelling force could come from the client, or future users, Xie believes, 'along the way we absorb and analyze different ideas, including [contradictory] opinions. The design process is similar to filtering noises ... and eventually [hearing them through] one channel, synthesized as a harmonic, clear sound.'

Xie's studies and practice have led her to design an inspiring project that sees the renovation and modernization of the Tangshan Phoenix Hill Park, located in Hebei Province, China, and originally constructed in the 1960s. The park's transformation preserves its existing uses but injects them with innovative compositions and contemporary materials. From analysing the site, Xie decided to weave the site's natural elements within its cultural context and adopt the concept of 'threading'. This meant opening up existing walls to establish sinuous connections, linking the users and the park's programme together. Xie considers the landscape to be in a constant state of flux, suggesting that

'each landscape architect or design team are only temporary participants in the design process'. Taking this 1960s park and rejuvenating it to form its current design demonstrates Xie's belief in the importance of creating projects with 'a good foundation', allowing future landscape architects to continue the design.

Reviewing the state of landscape architecture, with designers increasingly taking on global projects, and how local culture is often interpreted superficially or hastily, Xie offers her opinion that there are actually two types of 'superficial interpretations'. In the first instance, local culture can be represented by the 'symbolic approach'. In this case the 'symbolic features' become an important part of the tourism industry, as do the accompanying consumer goods. This 'economic logic', Xie believes, becomes the 'dominant design factor', and the designer has very little input. As she explains, 'the indigenous lifestyle and its symbolic system, under such logic, is de-constructed, dis-embedded and then re-configured', and thus, for Xie, this type of 'so-called local culture is doomed to be superficial'. An alternative approach utilizes local materials, but bases designs on an internationally recognized, contemporary style. And Xie acknowledges the prevalence of this approach, explaining: 'I realize that, with the large picture of globalization in mind, this type of homogeneous design result is somehow inevitable.' As this design method exists globally, it reflects the fact that, no matter where you are, people have the same problems that need similar solutions. 'The traditional concept of the local culture,' Xie reflects, 'has lost its foundation' due to migration, modernization and 'eventually become exhibits in a museum ... decorative elements in architecture or just tourism products'. Xie implores designers to 'avoid solely emphasizing the "uniqueness" of a local culture', but through analysis of new challenges and lifestyles 'to come up with constructive solutions to correspond to the homogeneous trends'.

Xie's Xiamen Haicang Central Public Green and Landscape Design, expected to be completed in 2018 and located in Fujian Province, China, is an extensive, long-term and highly complicated project. These factors have led to an open-ended design that can adapt to a dynamic method of dealing with undefined, ever-changing circumstances during the design and construction process. Measuring 2,890 hectares (7,141 acres), the large-scale public landscape will provide for a variety of public spaces of differing sizes while enhancing its environmental function. Xie believes this design will 'provide a positive, mixed-mode solution to complicated social and environmental problems caused by the rapid urbanization of China'. Importantly, Xie advises that, 'When we are under the obligation of inheriting our past, we should also be responsible for the future by constructing a more substantial, more open and more optimistic foundation at present.'

Xiao Ying Xie, View Unlimited Landscape Architecture Studio CUCD Beijing, China

'Xiao Ying Xie demonstrates a humbleness in dealing with the natural environment while maintaining creative freedom, fostering unique connections with her landscape audience and inspiring them to explore the excitement of the natural world.'

Xiaowei Ma on Xiao Ying Xie

Xiao Ying Xie, View Unlimited Landscape Architecture Studio CUCD

Xiamen Haicang Central Public Green and Landscape Design, Haicang District, Xiamen, Fujian Province, China (2018)

This large-scaled, mixed-mode urban landscape has a dynamic design that responds to China's rapid urbanization with integrity. The project is made up of three parts: the public space surrounding the Xiamen Southeast Shipping Center, Dapinghshan Park with views over Xiamen Harbour and Cai Jian Wei Forest Fitness Park.

Xiao Ying Xie, View Unlimited Landscape Architecture Studio CUCD

Tangshan Phoenix Hill Park Renovation, Tangshan, Hebei Province,
China (2008)

This landscape reconstruction project rejuvenates an existing park. In analysing
the site's natural elements and cultural makeup, the project has adopted the
concept of 'threading' and in doing so has opened up the existing walls to establish better connectivity and to provide organic linkage throughout, consequently
refreshing the park with a modern aesthetic.

Adrian McGregor,
McGregor Coxall
Sydney, NSW, Australia

A landscape architect and urban designer, Adrian McGregor is the founder and managing director of McGregor Coxall, a Sydney-based design studio. Born in Newcastle, NSW, Australia, he spent his youth surfing before enrolling to study landscape architecture in Canberra in the mid-1980s. Following graduation he travelled to North America and the United Kingdom where he worked on a range of environmental projects. In 1998, he founded his firm in order to focus on the pursuit of a sustainable design ethic. Since then, his practice has received more than fifty prizes and awards, including the TOPOS Landscape Award 2009 in recognition of its environmental design work. In addition to his studio work, McGregor has been a visiting critic and lecturer at numerous universities, and in 2006 established Biocity studio. The studio is a creative think tank which 'explores new technologies and urban design principles' to create new models for urban planning that considers cities to be complex ecosystems. McGregor demonstrates a passion for creating better future cities through environmental sustainability and innovative design.

Ballast Point Park, in Birchgrove, NSW, Australia, is McGregor's choice of one his own recently built parks to spend the day in. Located on a former industrial site and situated on a prominent headland projecting into Sydney Harbour, the design uses the latest sustainability principles to minimize the project's carbon footprint and rehabilitate the ecology of the area. The completed design respects the site's historical layers while updating it to include site-wide storm water biofiltration, recycled materials and wind turbines for on-site energy production. McGregor earmarks this Sydney park as a place he would visit, particularly on New Year's Eve, as it is a 'key vantage point for viewing the fireworks and experiencing the festivities'. Not only has the park become 'a dramatic theatre [from which to view] the city's most popular event of the year', but it has become a regionally significant urban park.

McGregor's inspiration for his contemporary, environmentally sustainable designs comes from the Australian bushland landscape and its corresponding naturally occurring plant communities. It also comes from the world's public spaces and the European renaissance towns, as he explains that 'The environmental and cultural legacy of these places has influenced the way I view cities and natural landscapes.' In discussing how his designs evolve, McGregor remarks that 'Some of my design is intuitive and defies any established process.' The remainder is derived through meticulous analysis and scientific data collated during a thorough interrogation process. 'Much of my work evolves through iteration and can morph into various outcomes throughout the process,' McGregor explains.

Regardless of the process, McGregor's projects sympathetically respond to the site's strengths while greatly improving on weaknesses. Little Bay Cove, like Ballast Point, was established on polluted land. In this case it was a site of 17 hectares (42 acres) contaminated with asbestos, located in Little Bay, NSW, Australia. Here, McGregor Coxall prepared the public domain masterplan and construction documentation for this 459-dwelling residential neighbourhood. The layout features houses situated in a way that respects the coastal topography, two public parks and a central ecological corridor. Brand Park, an essential element of the Little Bay Cove project, is the primary open space for the neighbourhood and contains a pedestrian network of scenic lookouts, concrete pathways, suspended steel access stairs, weir bridges and elevated boardwalks. The site is organized around a curving, 100-metre (328-foot) long, elevated walkway constructed from recycled timber and steel, which provides access from the park terrace to a lower part of the site.

McGregor's Biocity studio engages with what he believes are today's most pressing design issues – global population growth and the subsequent rapid expansion of cities. As he explains, 'Cities have now become the primary habitat for the human species and the sustainability of urban settlements is the key area that landscape architecture must engage.' The studio acts as a 'research vehicle' to examine the interface between landscape architecture and cities. 'The Biocity studio research explores new technologies and urban design principles to establish a framework for prosperous city futures. The ongoing development of the Biocity model is intended to develop strategies for the creation of better cities,' McGregror explains.

McGregor's Parramatta City masterplan proposes regenerating 31 hectares (77 acres) running along Parramatta River foreshore in New South Wales, Australia, to create a series of high-quality public realm spaces together with new building development. Seamlessly weaved together, the new development will create a network of accessible dynamic spaces. The River Square, the project's unifying element, will establish direct connections to adjacent river corridor, including Parramatta Square – the area's new public space. Tying the entire development together will be a series of vibrant focal nodes, including new cultural landmarks, event areas and multifunctional terraces. Indicative of his designs to date, when asked how he would like to influence future generations, McGregor feels, 'the greatest influence that we could impart is to leave a legacy of important projects that challenge the status quo'.

17/17

Favourite plants

1 Australian honeysuckle (*Banksia*)
2 Spinifex (*Triodia*)
3 Grass tree (*Xanthorrhoea*)
4 Gymea lily (*Doryanthes excelsa*)
5 Melaleuca

Favourite trees

1 Rose gum (*Eucalyptus grandis*)
2 Smooth-barked apple (*Angophora costata*)
3 Cabbage tree palm (*Livistona*)
4 Australian barrel (*Brachychiton rupestris*)
5 Snow gum (*Eucalyptus pauciflora*)

Favourite contemporary artists

1 Richard Serra
2 Jaume Plensa
3 Anish Kapoor
4 Jack White
5 Ai Weiwei

Favourite natural landscape

Australian beach dunes

Completed in 2014, this masterplan proposes a world-class public domain and new high-quality collection of buildings through the regeneration of the Parramatta River foreshore. New and existing features are weaved together through a network of active spaces, including multifunctional terracing and event zones, while the key unifying element, River Square, establishes a direct connection to the area's new public space, Parramatta Square.

Ballast Point Park, Birchgrove, NSW, Australia (2009)

Previously used as a quarry and later as an industrial site, this park's design peels back the layers of its diverse history to create a sustainable landscape. Located on a prominent headland jutting out into Sydney Harbour, the rehabilitation of this the contaminated landscape has created a valuable urban park featuring site-wide storm water biofiltration, recycled materials and wind turbines.

177

Little Bay Cove, Little Bay, NSW, Australia (2014)
McGregor Coxall created the public domain masterplan for this 459-dwelling residential neighbourhood, which includes two public parks and a central ecological corridor. The site falls to a constructed wetland where the neighbourhood's key open space, Brand Park, is located. The park features scenic lookouts, suspended steel staircases, weir bridges, boardwalks and a curving, elevated walkway made from recycled timber and steel.

Favourite plants

1 Palmilla
  (*Lophosoria quadripinnata*)
2 Vochi-Vochi (*Mitraria coccinea*)
3 Amancay (*Alstroemeria aurea*)
4 Digüeñe (*Cyttaria espinosae*)

Favourite trees

1 Quillay (*Quillaja saponaria*)
2 Arrayan (*Luma apiculata*)
3 Roble beech (*Nothofagus obliqua*)
4 Coigüe (*Nothofagus dombeyi*)
5 Monkey puzzle
  (*Araucaria araucana*)

Favourite materials

1 Local stone
2 Recycled timber
3 Precast concrete
4 Cor-Ten steel

Favourite natural landscapes

'I'm in love with the Chilean
terrain.'
1 Torres del Paine National Park
2 Atacama Desert

Following a degree in architecture and urban design from Universidad de Chile, and a Master of Landscape Architecture, from the University of Pennsylvania, Francisco Allard has gone on to work both in the United States and Australia. As an associate director at McGregor Coxall, Allard worked on large-scale projects such as the design of the Parramatta River City masterplan (see page 173), located in Parramatta, NSW, Australia. Now based in Santiago, Chile, where he is general manager of Urbanica, Allard's design focus is on the environmental and social opportunities present in each project.

When asked how to best resolve today's most pressing issues for landscape architecture, Allard explains that in order to address environmental issues such as climate change, overpopulation and the high demand for open space 'we need to design "suprastructures" not infrastructures, which can environmentally perform while creating a tighter social network … consequently generating value to society … [by expanding] the effects that a specific structure can achieve.' Allard strongly believes that landscape architects play a pivotal role in creating 'performative structures' that will enhance the environment and maximize social interaction.

Allard's design process reflects this ambition of creating spaces that best resolve the issues of environmental enhancement and social interaction. By starting with the site's setting, reviewing its topography, hydrology, and so on, he is best equipped to create strategies that work with the site's natural setting, and thus augment existing environmental conditions. This improvement, Allard believes, plays a vital role in the site's larger context. In interpreting the site's social spectrum, Allard uses 'the community's aspirations and needs [as] a tool to query the project's brief and amplify its outcome', while technically, Allard employs engineering solutions that can be used as an innovative tool to deepen the creative process.

Throughout the process, Allard uses collaborators from a variety of backgrounds (from geographers to economists) in order to push his designs to achieve the best possible outcome. Ensuring that nothing is taken for granted, these collaborators are brought in early to address the 'questioning stage' of a project. When asked with whom he'd like to collaborate more in the future, Allard's response highlights the benefit of working with a specialist very clearly: 'I would love to work with more artists and sociologists, as these two fields can bring deeper layers and meanings to a project. From the artist we can input a wider significance to the design; and from the sociologist we might be able to embed a deeper social interaction.'

One of Allard's future projects, TAHI Iquique, Alto Hospicio Cableway, for the city of Iquique located in the northwest corner of Chile at the base of a coastal cliff, is a system of cable cars that will act as public transportation. The cableway system will reconnect the city with a large development area of predominately low-income housing, located on a plateau above the city at the top of the cliff. Working with Nueva Via consulting group, Allard has developed a system of cable cars that will connect the two parts of the city in less than fifteen minutes. Staying true to his design ambitions, Allard would like to take advantage of a naturally occurring phenomenon in this area called the *camanchaca* (dense morning fog) and harvest the suspended water 'as many plants and fauna have been doing for centuries on the cliff faces around the north of Chile'. In his proposal the pylons and cableway act as 'fog water' harvesters, providing water for the cliffside's endangered ecosystem, while the base of every cableway station provides a green public space with community services, activating social interaction and offering panoramic views of the ocean.

The urban transportation scheme which Allard designed for the city of Iquique reflects his design ambitions as well as what he believes is needed from the future of landscape architecture. For Allard, it is only through embracing the environment and the community 'as our most powerful allies' that we 'can build a stronger and healthier society'. And this applies to the future of landscape architecture in South America as well, where, although traditionally 'there is a strong relationship between the way of life and the territory', there is a danger of this becoming 'lost in the turmoil of urbanization'. As a result, Allard observes that within South American landscape architecture there has arisen 'a new pledge for open space, sustainability and acknowledgment of the native roots'.

Allard is acutely aware of the necessity to create both ecologically and socially adaptable developments, not just in South America, but on a global scale. Allard's positive attitude to the important possibilities of landscape architecture can be seen in his vision for the successful future of the industry: 'Although the [indefinite nature] of our profession has always been seen as a weakness, it will become its tool for success. Our capacity to adapt, but also to understand living systems, will allow us to develop morphing and staging processes instead of designing fixed outcomes, merging active processes with design visions that are resilient to time and change.'

Francisco Allard,
Urbanica
Santiago, Chile

'Francisco's exploratory work in urban design is underpinned by a strong desire to make significant impacts on social, economic and environmental issues.' Adrian McGregor on Francisco Allard

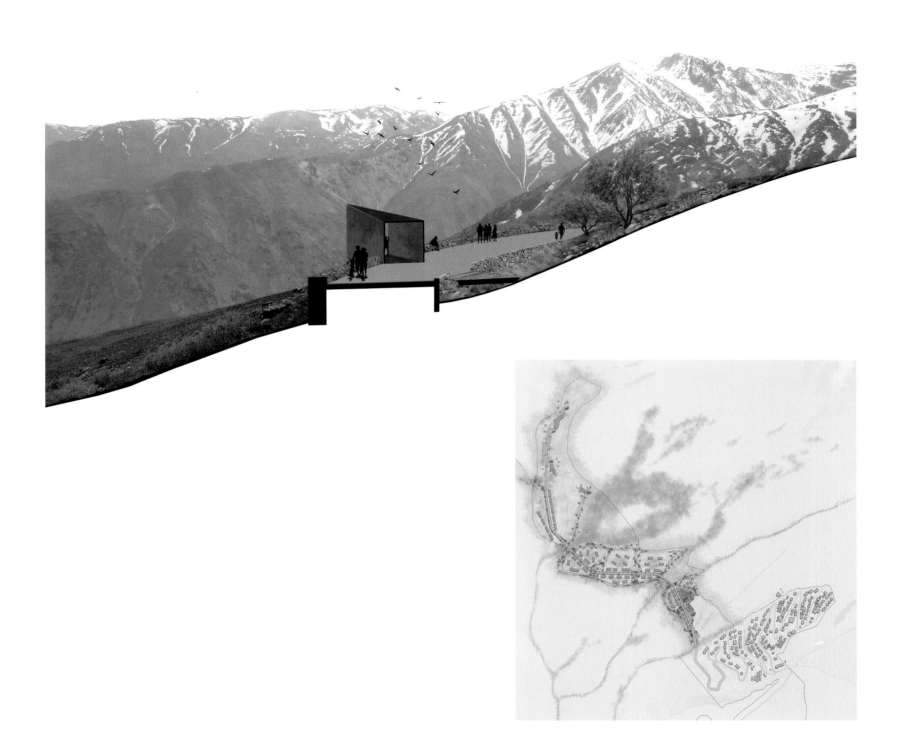

Francisco Allard, Urbanica

Manantiales Masterplan, Region Metropolitana, Chile (2030)

This masterplan project, located in the Andes Mountains near Santiago, extends the small ski resort town of La Parva. In addition to enhancing the site's ecological processes, the design creates a new town centre and centrally locates new building developments while minimizing visual impact. At the site's perimeter, an elongated promenade, complete with lookout shelters, playgrounds and open classrooms, is proposed.

Francisco Allard, Urbanica

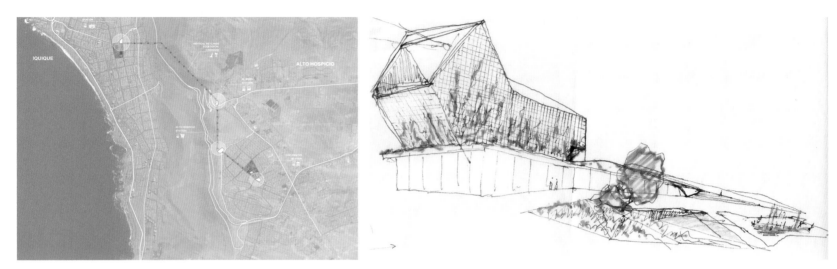

TAHI Iquique, Alto Hospicio Cableway, Región de Tarapacá, Chile (2020)

This project provides a new cable car transportation system that will reconnect the centre of Iquique to the upper plateau at the edge of the Atacama Desert. The proposal includes pylons and cableway stations designed to harvest fog water for use in irrigating endangered, fragile ecosystems, while the base of each station provides a green public open space.

Teresa Moller, Study of the Landscape, Teresa Moller and Associates
Santiago, Chile

Teresa Moller has accredited the birth of her career to her deep desire to help people and a profound passion to work with nature. Having studied at the New York Botanical Garden the Bronx, New York, and then at the Instituto Profesional de Ciencias y Artes (INCACEA) in Chile, for the past twenty-seven years Moller has realized numerous internationally celebrated projects. Her design philosophy is based on her respect for the site's existing elements combined with a complimentary, almost sculptural, refinement. Beyond her studio work, which includes private, public, corporate and institutional projects in Chile and abroad, she has also lectured extensively around the world. Widely published, Moller currently resides in Santiago, Chile, where she works in the studio she founded, Study of the Landscape, Teresa Moller and Associates, which specializes in landscape design and construction. Currently, she is working on projects in South America, Australia and Asia.

Spending her childhood in Chile's incredibly diverse terrain has certainly influenced her ability to respect, yet elegantly enhance, the landscape she touches. Moller herself acknowledges the fact that she derives inspiration 'from nature and architecture', explaining that, 'My work is about bringing both together and inserting people into nature'. Located 150 kilometres (93 miles) north of Santiago on a headland that juts into the sea, Moller's Punta Pite certainly does just that. The project features a footpath that embraces the character of the topographically rich site, while encouraging people to walk through the coastal landscape. Moller left the path untouched where the natural landscape allowed people to walk with ease, and where steep cliffs made walking difficult, a path or staircase was constructed. These architectural aspects were built from hand-cut granite, the same material as the cliffs themselves. Moller purposely omitted directional signage, allowing people to create their own journey as they meander through the awe-inspiring scenery. The landscape's poetic expression surrenders to the surrounding geography while providing visitors with the opportunity to reconnect with the rugged coastline.

Idiomatic of her design development, Moller explains that her creative process evolves through 'being in the place for as much time as possible and finding what is there for me ... to bring to people'. Moller's Casablanca II project, located in V Región de Valparaíso, Chile, is a landscape in which Moller has clearly spent a great deal of time, enabling her to create spaces that reawaken a visitor's experience of a productive landscape. The site's previous use had been for agriculture, and when Moller arrived, she explains, she saw that 'the flat valley floor was scarred with access roads and farm paths that seemed messy' and farmed fields 'seemed to cut and jar with the landscape'. She immediately decided to create a sympathetic and 'clean landscape'. Discovering that the land had been previously cultivated in a 'large circular form' greatly informed Moller's design direction for this project.

In this case, Casablanca II, sitting high upon a hill above, is linked to the valley floor with a spectacular stone staircase. The water trickles down these stairs into rills that flow through a *Casuarinas* forest in the valley below, and finally into the circular lake. After pruning the existing trees, Moller allowed them to grow and develop before evolving her design further. As well as the lake, crop fields and gardens, Moller's design included the planting of large vineyards, olive trees (for olive oil) and lavender. Although set over 46 hectares (114 acres), it is the simple gestures in this landscape which give it its beauty.

The sculptural quality of Moller's designs is no doubt related to her favourite contemporary artists who include Isamu Noguchi, Richard Serra, Donald Judd, Pilar Ovalle and Marcela Correa. Moller's Tierra Atacama landscape, located in an oasis town in the Atacama Desert in northeastern Chile, provides an example of her work's sculptural qualities. Enveloping the Hotel Tierra Atacama, the landscape transforms this part of the driest desert in the world into a small oasis miraculously producing food crops. The project seeks to find beauty in agricultural production in the desert, drawing inspiration from the traditional farming methods of the area. A wooden boardwalk takes visitors around the site, through stands of native Chilean palo verde (*Geoffroea decorticans*) trees to the cultivated land planted with sunflowers and corn. At the end of this elegant boardwalk stands a large and majestic carob tree (*Algarrobo*), under which simple wooden decks serve as rest points to take in the surroundings.

When asked what tools Moller uses to create her ethereal designs she responds, 'my heart'. She would like to influence future generations of landscapes architects by, in her words, 'showing them that our work is about caring for our planet and people, more than ourselves'. Her response to what she would do to make better cities of the future is simple: plant 'trees instead of paving', and albeit subtle, Moller's designs create seemingly intrinsic landscapes through her sophisticated and native planting palette, establishing an almost spiritual connection to the site combined within a contemporary aesthetic. Somehow, Moller's seemingly natural landscapes, clearly altered by human design, give the appearance of something that has existed for thousands of years.

Favourite plants

1 Orange glory (*Alstroemeria*)
2 Blue nasturtium (*Tropaeolum azureum*)
3 Broom (*Baccharis*)
4 Myrtle (*Myrtus communis*)
5 Chaura (*Gaultheria mucronata*)

Favourite trees

1 Southern beech (*Nothofagus*)
2 Common olive (*Olea europaea*)
3 Quillay (*Quillaja saponaria*)
4 Chilean acorn (*Cryptocarya alba*)
5 Pepper (*Schinus latifolius*)

Favourite materials

1 Stone
2 Water
3 Wood

Favourite contemporary artists

1 Isamu Noguchi
2 Richard Serra
3 Donald Judd
4 Pilar Ovalle
5 Marcela Correa

Casa del Mar, Los Vilos, IV Región de Coquimbo, Chile (2005)

Located in the north of Chile, this design blends a residential home into its native setting through the use of natural materials and endemic vegetation. At the front of the house, a triangular headland overlooks the Pacific Ocean. Covered in soil and silt, the headland was cleaned to reveal a textured, russet-coloured stone. Here, a wooden path leads to a sunken fire pit.

Punta Pite, Zapallar, V Región de Valparaíso, Chile (2005)

Located on a headland that juts into the Pacific Ocean, this footpath embraces
the character of the site and encourages people to traverse the coastal landscape.
Much of the landscape remains untouched, but where steep cliffs made walking
difficult, paths and stairs have been constructed from hand-cut granite, the
same material as the cliffs themselves.

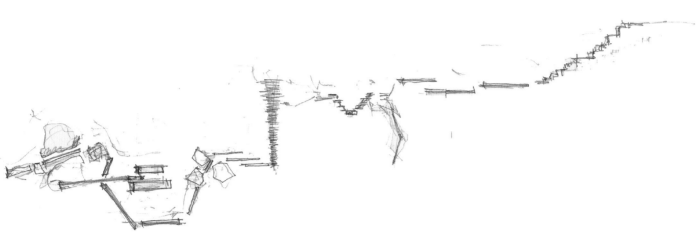

Casablanca II, Casablanca, V Región de Valparaíso, Chile (2007)

This project strips back the layers of agricultural history to create lush gardens surrounding a residential home. The house, sitting on the hill above, is linked to the valley floor with a spectacular stone stairs. Water trickles down them into water channels that feed into a circular lake. The design also features productive vineyards, olive trees and lavender fields.

Tierra Atacama, San Pedro de Atacama, II Región de Antofagasta, Chile (2008)

Located in an oasis town in the Atacama Desert, this project transforms part of the driest desert in the world into a landscape for producing food crops. Drawing inspiration from local farming methods, the project seeks to find beauty in desert agricultural production. A wooden boardwalk takes visitors through the site, ending in a decked area under a large carob tree (*Algarrobo*).

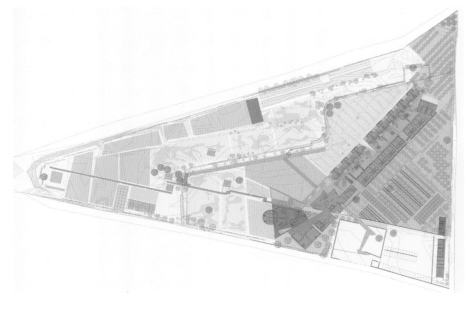

Favourite plants
1 Lewa star flower
   (*Conostomium quadrangulare*)
2 King's lily (*Lilium regale*)
3 Bullwort (*Ammi majus*)
4 Egyptian carissa (*Carissa edulis*)
5 Milkweed (*Kanahia laniflora*)

Favourite trees
1 Silk (*Albizia*)
2 Fever (*Acacia xanthophloea*)
3 Musine (*Croton megalocarpus*)
4 Cape chestnut
   (*Calodendrum capense*)
5 Aromo (*Acacia caven*)

Favourite materials
1 Natural stone – like granite
2 Rough cut marble
3 Limestone
4 Decomposed granite
5 Good soil

Growing up in Kenya allowed Chloe Humphreys to spend hours 'on safari' observing and admiring the surrounding nature. After initially studying at the Glasgow School of Art, Humphreys returned to her 'true love' – landscape design – studying both in Glasgow, Scotland, and London, England. She then went on to work with Steve Martino in Phoenix, Arizona before working with Teresa Moller in Santiago, Chile. In 2014, Humphreys returned to Kenya, setting up her firm, The Landscape Studio, where she designs delicate landscapes that relate culturally and environmentally to their native settings.

As her designs might suggest, Humphrey's takes inspiration from natural landscapes and 'observing how man interacts with nature'. Her work is seemingly unobtrusive yet strikingly established. Her project Delia's Memorial Lily Garden, located in Kenya's Isiolo District, was built as a memorial to Delia Craig, a woman who spent her life living in the Kenyan bush. The subtle design comprises a stone wall bench situated within the sloped hillside surrounded by tall white squill (*Drimia altissima*), an indigenous lily. Twice a year, with the seasonal rains, the mass-planted lilies bloom, bringing life and reflection to this serene location. Humphreys makes the principles underpinning her design process clear when she says that '... the key to all my work is observation, seeing what naturally occurs on the site and seeing how we can use that in the design'.

Her works are site specific and vary according to the location of each project. In the early stages of her designs she travels to the site, where she develops sketches and thoughts that help her to outline the project's design direction. Once this has occurred, she returns to her studio where her research on the site's 'indigenous species and cultures' is balanced with both the client and consultant's needs in order to create the design. This is the case with her project located in the savannah in northern Kenya where the 'simple intervention' of a stone-edged, circular lawn has been situated in the perimeter landscape surrounding the Lewa House Lodge. Built in 2014, the subtle 20-metre (65-foot) diameter circle provides an area from 'which to watch the game, the stars, the sundown as well as enjoy lying in close proximity of the beautiful textures of the African savannah grasses'.

Significantly, when responding to the question of today's most pressing global issues she believes that the 'lack of green spaces, especially in cities', is a concern that must be addressed in Africa. Equally, outside of cities, it is the 'preservation of natural landscapes' that must be prioritized. The vitality of 'good design' is something, she feels, which needs to be put forward and which developers need to take on board. Through the work of her studio, Humphreys' projects make use of indigenous species, where possible, so as to 'preserve some of the amazing natural flora (and fauna) that grows naturally in East Africa'. As seen with Delia's Memorial Lily Garden, the use of indigenous plant species will also decrease the amount of irrigation needed in order to create beautiful landscapes.

The experience of working in three continents – Africa, as well as North and South America – has allowed Humphreys to take on and deal with a variety of landscapes, teams and projects. When asked what she believes the future of landscape to be, she states that the role of landscape architecture is becoming increasingly important. In a world already full of built form, she feels that future landscape projects should look 'more at naturally occurring ecosystems and respecting the balance of nature while maintaining beautiful and simple design'. And as the world becomes smaller due to urban sprawl, Humphreys would like to see a return to the 'more local concept of producing food'. 'Self sufficiency,' she says, 'is core for truly providing for a healthy relationship between man and nature.'

Humphreys does not limit herself to the broader landscape, and her work involving traditional African pottery includes pieces that employ materials to create simple forms for use as planters or sculptures in the garden. However, in keeping with her minimalist concepts, elements of her designs border on artistic introductions to landscape – reflecting her work with Teresa Moller.

Her future work in Tanzania, where she is developing a hotel project in Dar es Saalam, is both inspired by and respectful of the local landscape character. This approach exemplifies her advice to future generations whereby she believes one should take a 'light hand' in designing the existing landscape. She believes that one should 'never mimic nature, she will always do it better than you'. Collaborating with her husband, Michael, Humphreys' project in Tanzania has drawn inspiration from the local 'Swahili style', a style itself influenced by Persian and Arabic culture, injecting simple, but lush planting combined with reflecting pools to create elegant spaces surrounding the Serena Hotel. Humphreys' design aesthetic and respect for the local culture and flora and fauna well places her to create refined landscape architecture projects in Africa which both sustainably enhances ecology while providing socially relevant spaces. This design attitude will hopefully help Humphreys fulfill her wish of convincing future developers to introduce more sustainable green spaces and parks into African cities.

18/18

Chloe Humphreys, The Landscape Studio Nairobi, Kenya

'Chloe is a special and sensitive person who is very much in touch with art, nature and culture, making her a great designer – I can't wait to see how her work evolves with time.' Teresa Moller on Chloe Humphreys

Chloe Humphreys, The Landscape Studio

Lewa House, Lewa Downs Wildlife Conservancy, Kenya (2014)

Designed as a place to enjoy the northern Kenyan savannah, this project comprises the simple intervention of a circular lawn with Tanga yellow stone edging along its perimeter. Located on the grounds of the Lewa House, a lodge house on Kenya's Northern Frontier, the site provides a quiet area from which to admire the wildlife, skyline and textured African savannah grasses.

Chloe Humphreys, The Landscape Studio

<u>Delia's Memorial Lily Garden</u>, Isiolo District, Kenya (2014)

This seat and wild lily garden were built as a memorial for Delia Craig, a woman who spent her life in the Kenyan bush. Made from on-site materials, the memorial comprises a dry stone wall seat nestled against an existing rock kopje (rock outcrop) and indigenous lilies planted en masse. The lilies bloom twice yearly with seasonal rains.

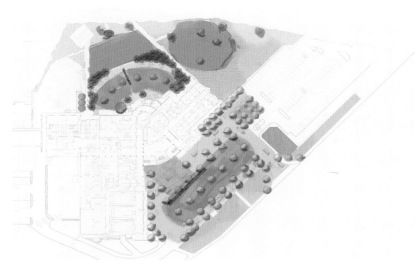

Dar es Saalam, Dar es Saalam, Tanzania (2016)

Inspired by the Swahili style, which draws from Arabic and Persian influences, these gardens in Dar es Saalam in Tanzania provide a luscious backdrop to the Serena Hotel. The design includes dramatic reflective pools, lush tropical planting used to define main garden areas and a formal frangipani forest at the hotel entrance.

Catherine Mosbach, mosbach paysagistes Paris, France

Catherine Mosbach creates world-renowned works through her firm, mosbach paysagistes, in Paris, France. Following a degree in landscape architecture from the prestigious L'École Nationale Supérieure du Paysage in Versailles, Mosbach went on to become the co-editor and co-founder of the contemporary landscape architecture journal *Pages Paysages* in 1987. That same year she established her eponymous practice and has since created many award-winning projects including Botanical Garden Bordeaux, France, which won the Rosa Barba Landscape Prize at the 3rd European Landscape Biennial in Barcelona. The same project was featured in the Museum of Modern Art's exhibition *Groundswell: Constructing the Contemporary Landscape* in New York City, in 2005, bringing her highly acclaimed landscape architecture projects to the attention of an international audience.

'Louvre-Lens Park', Mosbach replies when asked which one of her most recent works she'd like to spend the day in, adding that, 'This project addresses the question of compartmentalizing and de-compartmentalizing – what pertains to the realm of art, architecture, landscape, economics and history.' Rolling out over a site formerly used as a coal mine in Nord Pas de Calais, France, Mosbach describes this project as restoring 'a tingling to the skin. It sets it tingling in response to the different strata considered by mobilizing them together'. Through the re-colonization of plant life on top of what was once scarred land and the creation of depressions and mounds, reminiscent of slag heaps – a by-product of coal production – the project attempts to rebuild the land in context with its historical past. In doing so it restores the link between the 'skin' (the surface) and the 'depth' (resources). In Mosbach's words, 'It opens the door to [the] future by introducing the arts as mediators of all the ages and as bridges to new mentalities.'

Mosbach explains that inspiration for this museum park came mainly 'from biologic input'. Using nature, Mosbach has created spaces in which plant life can be used to help 'fix heavy metals in the soils [and/or] reduce ambient dust'. The design of the park transforms it into an evocative landscape through the creation of a series of perceived openings and closures. Mosbach took advantage of nature's healing qualities, most evident in her redesign of a 'vertical slice of schist soil', a product of mining activity, to form an enclosure open for colonizing moss. It can also be seen in the site's horizontal soil perforations, which are not only reminiscent of the shapes and forms found in mining activity, but also provide perfect habitats to remediate the soil, reduce air pollution and capture excess water for the micro gardens.

Mosbach's creative process relies on her ability to carefully test 'a place at different scales', in both 'what is visible and what is not immediately present'. She stresses the importance of redeveloping drawings and other visual interpretations to explore this process. 'Our mind is absorbed by so many questions,' she explains, 'that we need these tools to give us spontaneous contact [with our design] and an immediate look [into what they mean].' Throughout this process, Mosbach attempts 'not to be absorbed by the everyday stream, but to maintain a distance, to move from point to point and capture an exceptional power of life'. With Mosbach's Botanical Garden of Bordeaux, she has created a truly explorative landscape, which both questions and celebrates the phenomena of nature and culture in regards to humankind's relationship with the plant world. The garden is made up of seven modular structures based on the major functions of the garden: exotic (Urban Garden), ethnobotanic (Field of Crops©), ecological (Environment Gallery©), topical Aquatic Garden), Allée of Plants and Community Garden. How these modules have been explored can be seen with the example of Field of Crops©, which focuses on the action of scarifying the earth with vast crop-growing areas; and the Environment Gallery© which reveals itself as a landscape informed by the stratifications in the ground and the process of environmental transformation in terms of geology, soil and plant cover. The explorative nature of these spaces offers visitors a variety of different scales to explore while constantly introducing new landscape appearances and hence new potentials for interpretation and appropriation.

'We do not want to predict anything, we prefer [to] dream', Mosbach replies when asked about the future of landscape architecture. 'I dream that landscape architecture keeps humanity in connection with production, soil, seasons and human beings.' In doing this, Mosbach explains, we'll have a better connection to 'biological concerns', continuing, 'Our capacity for abstraction could become extremely dangerous when we lose the delicate reality of our biological life, and become ourselves a kind of device.' Mosbach's project, Phase Shifts Park in Taichung, Taiwan, explores this through a project that, in her words, 'tries to create an urban utopia by combining a lithospheric design [water, topography and soil] with an atmospheric design [heat, humidity and pollution]'. Acknowledging that the expectation 'to control both level atmosphere and lithosphere could be presumptuous', she sees this design as a 'fertile way' to shift the urban lifestyle. Her use of topography to capture rainwater, therefore 'nourishing the water table' and providing irrigation, together with planting to create an enhanced microclimate, will produce a park in which the community can escape the heat and rain, relax in a scene devoid of noise and pollution and be encouraged to have fun in the open air. This park's design exemplifies Mosbach's biological approach to design in a transformative and seductive way.

Favourite plants

1. Mosses
2. Ferns
3. Heather (*Calluna*)
4. Flax (*Linum*)
5. Rice

Favourite trees

1. Willow (*Salix*)
2. Poplar (*Populus*)
3. Birch (*Betula*)
4. Beech (*Fagus*)
5. Maple (*Acer*)

Favourite materials

1. Earth
2. Water
3. Sand
4. Concrete
5. Wood

Favourite contemporary artists

1. Gerhard Richter
2. James Turrell
3. Giuseppe Penone
4. Pascal Convert
5. Jérôme Boutterin

Phase Shifts Park (Jade Ecopark), Taichung, Taiwan (2017)

This 70-hectare (173-acre) park concept defines three parameters, heat, humidity and pollution, mapping them on site and creating a design that improves climatic conditions through the use of plants and trees and built structures. Within the framework sporting, recreation and play areas will be connected through a series of paths. The design is done in collaboration with Philippe Rahm and managed locally by Ricky Liu & Associates Architects + Planners.

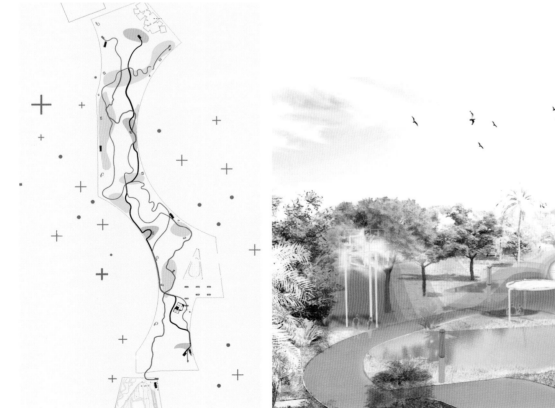

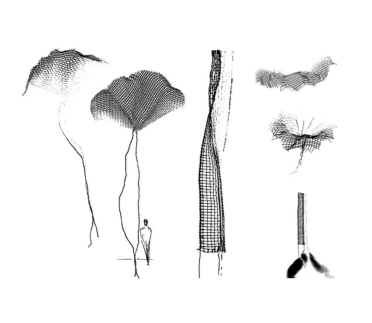

The Botanical Garden of Bordeaux, Gironde, France (2007)

Exploring humankind's relationship with the plant world, this project comprises seven gardens, two of which are featured here, the Field of Crops© and Allée of Plants. The Field of Crops© explores the cultivation of land for extensive crop use, while the Allée of Plants delicately places trees, asymmetric pieces of stone in grass and sculptural frames inhabited by climbing plants.

Louvre-Lens Park, Nord Pas de Calais, France (2009)

This park provides a serene foreground to the Louvre-Lens museum designed by architects Kazuyo Sejima and Ryue Nishizawa of SANAA. Located on a former coalmine site, the design draws inspiration from the shapes and patterns associated with the site's historic past. Only here, instead of heaps of coal, landforms have been created to embrace plant habitats, such as colonizing moss, aiding in soil remediation.

Favourite colour

Different shades of grey

Favourite plants

1 Evergreen ferns
2 Wild ginger (*Asarum europaeum*)
3 Horny goat weed (*Epimedium*)
4 Narrow-leaved mock privet
   (*Phillyrea*)
5 Corsican mint (*Mentha requienii*)

Favourite trees

1 Alder (*Alnus glutinosa*)
2 Storax (*Styrax*)
3 Wintersweet (*Chimonanthus*)
4 Hop hornbeam
   (*Ostrya carpinifolia*)
5 Tupelo (*Nyssa sylvatica*)

Favourite materials

1 Steel
2 Slate
3 Stoneware
4 Water
5 Black locust wood

With the belief that 'a beautiful landscape incites you to move, to look around and beyond the site itself', David Besson-Girard's designs seem to evoke a journey through time and space. Whether relaxing in a small garden in the centre of Paris or researching within the landscape he created for the Pôle Scientifique et Technique du Ministère de l'Écologie (the Centre for Research and Technology of the French Ministry of the Environment) in France, his work embodies an appreciation of 'the journey' in both large and small projects. Furthermore, his range of works, from private Parisian gardens to the landscape surrounding a memorial to the casualties from World War I, displays a skill with details that adapts easily between small- and large-scale productions. Indeed, Besson-Girard feels that 'attention to detail is fundamental to the expression of a project', and using the analogy of a written text, where 'a small spelling error or iffy punctuation can interrupt the flow and meaning of work', he explains that this high-quality detailing ensures projects are created that are designed to last, and that can be easily understood.

Based in Paris, and receiving his degree from the L'École Nationale Supérieure du Paysage in Versailles, Besson-Girard's background in earth sciences and landscape architecture has led to a career designing projects that are often involved in creating cultural symbols or have socially important expectations. Over the last decade he has lectured in Paris and at his alma mater in Versailles while designing high-profile projects with his firm. More recently, his designs have been selected for the Victoires du Paysage, a celebration of the industry's most outstanding projects.

Besson-Girard is often inspired when 'observing the transformation of the environment around the work site', and this natural and social transformation is something he aims to reveal in the forms of his work. In his design of the *pôle ville* (city section) surrounding the Pôle Scientifique et Technique du Ministère de l'Écologie, he created a pedestrian campus at the centre of the university site and on the roofs of the building designed by French architect Jean Philippe Pargade. The site around the building evolved to form a patchwork of functional land plots (parking, sports ground, and so on), composed as a mosaic of fields. The overall landscape's rolling form and fluidity makes it conducive to informal encounters and social interactions. Here, the continuity of spaces links users from the east and west pedestrian entrances to the square, upper garden and promenades.

With the rehabilitation of a former industrial site in 2009, the Gardens of a Former Cartridge Factory, located in Bourg-lès-Valence, France, Besson-Girard reorganized the exterior spaces to create twin gardens, which form a large courtyard when combined. Separated into public and private areas, the landscapes' rhythmic design, as Besson-Girard states, remains 'true to the spirit of Charles Fourier's utopian phalanstery as initially projected and built by Noël Sagnial (architect).'

At times working with culturally and socially demanding sites, Besson-Girard designs with the ambition of creating spaces that make better places to live. Re-establishing our relationship with the planet, he feels, is an essential part of architecture, landscape architecture and urban design – not just for individual 'city projects', but globally. Responding to the question of design issues today, Besson-Girard states: 'With the pressing ecological and economic challenges and ever more pervasive social interaction, the landscape architect plays a pivotal role today because we must lead the debate on culture and sensibilities in the choices made for developing man's living space on the planet.'

Currently working on the Gardens of the Notre Dame de Lorette International Memorial near Arras in Ablain-Saint-Nazaire, France, designed together with architect Philippe Prost, Besson-Girard has developed a sympathetic landscape design that responds to the surrounding landscape and the memorial that, in places, seems to float above it. Situated at the foothills of the Artois region of France, the architect, together with the typographer Pierre di Sciullo, has created a large, elliptical-shaped ring displaying the names of approximately 600,000 people who were killed in the Durant region in World War I. Accentuating the form of the hilly Artois region, the landscape design rolls out under the ring to delicately support the memorial, together paying tribute to life in 'an unfathomable dimension'. Inside the entrance, the landscape unfolds to provide unobstructed views of the inscribed walls, while flowers beds in the lawn accentuate its slope and bring colour to the space. Covering the centennial period from 2014 to 2018, the evolving plant cycle, itself a journey from grass to flowers to perennials, will reach its 'pinnacle of expression' to include red poppies, blue cornflowers and white forget-me-nots, specifically symbolizing the German, British and French troops who fought there.

Designing spaces with the aim of giving users a journey is not only something that Besson-Girard seems to design into his own landscapes, but it is something he envisions would make better cities for the future, remarking, 'I imagine a network of gardens. Small private gardens, terraces, vegetable gardens, all manner of personal expression spaces under heaven, but linked together by vast walking or cycling paths. These structures lead to large geographical and historical spaces in the territories surrounding the city. This layout lets the body exercise all its senses, to understand all the elements, the earth, water, the vegetation, man's dwellings. This will heighten our awareness of the geography, the history and the possible future of man's dwelling places on Earth.'

David Besson-Girard,
David Besson-Girard paysagiste
Paris, France

'David Besson-Girard's conceptual background gives him the freedom to move between tradition and modernity – introducing landscape architecture into contemporary life, independent of an international landscape style.' Catherine Mosbach on David Besson-Girard

David Besson-Girard, David Besson-Girard paysagiste

Exterior spaces of Pôle Scientifique et Technique du Ministère de l'Écologie, Campus Descartes, Marne-la-Vallée, France (2014)

The design surrounding this centre for research and technology creates a fluid pedestrian campus that encourages social encounters and impromptu meetings. The cohesive design links users from the site's eastern and western pedestrian entrances to the square, upper garden and promenades, while playfully planted roof gardens accentuate the curve and form of the building beneath.

David Besson-Girard, David Besson-Girard paysagiste

Gardens of a Former Cartridge Factory, Bourg-lès-Valence, France (2009)

The project redistributes the building's exterior public and private spaces into twin gardens which, taken together, form a large square courtyard. The gardens are formed of a crisscrossing paving pattern that creates a playful grid of planting textures, lawns, beds and trees. Running parallel to the main pedestrian path is a planted, linear waterway.

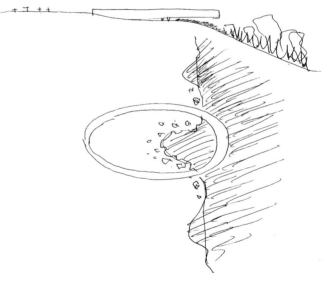

<u>Gardens of the Notre Dame de Lorette International Memorial</u>,
Ablain-Saint-Nazaire, France (2015)

Situated in the hills of the Artois region facing Flanders Fields, this ring-shaped
monument bears the names of 600,000 World War I casualties. The landscape
comprises a rolling stretch of land, accentuating the site's hilly relief. The opening
underneath the ring expresses the inability to completely enclose the land within
borders. The plants will evolve from a lawn to a perennial landscape.

Laurie Olin,
OLIN
Philadelphia, PA, USA

'Inspiration comes from the world and one's experience, from nature and having lived and travelled, things seen and heard, read and been delighted by,' Laurie Olin explains. Growing up in the wilds of Alaska, Olin describes this wilderness environment as a 'fabulous place to be a child with the woods and mountains, lakes and rivers, and streams, animals and interesting people who'd come to the edge of civilization'. Later, he 'fell in love with cities' like New York City and travelled to Europe, living, studying and working in Italy, England and France. Here, he describes: 'The art, food, historic gardens and parks, squares and piazzas, art and life of it all is a treasure trove of memories, great ideas, colours, forms, strategies, and yes, inspiration. So it's the caribou and Velázquez, the Jardin du Luxembourg and Bernini, Olmsted and Frank Lloyd Wright, aspen trees and André Le Nôtre. Inspiration is everywhere – and then in music especially, in one's favourite jazz solos memorized when young, in nocturnes and sonatas, or the grand chorales and symphonies, in erosion patterns and Native American baskets.'

A distinguished teacher, author and one of the most renowned landscape architects practising today, he has guided his studio through many of their signature projects, from the Washington Monument Grounds in Washington DC to Bryant Park in New York City. After studying civil engineering at the University of Alaska, Olin moved to Seattle to pursue architecture at the University of Washington where he was encouraged to focus on landscape by the American landscape architect Richard Haag. Today, Olin has served as chair of the Department of Landscape Architecture at Harvard Graduate School of Design, and, for the past forty years, taught at the University of Pennsylvania where he is Practice Professor of Landscape Architecture. In addition to receiving numerous accolades, Olin is the recipient of the 2012 National Medal of Arts, the highest lifetime achievement award for artists and designers bestowed by the National Endowment for the Arts and the President of the United States. He also holds the 2011 ASLA Medal, the highest award the American Society of Landscape Architects (ASLA) can grant to a landscape architect.

When asked about how his designs evolve, Olin responds 'Slowly'. Starting with the site, he assesses 'what is there and what isn't. I daydream and wander a bit, talk to people, ask them questions (not what do they want), but about other things, their hopes and about the place.' Olin notes there is a 'bit of digging into the history of a place, its ghosts. One tries to imagine what it is that people don't know how to ask for, can't quite imagine, but hope you will think of. I ask myself what would a child like, because

then I'd probably like it.' Important to this process is the site's climate and its nature, while the site's programme also needs to be accommodated on site, although, he explains, 'it is rarely the first thing'. His designs 'always start by drawing, doodling and sketching,' he reveals, before developing further through large 'cross sections, with people,' which he finds to be 'just as important to his design development as plans'. Then, simple models help him better understand a design's potential. Eventually the design develops into construction drawings on the computer, but, he explains, 'I never begin there. I'm fond of drawing full size construction details and making mock-ups of things.'

Reflecting on collaborations, Olin explains that he has developed several relationships 'that have gone on for decades', working on numerous built and unbuilt projects with various architects, including Peter Eisenman, Frank Gehry, Richard Meier, Norman Foster, Henry Cobb of IM Pei & Partners (now Pei Cobb Freed & Partners) and Bob Frasca of ZGF. 'One learns from and enjoys working with superb designers,' Olin explains. 'But one should not overlook the daily collaboration that goes on for years in an office from partners, associates, assistants and staff, the effort, trust and help one gets from others, their criticism and assistance, their insight and support.'

Citing 'the needs of the vast population of the world in terms of housing and a healthy environment – water, safety, resources, and community' as today's most pressing design issue, Olin explains that, 'Cities are the design problem. Cities are landscapes, albeit urban ones, and they need to be transformed into supportive places for people to live, for children and old people, for the poor as well as for the middle class and those with resources and power.' Paraphrasing the writer and publisher J B Jackson, Olin believes 'everyone should have an environment that is ecologically healthy, socially just, and aesthetically rewarding'. However, due to the 'scale and magnitude of urban growth', Olin is concerned by a lack of well-trained practitioners who are 'both broad enough and yet deeply technically skilled', believing that 'few existing nations or governments seem to be addressing the problem adequately at the current moment'.

For future generations, Olin recommends landscape architects 'embrace a "slow food" attitude toward their design and its processes … Many of the best things in life and design need a bit of time for us to consider and think about, to mull and perk. Remember that our work is equally about culture and nature, that it is not a science, but one of the arts – possibly the least understood and potentially the greatest of them all.'

Favourite plants

1 Siberian iris (*Iris sibirica*)
2 Peonies – especially dark, rich colours
3 Mountain laurel (*Kalmia latifolia*)
4 Lavender (*Lavandula*)
5 Oakleaf hydrangea (*Hydrangea quercifolia*)

Favourite trees

1 Coastal redwood (*Sequoia sempervirens*)
2 Horse chestnut (*Aesculus hippocastanum*)
3 Paper birch (*Betula papyrifera*)
4 Lebanon cedar (*Cedrus libani*)
5 London plane (*Platanus* x *hispanica*)

Favourite materials

1 Granite
2 Marble
3 Limestone
4 Tropical hardwoods – such as teak or Ipe
5 Birch ply

The Barnes Foundation, Philadelphia, PA, USA (2012)

Relocating Dr Albert Barnes's art collection to Philadelphia's Benjamin Franklin Parkway, the iconic collection is now more readily available to the public. Presented within an inspiring setting, the design employs the concept of a gallery within a garden and a garden within a gallery. The garden's various water features create a reflective and serene setting for contemplating the collection.

Simon and Helen Director Park, Portland, OR, USA (2009)

Developed entirely over a parking structure, Director Park has become a well-used public piazza with a range of amenities and activities. The park's large-scale glass and wood canopy shelters café seating areas and reinforces the site's architectural massing. The water feature includes arching jets contained within a semicircular basin and framed by curved wooden benches, which can be drained to accommodate diverse programming.

Together with a team led by KieranTimberlake, OLIN's design for the US Embassy in London represents democracy's core beliefs of transparency, openness and equality. The welcoming design employs exceptional sustainability principles to create a landscape that celebrates English gardens and parks as the setting for civic buildings.

OLIN collaborated with Peter Eisenman on the memorial's development within the context of its surroundings. The memorial site comprises 2,711 unadorned concrete steles and has been graded to create an uneven ground that, along with the steles, evokes a sense of insecurity, instability and loss of orientation. Trees are dispersed randomly as a testament to the fragility and persistence of life.

Favourite plants

1 Chinese bushclover (*Lespedeza*)
2 Thunberg spiraea
   (*Spiraea thunbergii*)
3 Rhododendron Oomurasaki
   Tsutsuji (*Rhododendron pulchrum*
   'Oomurasaki')
4 Ruscus bamboo
   (*Shibataea kumasaca*)
5 Koguma zasa
   (*Sasaella glabra* 'Minor')

Favourite trees

1 Japanese zelkova (*Zelkova serrata*)
2 Candyfloss
   (*Cercidphyllum japonica*)
3 Full moon maple (*Acer japonicum*)
4 Kousa big-bracted dogwood
   (*Benthamidia japonica*)

Favourite materials

1 Galvanized steel with an
   acid treatment
2 Black granite
3 Wood decking
4 Porcelain
5 Rocks

Born in Numazu-city, Japan, Toru Mitani obtained a Master in Landscape Architecture from Harvard University Graduate School of Design and a PhD in Architecture from the University of Tokyo. Having worked with Child Associates, Peter Walker and Martha Schwartz, followed by Sasaki Environment Design Office, Mitani went on to set up the landscape architecture firm 'studio on site' under the partnership of Hiroki Hasegawa, Chisa Toda and Yuuji Suzuki. He is currently a Professor of Landscape Architecture at Chiba University in Japan and his wide range of landscape architecture projects has received numerous accolades.

Taking inspiration from scenes of everyday life, such as observing weeds in a drain, the conditions of street trees and climate changes, Mitani builds a visual library of his 'design vocabulary'. These experiences, Mitani recognizes, offer a similar 'chemical reaction' as when he reads a piece of literature or views fine art. A process of categorizing these 'scenes' takes place in his mind for future use. Some of these impressions may well be evident in his project Okutama Forest Therapy Trail in Okutama Town, Japan, a trail and facilities project for a forest therapy programme. Mitani himself feels 'that this project is a dedication to the site itself instead of the space [being created] by myself'.

The 1,295-metre (4,232-foot) long trail, designed with Yuuji Suzuki, provides visitors with a calming walk through the forest, taking in the sights while improving health and well-being. Implemented with the advice of the Forestry and Forest Products Research Institute and Chiba University, the project takes on two aspects: the reuse of the cedar and cypress woodland and promoting welfare for the older generations who live in this hillside region in northwest Tokyo. 'The hillside and forest is an environment of a certain quality and all my [designs]; seats, tables, walkways, as well as architectural facilities, are just a key for people to realize various qualities of the natural environment.' The design reflects a sympathetic response to a mature landscape that has been redefined to create thought-provoking spaces for all to enjoy.

In response to how his design process evolves, Mitani admits that he is 'kind of a lazy person' when it comes to starting schematic design, 'because I know the waves of cost control will come soon'. In saying this, Mitani acknowledges that it is the budget that controls the design, and that it is up to the designer to realize the scheme within budget limitations. Mitani also believes that technical issues play an important role in design development.

With his Fudoki Garden at the Shimane Museum of Ancient Izumo, located in Izumo, Shimane, Japan, Mitani, together with Chisa Toda, designed a public garden surrounding the museum designed by Fumihiko Maki. The museum is dedicated to information and artwork about the nearby Izumo Shrine and the regions ancient history. The gardens themselves, measuring 5.6 hectares (14 acres), are nestled into the forest and hills of the Izumo region located in southwest Japan. The project's landform reflects the site's geological history while the 288-metre (945-foot) long path relates to local mythology. A seat and water feature at the end of the path offers a calming space to rest and listen to the sound of water.

Although Mitani's projects respond to their natural setting with apparent ease, it is the pressing global issues of 'rapid climate change' and the 'globalization of the economy' which, he believes, effect landscape architects the most. Reflecting that even though landscape architecture is 'based on locality', materials and details are often repeated in order to be more cost efficient, and damaged ecological systems, due to climate change, are not met with high-quality design standards, such as drainage, planting and disease prevention.

Mitani's masterplan proposal in a reclaimed landscape at the centre of Tokyo Bay, entitled Green Cross, comprises two types of 'green' – the wild and the urban. Designed together with Motoichi Nagasawa of Nihon Sekkei and Chisa Toda from studio on site, the 'forest-field' project, completed in 2014, is the first stage in the creation of a 'wild green future' for this 20-hectare (49-acre) reclaimed land. The first step in the project is a wooden windbreak which surrounds and protects the plant nursery while also providing a focal point to the vacant landscape, producing a 'new horizon' line set against a backdrop of Tokyo skyscrapers.

Designing a landscape in front of and overlooking Tokyo, it seems apt to ask Mitani what one thing he would do to create better cities for the future. In actuality, Mitani would like to create a place that is not designed for people, explaining that he would rather create a place for nothing. His only question is, 'Who would pay for such a project?' In regard to which aspect of historic landscape design would most likely offer inspiration for his future designs, Mitani replies: 'A feeling of the sublime when I rambled alone under the large sky at the Castle Howard garden, a witness of infinity on the axis in Vaux-le-Vicomte, a sense of nothing when I sit at the edge of the wooden terrace of Daisen-in, Daitokuji, those aspects of masterpieces show me the fundamental role of landscape architecture, that is the solitude of human beings in the eternity of the world ... Those aspects have always [guided] my design concept in any kind of project and I believe they will do so in the future too.'

Toru Mitani,
studio on site
Tokyo, Japan

'Toru Mitani is a remarkable and brilliant designer, one whose work has dealt with essences, form and spirit ever since his student days – a poet of the landscape, as tough as he is clear and gentle.' Laurie Olin on Toru Mitani

Toru Mitani, studio on site

Fudoki Garden at the Shimane Museum of Ancient Izumo, Izumo, Shimane, Japan (2006)

Designed by Toru Mitani with Chisa Toda, these gardens surround the Shimane Museum – a museum about the Izumo Shrine and the region's history. The site's landform responds to the area's geological history and includes a 288-metre (945-foot) path that culminates in a seat and a small fountain.

Okutama Forest Therapy Trail, Okutama Town, Tokyo, Japan (2010)

Designed by Toru Mitani and Yuuji Suzuki, this project's concept creates a 'forest living room', expressed with trails, plazas and architectural facilities. With advice from the Forestry and Forest Products Research Institute and Chiba University, this design's trail network forms part of a forest therapy programme. The trails include seating areas for relaxation and contemplation constructed from recycled cedar and cypress.

Toru Mitani, studio on site

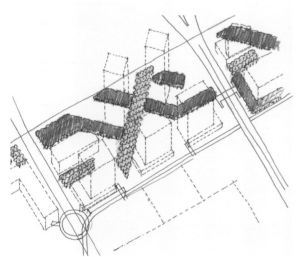

Green Cross, TOYOSU 22, Toyosu, Tokyo, Japan (2014)

Designed by Toru Mitani with Chisa Toda of studio on site and Motoichi Naga-sawa of Nihon Sekkei, this design sits on reclaimed land in Tokyo Bay. The project's masterplan reclaims 20 hectares (49 acres) using the concept of the 'Green Cross' – the urban (pink) and the wild (green). The 'forest-field' structure is the first part of the project; the wood structure surrounds the plant nursery, and acts both as a windbreak to protect them and a focal point for the vacant lot.

Jacqueline Osty,
Atelier Jacqueline Osty & Associés
Paris, France

'*Le paysage du quotidian*' (the everyday landscape) is what Jacqueline Osty predicts future landscape architects will create. Celebrated for her ability to translate landscape as structure with a strong architectural feeling, Osty has worked on many urban design projects in most of France's major cities. Prior to founding her firm in 1983, Osty studied landscape architecture at the distinguished L'École Nationale Supérieure du Paysage de Versailles. Since then Osty has developed a very contextual and sensitive approach to the site, working back and forth between large- and small-scale details, and in doing so treating each project like a fine piece of weaving. Osty's award-winning designs work across a range of landscape types, from large public parks to urban spaces and restructuring. In addition to her studio work, Osty is a Professor of Landscape Architecture at L'École Nationale Supérieure de la Nature et du Paysage in Bloise, France.

Osty sees landscape architecture as a transformative process that must result from careful consideration and analysis of a site's various data. As she explains, 'It is the territory that provides the components, and thus you must pay attention to the territory before transforming it.' Osty always takes inspiration from the site's context. For Martin Luther King Park, situated in Paris, it was the site's former railway history that informed the design's linear nature, together with the adjacent nineteenth-century Square des Batignolles, designed by French landscape architect, Jean Charles Alphand, which enlightened Osty on 'the way to conceive pieces of nature in a dense urban context'. Located in the future neighbourhood of Clichy Batignolles in Paris, it is here, Osty reveals, she would choose to spend 'a beautiful autumn day … to be in a natural surrounding where seasons are fully expressed, while contemplating the Parisian skyline'. Such inspiration allowed Osty to take a reasonably small site (in comparison to the size of Paris) and, in her words, create a 'landscape frame of great poetry, allowing different generations of different social classes to use this place side by side and to contemplate the living world right at the heart of the big city'.

Throughout the sustainably designed park, three themes have been developed in a contemporary plurality and with a progressive approach: the theme of seasons that creates multiple ecosystems, the theme of water used as a recreational or an ecologically precious component and the theme of the body that results in multiple sporting activities and recreational uses. In allowing the site's attributes to inspire her design, Osty's work delivers clear and simple lines overlaid with the richness and textures of materials and history to give her designs a depth of space and time.

Describing her favourite colour as 'the colour of the sky, and so of the sea', it comes as no surprise that of her recent works, Osty would choose to visit Sables d'Olonne seafront. Located in Vendée, France, she would visit in the summer 'to contemplate the line of horizon of the Atlantic Ocean, walking along the promenade, between two worlds: the animated seaside town and the colourful nonchalant beach'. In most coastal towns, the waterfront has long been the major axis of movement. In the reclamation of this waterfront, Osty's design allows pedestrians to move seamlessly and with ease along the bay from the port and transversally from the city to the beach, giving emphasis to the abundant plants and creating a shared space for pedestrians as well as reduced vehicular traffic. In doing this Osty does the one thing she feels would make the cities of the future better: 'create links'. In designing future cities she would like to 'create links between the parts which are separated from one another, ensuring continuities, bringing near and far closer [and connecting] history and geography, past and present'.

'My creative process is a progressive mental construction, very slow,' Osty explains, 'The information can be technical, cultural, aesthetic or emotional … from the head to the hand, I draw the intuition.' The transformation of the Zoological Park of Paris encapsulates Osty's ability to intuitively do just that. The park is a scenography of viewpoints, which erases physical boundaries, creates the illusion of depth and highlights perspectives within the park. The landscape is composed of screens made of vegetation and topography, theatrically creating a park that is sympathetic to animal welfare while providing an immersive experience for visitors. Through the creation of biozones that mirror biodiversity threatened by global issues such as deforestation and global warming, the park also addresses what Osty believes is one of today's most pressing design issues: the 'preservation of our planet and the diversity of natural habitats'. However, Osty highlights a second global issue: 'the landscape must [also] be considered in its cultural dimension, and not only the environmental. The transversal dimension of landscape includes a global vision in urban habitat as well as in the countryside, in everyday places as well as remarkable places. The landscape constitutes an essential element of the individual and social well-being.'

With influences that include the painter Paul Klee and the movie director Michelangelo Antonioni, one can imagine how Osty's clean-lined, highly contextual designs develop into a patchwork of complementary spaces that provide a platform from which to appreciate the beauty of nature.

Favourite colour

'The colour of the sky, and so of the sea.'

Favourite plants

1 Peonies (*Paeonia*)
2 Lindheimer's beeblossom (*Gaura*)
3 Grasses
4 Rockrose (*Cistus*)
5 Foxtail agave (*Agave attenuata*)

Favourite trees

1 Palm
2 Oriental plane (*Platanus orientalis*)
3 Willow (*Salix*)
4 Oak (*Quercus*)
5 Shadbush (*Amelanchier*)

Favourite materials

1 Concrete in a light colour
2 Steel
3 Golden gneiss
4 Black basalt
5 Green stone

Favourite natural landscape

The desert

By unifying the paved surfaces from beach edge to building edge, this design has created a broad promenade that allows pedestrians to easily move between the city and beachscape. Paving patterns have defined extended pedestrian zones and reduced vehicular traffic. In addition to planting beds, seating areas and shade structures, a neutral colour palette and flush surfaces define this elegant promenade.

Martin Luther King Park, Paris, France (2007)

Situated on a former railway platform, this park gracefully stitches into its urban setting through paths extending into the adjacent neighbourhoods and green spaces. Developed on sustainable principles, including recycling site materials, implementing responsible water strategies and creating diverse ecosystems, the park provides both recreational areas and intimate spaces within a park that enhances biodiversity and offers seasonal interest.

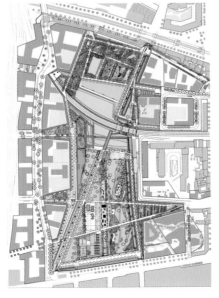

Located on a former coal storage wasteland on the banks of the Seine River, this site has gone through a re-naturalization process whereby more than 100,000 young saplings have been planted. Organized to accommodate large and small festivities, the park maintains the site's character as an industrial port by incorporating railway tracks, recycled concrete and paving stones within the overall design.

Paris Zoological Park, Paris, France (2014)

The transformation of this zoo responds keenly to today's ecological concerns. Comprising biozones that represent biodiversity affected by issues such as deforestation and global warming, the project is guided by design principles that put animal welfare and visitor experiences first. The result is a 'sceneography' of viewpoints, adding the illusion of depth, and framing plants, topography and animals.

Favourite colours
1 Pastel orange RAL 2003
2 Yellow grey RAL 7034
3 Cement grey RAL 7033
4 Grey white RAL 9002

Favourite plants and trees
1 Strawberry (*Arbutus unedo*)
2 Edible fig (*Ficus carica*)
3 Papaya (*Carica papaya*)
4 White frangipani (*Plumeria alba*)
5 Wild strawberry (*Fragaria vesca*)
5 Chinese mahogany
  (*Toona sinensis*)
6 Bagras (*Eucalyptus deglupta*)
7 Kentucky coffeetree
  (*Gymnocladus dioica*)
8 Japanese zelkova (*Zelkova serrata*)
9 Flamboyant (*Delonix regia*)

Favourite materials
1 Black locust wood
2 Brick
3 Hainaut blue Belgian limestone
4 Painted steel
5 Paint

Bertrand Vignal founded BASE with Franck Poirier and Clement Willemin in 2000, and the company now has a team of thirty-five landscape architects, architects and engineers, with offices in Paris, Lyon and Bordeaux, France. Currently working on large-scale urban territories, predominantly in the south of France, Vignal also has projects in exotic islands, such as Nouméa, Réunion Island and French Antilles.

Selecting from his more recent projects, Vignal recommends a visit to his recently completed Park Blandan, in Lyon. A celebration of multiplicity, this 20-hectare (49-acre) park provides almost everything you could imagine for an outdoor day of fun, from bespoke playgrounds with a dynamic combination of colour and materials to fitness and sports facilities, to quiet spaces and immersive green ambiances. And yet it is the intensity of the surrounding community, in particular the vitalizing attitudes of children and teenagers, that provides the urban park's all-important animation. In fact, people's ideas and actions are paramount to much of BASE's work, who admit to putting humans at the heart of their design philosophy, and Vignal clearly understands our fascination with people watching in parks, urban spaces and on the street.

Indeed, the dynamics of 'the street' provide an important source of inspiration for him; he lists 'steps in a pedestrian street' as one of his favourite sounds, alongside 'trees cracking, frogs at night and Italian crickets'. Considering this, their current project for Bordeaux Zoo in France might seem fitting. One of the elements in the design that BASE are currently working on is entitled Ville Animale; this 'animal city' imagines a streetscape where animal-watching visitors can walk past hotels for insects and small animals. 'We are trying to match animal environments with visitor features and even positions, creating mirror effects and extended experiences of strangeness', Vignal explains.

With this emphasis on observing the theatre of nature, it's no surprise that the company also take their inspiration from movies, art exhibitions and travelling – Vignal travelled extensively before living in Venezuela for some time, where he studied urbanism and tropical vegetation. A wealth of cultural experience and inspiration no doubt informs his belief that 'the work of landscape architecture is an exercise in storytelling, escape and imagination, while staying focused on the cutting edge'. This balance between creativity and the cutting edge underpins much of Vignal's numerous projects. However, for Vignal it is vital that the landscape itself provides the starting point for any creative process, and that ego or dogma do not inform decisions.

Vignal likens the company's design process to 'a game of hide and seek'. Having taken their cue from the site itself, they compare each other's vision, mapping ideas to the site's dimensions and the necessary programme until the project begins to reveal itself. 'Mostly, the project is already there from the start, in front of our eyes, but at first we can't see it.' Pointing to simplicity and clarity as key factors in keeping things on the right track, Vignal explains: 'We try to make it rise by itself in a simple, elegant and obvious manner. If just one out of three is missing, it might turn out expensive, pretentious and messy.'

Vignal believes 'Landscape architecture is not done yet. A lot still has to be shared, invented and upgraded. The profession is a very recent one indeed, and in a way that is one of its main interests. What we try to share with our team is energy, and the ability to see design as a way to set oneself free, rather than to torture oneself with ego, comparison and performance issues. Landscape is a vivid and complex matter, but one can always [succeed] with simplicity and authenticity.'

Having studied biology and architecture before studying landscape architecture at the L'École Nationale Supérieure du Paysage in Versailles, France, Vignal understands the importance of collective intelligence when considering the vast possibilities that stem from the many different practices of landscape architecture. While the relationship with the client is paramount, he acknowledges the need for close collaboration with architects and specialists in engineering, ecology and lighting design to ensure success. 'We particularly appreciate light design and ecology, because they can provide a whole new dimension to a constructed project,' he explains. And as he finds himself working more and more on large-scale urban productions, exposing him to issues of economy and housing, it is essential for Vignal that programming and landscape architecture work together to ensure that geography, sustainability and spontaneity guide a design's development.

In terms of sustainability, Vignal believes that because of its vital and social functions, and 'because it allows people to get together', food will become an increasingly important consideration in the construction of city spaces in the future: 'There are hundreds of possibilities to eat, make food, grow food, cook and share these together outdoors, possibilities that we can't always imagine right now, and that may have multiple ecological, political, human and social dimensions.'

Bertrand Vignal, BASE
Paris, Lyon and Bordeaux, France

Bertrand Vignal, and his dynamic team at BASE, inject aesthetic and ecological value into their designs, and in doing so create high-functioning urban projects and landscapes that adapt to meet the evolving needs of the surrounding communities and cities.'

Jacqueline Osty on Bertrand Vignal

Bertrand Vignal, BASE

Park Blandan, Lyon, France (2013)

Located on an old barracks site, this design introduces a contemporary urban landscape into the centre of Lyon. The urban park combines the site's historical remains with creative solutions to construct diverse spaces, including playgrounds, skate parks and sports grounds, merging cutting-edge play equipment with an historical aesthetic.

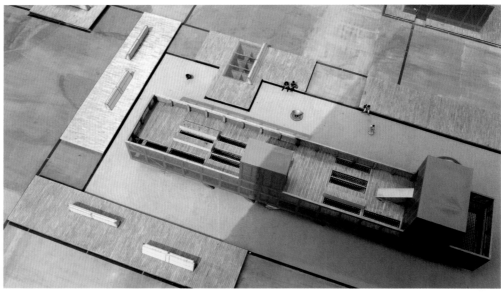

Bertrand Vignal, BASE

Lormont Génicart Sud, Lormont, Gironde, France (2014)

Located within a housing estate from the 1960s, this project uses traffic-calming measures to transform the area into a car-free zone featuring newly created urban spaces, plazas and sporting grounds. One unique feature is a large seated plaza area orientated on a mosaic of deck and paving materials, at the centre of which is a vibrant play structure containing hidden passageways and rooms.

Myungkweon Park, GroupHAN
Seoul, South Korea

After graduating as a landscape architect from Seoul National University, Myungkweon Park describes Korea during the 1990s as a time when the public viewed landscape design as either gardening for the privileged or monumental government projects by civil engineers. It was at this point that he decided to pioneer a whole new industry of landscape architecture in South Korea for the general public, and his humanistic and design-oriented approach to large-scale residential projects was enthusiastically accepted. Over the next two decades, Park's firm, GroupHAN Associates, designed over five per cent of the built area of the city of Seoul, including the first ecological park in Seoul and winning numerous prestigious competitions, beginning with the Han River Historic Waterfront and including the Seoul Grand Park and Baegot New Town Parks. From 2008–10 Park was a visiting scholar at Harvard Graduate School of Design.

'For a long time my inspiration for design came from my childhood memories in the village where I grew up,' Park explains. 'The soaring pine forest with thick morning fog, a crystal-clear creek full of small creatures and birds, a narrow path meandering through the grassy field ... those images and experiences of a pre-industrial, agricultural landscape deeply affected my perspectives and design language.' Influenced by these landscapes, Park attempts to create spaces with 'ample opportunities for play and exploration' while bringing nature back to densified urban centres. More recently, Park has become inspired by 'historical literature, traditional philosophy and folk art, or its contemporary interpretation'. When asked how the designs develop at GroupHAN, Park says, 'We talk a lot.' The GroupHAN creative process involves a collaborative charrette approach whereby everyone can offer ideas towards the design of the project. His office features people from a range of professions, including graphic designers, hydrologists, engineers, ecologists and of course landscape architects, and the diverse backgrounds, memories and stories help increase the number of possible suggestions. Park believes a 'landscape architect is not an artist or engineer ... we're moderators whose strengths are understanding the human scale and experience'. Operating without hierarchies, everyone who works on Park's projects – from within the company or outside of it – has the ability to voice their ideas or concerns. As Park summarizes, 'It's not the person who knows more or has longer industry experience that makes the difference. It's the person who has a great idea and can execute the communication of that idea.'

Located in Siksa-dong, Goyang, South Korea, Siksa New Town Parks is one of Park's recently built projects and highlights his ability to construct an explorative landscape packed with nature in a densely populated setting. Built on a former brownfield site, the extent of this project was made possible because of Park's close relationship with the client, allowing his firm to contribute to the decision-making process of the site, such as allocating land use and transportation. With an overall vision for ecological restoration and urban green infrastructure, Park was able to convince the client to, in his words, 'invest a significant portion of the development cost in the reintroduction of once-forgotten streams passing through the site and an extensive bioswale network supported by cutting-edge rainwater recycling facilities'. The water is not only used for storm water management and ecological restoration, but also features in wading pools, seasonal ponds and a water playground. Siksa New Town is a prominent example of how a high-density development can integrate green infrastructure as a core value and create livable communities.

According to Park, both the environment and social effects of global climate change provide some of today's most pressing design issues. However, while acknowledging that 'technology can be developed within a relatively short time frame to address specific environmental issues', he stresses that 'people's mind and habits do not change as quickly as the technology advances'. Comparing it to the time taken for people to fully understand the technology behind such things as electricity and cars, Park would like to see landscape architects work on 'energy efficient design, rainwater reuse and carbon dioxide mitigation' in such a way that it is integrated 'comfortably' into people's everyday lives. Forming a part of Baegot New Town Parks masterplan in Siheung, South Korea, Brackish Water Park explores this idea through the creation of a landmark green space, located where the sea and the city come together. Due for completion in 2016 and located on a former landfill site, the park is designed to be, in Park's words, 'full of extraordinary nature and experimental thinking'. With a dramatic sea level change, ranging up to 8 metres (26 feet), 'it will be very interesting [to see] how we manipulate this natural phenomenon to create a unique place with sublime beauty'. Park intends to harness the site's natural characteristics by creating a brackish ecological pond where salty seawater meets freshwater – creating a habitat for animals and plants to populate. The park's planting also aims to shelter visitors from the scorching sunshine and salty winds, offering an enjoyable environment for the community to explore a child-like sense of adventure within a natural setting.

Regarding the future of landscape architecture, and reflecting his idiosyncratic design approach, Park explains, 'People should coexist with nature. Aesthetics should coexist with efficiency. Environment should coexist with health.' Furthermore, Park believes 'The future of landscape architecture is unlimited. We're living in an age where the landscape architect has never had a more important role.'

Favourite plants

1 Fountain grass (*Pennisetum alopecuroides*)
2 Broadleaf liriope (*Liriope muscari*)
3 Winter jasmine (*Jasminum nudiflorum*)
4 Korean barberry (*Berberis koreana*)
5 Curvedutricle sedge (*Carex dispalata* 'Boott' var. *dispalata*)

Favourite trees

1 Japanese red pine (*Pinus densiflora*)
2 Bamboo
3 Bastard tamarind (*Albizia julibrissin*)
4 Crape myrtle (*Lagerstroemia indica*)
5 Japanese white birch (*Betula platyphylla*)

Favourite natural landscapes

1 The valleys in Bukhansan National Park, South Korea
2 Yosemite National Park, CA, USA
3 Vancouver Island, BC, Canada

Munhwa Broadcasting Corporation Headquarters, Sangam-dong, Seoul, South Korea (2013)

Located in Seoul's Digital Media City, this large urban plaza enriches the city's urban fabric by combining hard landscape and planting elements to create a vibrant public space. Graphic paving patterns orientate pathways and highlight the site's social nodes. Lush vegetation, bespoke furniture, art and fountains enliven the plaza and draw the city inwards.

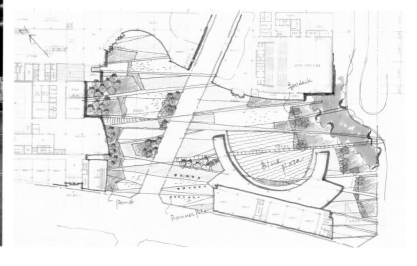

Siksa New Town Parks, Siksa-dong, Goyang, South Korea (2010)

This park provides exemplification of how a high-density development can integrate green infrastructure in urban communities. Dense, lowland urban areas are often susceptible to flash floods due to poor planning. This park collects and recycles 454 million cubic metres (120 billion gallons) of rainwater each year while offering a verdant landscape featuring wading pools, seasonal ponds and playgrounds.

Baegot New Town Parks, Baegot New Town, Siheung, South Korea (2016)
This 57-hectare (141-acre) park is located at the junction of the city and the sea.
Taking full advantage of the site's natural characteristics, a brackish ecological
pond – comprising seawater and rainwater runoff – provides a central focus for
the design. Elsewhere, the introduction of vegetation has created an enhanced
microclimate where visitors can escape the heat and humidity.

'Architecture is basically about addition and stability, while landscape is about transformation and change,' Yi Kyu Choe remarks. Recognizing that a building can start from nothing, but landscape architects 'are perplexed when they are given a tabula rasa', he sees the profession more as a 'social movement', as opposed to art, which is 'basically an individual endeavour'. Choe is a South Korean-born landscape architect who is now based in New York City where he is the founding partner of the Unknown Practice, a firm dedicated to research and the implementation of creative urbanism in physical and cultural formats. After receiving a Master of Landscape Architecture from the University of Toronto and a Bachelor of Arts and a Master of City Planning from Seoul National University, Choe worked for various companies, including GroupHAN Associates NYC, before setting up his own firm.

When Choe thinks about the future of landscape architecture, he believes 'we should look at the past', explaining that, 'The twentieth century was an era of abundance and ruthless economic growth, but we now face an age of expensive natural resources and an increasing elderly population.' In order to deal with these challenges, Choe believes that 'agile interventions like tactical urbanism are good, but we don't have to be confined to what can be done now'. In fact, Choe believes we need a 'fundamental change', such as returning to early visionaries, like Frederick Law Olmsted, when landscape architecture and urban planning were not separate. '[Olmsted] changed the way we occupy spaces and build cities.'

Due to be completed in 2024, Overpeck Park, in Bergen County, New Jersey, is one of the firm's most recent projects. Measuring 328 hectares (811 acres), this large park is similar in size to Olmsted's own Central Park in Manhattan. A brownfield site, with a large volume of water at the centre, Choe plans on establishing a 'world-class public space' and describes it as 'a Versailles in Jersey'. Located in an ethnically diverse neighbourhood, the design aims to create a park that will meet the needs of its community while also offering them the opportunity to contribute to, and thus take ownership of, it. Comparing it to André Le Nôtre's Versailles where trees and plants were brought in from all over France, Choe, too, wants to incorporate trees and plants native to the residents' home countries, diversifying the plant life and enriching the community's park experience.

Living in New York City allows Choe to draw on one of his inspirations – the 'streets'. Walking the streets and photographing them allows Choe time to complain, praise and cherish 'what works and what doesn't, what is timeless and what is obsolete, or what is beautiful and what is ugly'. In addition to the reality at ground level, Choe is also inspired by the satellite images on Google Earth which he feels 'tell a story about how cities are structured and how nature flows'. But his 'strongest inspiration', he explains, comes from conversations with fellow designers and writers. In his words, good design actually comes not from the brain, 'but from somewhere between the lips'. Although, reflecting on his time in design school, he remembers a professor telling him 'let your hand design, not your head'. Choe's creative process steers away from visual references, often leading to a 'tweak of existing work', or retrospectively creating a concept after a design, and instead focuses on the site's needs and understanding them clearly. This, he believes is 'the difference between happy, fulfilled design and miserably iterative, unending work' .

Choe's Heliofield project, at Fresh Kills Landfill, New York, shortlisted for the 2012 Land Art Generator Initiative competition, questions the conventional approach of placing utility-scale photovoltaic cells in a barren site created by clearing nearly all 'traces of plant and animal life' for ease of installation and maintenance. Choe explains that 'this practice effectively creates a site that is, in ecological terms, a monoculture'. Heliofield aims to establish sustainable relationships between renewable energy technology and the land they inhabit. Normally installed in a manner that is generally 'unsympathetic to site conditions', this proposal aims to create a reciprocal relationship between energy infrastructure sites and local ecology. As Choe explains, 'Heliofield generates power through its technology but gains resilience through biodiversity.' This project touches on the subject that Choe believes is one of the most pressing issues facing landscape architects today: 'energy'. Referencing the tragedy at Fukushima in Japan, Choe would like to see a transition from nuclear power to 'safer and more renewable sources of energy'. But as with Heliofield, large-scale solar or wind installations need to address ecological issues.

When asked about this future legacy, Choe reflects that 'as a designer, I also want to make a masterpiece. But, my version of a masterpiece is not something totally experimental, avant-garde or utterly precious. To make an analogy, less like a BMW, and more like a Honda Civic kind of masterpiece.' Choe's design is 'based on deep understanding of human comfort, urbanism and balance'. He wants to be remembered 'as a designer who made thoughtful landscapes and cities'.

22/22

Yi Kyu Choe, Unknown Practice New York, NY, USA

'I always encourage young designers to compete on an international stage and learn global markets if they want to be an industry leader. Yi has the guts to enjoy the challenge while his achievement in New York is quite remarkable.'

Myungkweon Park on Yi Kyu Choe

Yi Kyu Choe, Unknown Practice

Heliofield, Fresh Kills Landfill, NY, USA (2012)

The conventional approach to renewable energy is to locate it in an isolated area, devoid of all plants, animals and humans, easing the installation process and maintenance. This often means removing existing woodlands or planting areas. Receiving Honorable Mention in the 2012 LAGI (Land Art Generator Initiative) competition, this project looks towards establishing a relationship between technology and landscape.

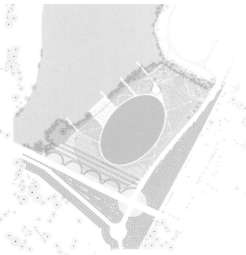

CITY VS PARK   CITY = PARK

Yi Kyu Choe, Unknown Practice

Overpeck County Park, Bergen County, NJ, USA (Phase 1: 2024)

Located in the metropolitan New York City area, northern New Jersey, this park aims to transform this former brownfield site into an exceptional public space. To enrich the site, the landscape proposals include adding trees and plants from the Bergen County residents' home countries. Similar in size to New York's Central Park, this project aims to bring together people from different social and economic backgrounds.

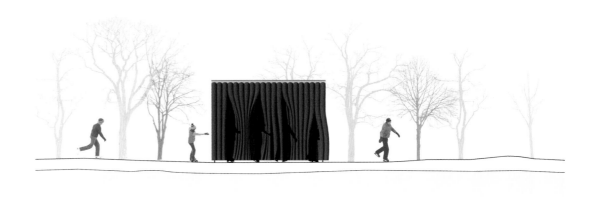

Woolhaus, Assiniboine River, Winnipeg, Manitoba, Canada (2013)

Located on the world's longest natural outdoor skating trail, this project sees the installation of a shelter and art piece in Winnipeg, Canada. Its location on top of a frozen river influenced the project's choice of materials – woollen tubes. Like a warm sweater, this material surrounds the structure, holding warmth inwards, while its translucent roof allows warm sunlight to penetrate its interior.

Martin Rein-Cano, TOPOTEK 1
Berlin, Germany

Through the work of his firm TOPOTEK 1, Martin Rein-Cano addresses social and cultural issues through bold and captivating designs. Born in Buenos Aires, Argentina, Rein-Cano studied art history at Frankfurt University before training in landscape architecture at the Technical Universities of Hannover and Karlsruhe. After working for the office of Peter Walker and Martha Schwartz in San Francisco, Rein-Cano set up his firm in Berlin in 1996. Among numerous awards, TOPOTEK 1 recently received a Gold Medal for their striking project, Superkilen, in Denmark from the International Olympic Committee IOC/IAKS Architecture Award.

Rein-Cano believes landscape architects are 'chiefly responsible for addressing social and cultural issues'. He believes that public spaces 'have to seduce and play with their users, to open them up and give them the feeling that they can achieve things that they might not attempt elsewhere. Public spaces should also reflect their cultural surroundings as well as become generators of culture in and of themselves.' In his own designs, Rein-Cano addresses these issues by reviewing the site's context, determining whether to prioritize the social-cultural context rather than the built, and with an open mind works out the best solution in the most experimental way.

Having spent a great deal of time analysing diverse landscapes and communities, it's perhaps unsurprising that among his favourite sounds, Rein-Cano lists 'Languages that I like the sound of but don't understand, such as Hebrew and Arabic [and] murmurs in general, such as semi-recognizable sounds deciphered between being awake and dreaming.' With Superkilen, an urban park located in one of Copenhagen's most dynamic and multicultural districts, Rein-Cano created an incredibly evocative space that provides an alluring focus for the surrounding community. This design celebrates diversity while creating a public space with its own identity. With local residents selecting the park's objects, Superkilen gives the area a vibrant community space which embraces multiplicity. In Rein-Cano's words, 'There are just so many things that Superkilen offers which you wouldn't find in any other open space.'

Rein-Cano's influence is generated 'through the collage of experiences, interactions and collaborations that are my everyday life ... This experiential and interactive dynamism inspires my work.' He sees it 'as a chain, or a net of influences generating endless sources and maps of motivation'. Rein-Cano finds that it is criticism and input from other disciplines which adds the most value to his projects, explaining that if there 'is no such cross-pollination between roles then it becomes a mere addition of qualities, which defies the purpose of collaboration'.

Rein-Cano explains his creative process as evolving in one of two ways: 'Either it starts with a brainstorm session leading to a straightforward and great idea ... often incredibly simple, and easily translated into reality ... or the brainstorm ends clouded with uncertainty and insecurity – where the destination is unknown.' This latter (and more frequent) outcome requires Rein-Cano to 'sculpt the concept' through a process which he calls 'thinking in form' until a 'specific direction and structure' is achieved.

With the UNESCO World Heritage Cloister Lorsch in Germany, one of the first Christian settlements above the Alps, Rein-Cano describes a place where, while little of its original structure remained, its 'greatest presence was somehow its immense absence'. Here, the central design idea is to make the 'monastery's former existence legible'. What is considered to be the extent of the waned monastery is retold through topographic transcript; the outlines of the church, the walled entrance court, and the conclave and cloister are defined and represented by a raised terrain. In this way, Rein-Cano comments, 'the imprint of lost architectural volumes generates absence legible in space'. The completed design offers visitors a truly poetic and sensual landscaped composition.

'I always say that landscape architects act as though they need to wait to be asked to dance, rather than ask themselves,' Rein-Cano remarks when asked about how he'd like to influence future landscape architects. 'I would like us to take a step forward, grab leadership, show our pride and become real contenders; interacting with new typologies of space, not only with "do-gooder" projects but concentrating more on the social context, creating beauty to encourage social interface. I'd like for the formal outcomes of landscape architecture – the quality of the design – to be as bold as the narratives they are built on.'

The experimental design for the Le Croissant in Paris intends to do just that. Drawing from garden design's long history of fitting foreign elements into landscapes in order to define spatial character, TOPOTEK 1 intends to make use of a collection of exotic, quirky and re-contextualized objects from around the world. These include a circular-shaped table-tennis table, a hat rack and even trees which have been selected for their atypical shapes and colours. As Rein-Cano explains, the project is an 'eclectic approach to public space as a collection of diverse programmes and objects that resembles, for me, places in society that are not clearly defined with one identity but with several identities – as are globalized societies. The Parisian context is one of grand scales and rationalized structures, through the collection of objects [the design intends] to bring the landscape down to an intimate, emotional and human scale.'

Favourite plants

1 Ferns
2 Tulips (*Tulipa*)
3 Irises
4 Roses (*Rosa*)
5 Rhodendrons

Favourite trees

1 Cedar (*Cedrus*)
2 Beech (*Fagus*)
3 Plane (*Platanus*)
4 Palm
5 Cherry (*Prunus*)

Favourite materials

1 Paint/colour
2 Brick
3 Bronze
4 Textiles
5 Asphalt

Favourite contemporary artists

1 Rebecca Saunders
2 Peter Fischli & David Weiss
3 Rosemarie Trockel
4 SUPERFLEX
5 Anish Kapoor

Dissolved as a monastery in 1557, little remains of the original Benedictine Abbey, now a World Heritage Site. This project's design makes the monastery's lost volumes and former existence perceivable on the ground plane. In this case, the church's outline, walled entrance court, concave and cloister are represented above ground by a raised slope, some 35 centimetres (14 inches) high, imprinting the structure's lost dimensions above ground.

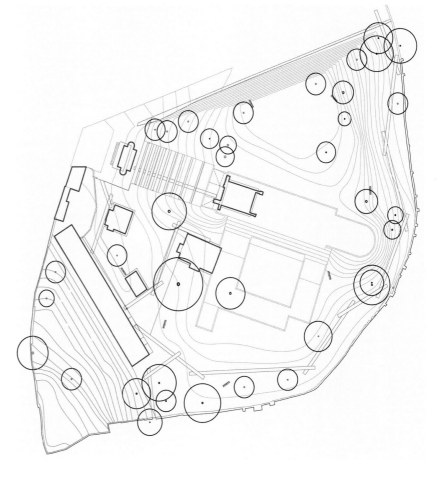

Located in a culturally diverse neighbourhood in Copenhagen, this design makes dynamic use of colour, graphics and objects to create a thriving urban park. Local residents aided in the design process, creating a park that includes objects and ideas that represent the community's interests. The park champions diversity while creating a strong community identity.

The Big Dig installation plays on the childhood saying that 'if you dig deep enough you'll end up in a foreign country'. This 10-metre (33-foot) wide excavated concrete shell is blanketed in artificial grass. Sounds from around the world – such as commuters in New York City, Argentinian cows grazing and the streets of Berlin – are broadcast from the bottom of the hole.

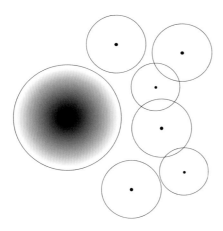

Le Croissant Nanterre, Paris, France (2016)

This crescent-shaped park will be situated in an area of Paris characterized by mixed architectural styles. This park's concept draws on garden design's history of utilizing foreign objects in order to create spatial character. Here, collections of quirky, exotic and re-contextualized objects, such as uniquely shaped trees or a recycled highway ramp used as an outdoor terrace, will be brought together to create an eclectic park.

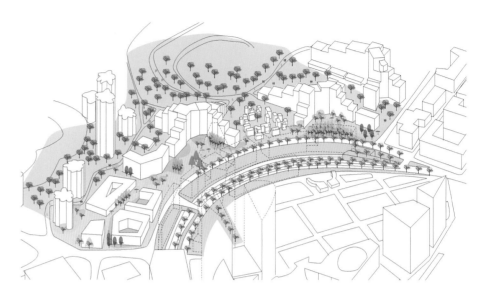

Favourite plants

1 Elderberry (*Sambucus*)
2 Cordgrass (*Spartina*)
3 Bluestar (*Amsonia*)
4 Joe Pye weed (*Eupatorium*)
5 Stonecrop (*Sedum*)

Favourite trees

1 Beech (*Fagus*)
2 White oak (*Quercus alba*)
3 Sumac (*Rhus*)
4 Kentucky Coffeetree
  (*Gymnocladus dioicus*)
5 Indian bean (*Catalpa*)

Favourite contemporary artists

1 Sarah Sze
2 Maya Lin
3 Richard Serra
4 Richard Misrach
5 Julie Mehretu

Favourite natural landscape

The islands of the
Chesapeake Bay, USA

Since founding the New York City-based landscape architecture and urban design firm SCAPE in 2005, Kate Orff has advanced projects of all scales: from harbour-wide planning efforts for the NYC Coastal Protection plan, to on-the-ground ecological investigations such as marine habitat pilot installations in the Gowanus Bay, New York. Orff's work bridges design, science and activism to redefine the role of the landscape architect in the age of climate change. In addition to running a studio she is also an author and editor as well as an Associate Professor at Colombia University where she teaches graduate design studios and interdisciplinary seminars focused on sustainable development, biodiversity and community-based change. Orff herself has been named a United States Artist in 2012 and a National Academician in 2013 while SCAPE has received numerous awards for its built work and the advancement of social and ecological innovation. In 2014 SCAPE's Living Breakwaters project at Staten Island, New York, was selected as a winner of the US Department of Housing and Urban Development's Rebuild by Design Competition and as the winner of the Buckminster Fuller Challenge – the highest award offered for socially responsible design.

Based on her own 'spatial biography' – something that varies according to place of origin, preferences, and so on – Orff states that her 'dream space – at least a good dream – is the shallows and shoals of the Chesapeake Bay [Maryland, USA]'. Having grown up near Annapolis, Maryland, on the Severn River 'with a very close cultural connection between neighbourhoods and the network of rivers, inlets and bays', she explains that 'when I'm designing in the New York Harbor, I'm probably bringing that "spatial biography" into play – the way that Annapolis is still so culturally connected to its Bay context, and aiming to create micro-connections within a regional ecology that brings water, animals and people closer together'. While deeply influenced by this type of natural landscape, in her childhood Orff also experienced the 'prototypical suburban landscapes of America – not necessarily a nightmare, but maybe a bad dream'. These 'residual landscapes' of America are also a part of her spatial biography and a lot of her design work 'develops with both these utopian natural landscapes and dystopian urban or sub-landscapes in mind'.

One might surmise that Orff's research-driven creative process begins with the site's context in order to understand the cycles and processes of the living things that inhabit the landscape. Orff combines the layers of information to 'create new feedback loops, habitats and human experience'. This can be seen with SCAPE's Oyster-tecture project, a part of the *Rising Currents* exhibition at the Museum of Modern Art in New York, NY, in 2010, which proposes to 'nurture an active oyster culture that engages issues of water quality, rising tides and community based development' around the Gowanus Canal in the New York City Inner Harbor. An open framework for the growth of native oysters and marine life is constructed from a field of piles and a web of 'fuzzy rope' that supports oyster and mussel growth and builds a layered 'landscape mosaic'. By taking advantage of the biotic ability of oysters, mussels and eelgrass, the new reef will attenuate waves and clean millions of gallons of harbour water. The design aims to create a regional park along the New York Harbor edge, generating a catalyst for the city's future waterfront use.

'The twenty-first century is the century of the landscape architect,' Orff states when asked about the future of landscape architecture. Orff believes that landscape architects are uniquely placed to bring together the disciplines of design, science and 'community-based processes' to deal with 'complex environmental, social and political issues'. By working more strategically, rather than at 'surface level', landscape architects are well poised to readdress the public realm, beyond creating a 'spruced-up plaza', by resolving 'atmospheric, hydrological and social fragmentation crises'.

In asking Orff what one thing she would do to create better cities of the future, her response that she would 'densify cities' may seem surprising. In fact, what she's proposing is limiting urban sprawl into the countryside and densifying city centres. 'As a landscape architect,' Orff explains, 'I'm interested in improving habitat and expanding the countryside into a thicker and more diverse mosaic and creating escape routes for wildlife to facilitate what surely will be an exodus of movement and shifts in migration patterns for survival.' In the aim of creating spaces with dual purposes in order to maximize their potential, SCAPE created Pave Academy in Redhook, Brooklyn, NY. More than a 'typical' play area for students, the design for this new school playground provides a multifunctional space for both the school and surrounding community. Colourful pavers and lush planting beds create inviting spaces for outdoor learning and community recreation. The park's publicly accessible landscape serves both as a school playground and community gathering space, demonstrating the benefits of a new, dual-use school playground typology.

Moving forward, Orff would like to 'motivate landscape architects to move away from the typologies of the plaza and the park – typical products of the modern city-building era – to create new edge and corridor landscape conditions'. She believes that future landscapes will need to engage 'the edge, the rooftop, the vertical facade and other interstitial, often overlooked spaces'. SCAPE's work does just this as it combines a 'unique matrix of science, design, site and serendipity' to create inspiring works.

Kate Orff,
SCAPE
New York, NY, USA

'Kate has the unique ability to interweave the larger ecological picture with the intimate landscape experience. Rich in research and sharp in focus, her far-reaching and systemic approach intertwines public environmental infrastructure and social engagement to create stimulating public spaces.'

Martin Rein-Cano on Kate Orff

Kate Orff, SCAPE

Pave Academy, Red Hook, Brooklyn, NY, USA (2013)

This urban play area sets the stage for a colourful landscape that assigns a new typology to school playgrounds. Open for both the school and the community to use (during non-school hours), this playground provides an energetic combination of colourful pavers and textured planting beds to create a multifunctional space for both outdoor learning and play.

Kate Orff, SCAPE

Glen Oaks Branch Library, Queens, NY, USA (2012)

This project integrates planted plazas with porous materials to create an urban hardscape that naturally deals with rainfall. A thin layer of soil under the bluestone paving filters rainfall and creates a 'planter-box' effect. Sumac (*Rhus glabra*) is planted into this thin crust and frames the plaza space. Rainwater collection from the rooftop is used to irrigate plants.

241

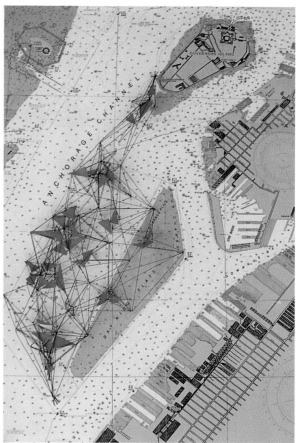

Oyster-tecture, NYC Inner Harbor, Gowanus Bay, NY, USA (ongoing)

This project proposes nurturing an active oyster culture that addresses issues of water quality, rising tides and community-based development in the area surrounding Brooklyn's Red Hook and Gowanus Canal. The proposal uses an open frame made from piles through which a fabric of 'fuzzy rope' is woven. Here, native oysters and marine life grow and develop and, using their biotic abilities, clean Harbor water.

Yoji Sasaki, Ohtori Consultants Environmental Design Institute
Osaka, Japan

A leader in the field of modern landscape architecture in Japan, Yoji Sasaki is a landscape architect with over forty years of experience in practice and teaching. After graduating from Kobe University, Sasaki received a Master of Landscape Architecture at Osaka Prefecture University. Between 1987 and 1989 Sasaki moved to the United States where he studied landscape architecture as a Research Associate at University of California Berkeley and Harvard Graduate School of Design. At present, Sasaki is a Professor in the Department of Environmental Design at Kyoto University of Art and Design, and the design adviser of Ohtori Consultants Environmental Design Institute. Throughout his career Sasaki has won numerous design competitions including Saitama Keyaki Plaza, Roppongi Hills, Niigata Station Plaza, and other international projects including Republic Polytechnic Campus, Hannam the Hill, also receiving the Japanese Institute of Landscape Architect's JILA Prize.

Of his most recent works, Hannam the Hill in the heart of Seoul, South Korea, is one which Sasaki would choose to spend the day enjoying. 'Because in a multicultural environment,' he explains, 'I created a design in harmony with nature and culture.' Hannam the Hill is a residential complex that was designed with the concept of 'showing invisible nature'. The project creates new possibilities for Korean modern residential landscape. Taking inspiration from the countryside village landscapes and traditional pottery, Sasaki explains he learned 'the texture and colour of materials and planting combinations'. This can be seen in the water plaza, which features a steep embankment that has been cleverly converted into a waterfall wall. The wall's rhythmic pattern represents an abstract form of layered strata and provides a textured surface for the water to fall, enhancing its visual and auditory qualities. Art sculptures have been situated inside and outside of the site, converting the entire site into a sculpture park. Elsewhere, elegant and clean-lined elements such as the entrance gate and the bridge take inspiration from the white porcelain found in Korea. Overall, Hannam the Hill achieves a modern expression as a culture in harmony with the natural landscape.

Sasaki believes 'the role of the landscape architect is to give the silent landscape three-dimensional words, and to let it speak'. And in order to do this, Sasaki explains, he follows three principles: 'show the invisible nature', 'express it as a form of relationship between people and nature', and 'place making, which is made by people'. With the rooftop garden courtyard design at Sakuradia Condominium in Saitama-city, northern Tokyo, Sasaki made a space which allows people to reconnect with the natural environment. Sitting on top of the structure, the loading conditions for the garden were severely restricted, making it impossible to plant large trees. In order to avoid a monotonous landscape, Sasaki created diversity through layering. Here, the layering allowed the residents to participate in various activities at the same time, creating a magnetic field of space configuration offering many levels of communication.

Sasaki likes to collaborate 'with people who share the [same] landscape image'. Over the years this has allowed for collaborative design competitions with architects including Shigeru Ban and Fumihiko Maki. Recently he collaborated with Maki on the design of the new Republic Polytechnic campus in Singapore. Located in the woodlands, within a suburban neighbourhood in northern Singapore, this site hosts over 14,000 students. Acknowledging the site's sloping landscape and the adjacent regional park, the design intends to express sensitivity to the context while developing a 'campus in the park'. True to his design ambitions, this design succeeds in creating a campus replete with natural experiences.

Set to be completed in 2023, Sasaki's new Bandai Plaza is located at the entrance of Niigata Station in Niigata, Japan. Acknowledging the site's history and the city's famous trees, the design intends to express sensitivity to its context and develop a new sense of place as a 'station plaza under the forest of willow'. Unlike a typical Japanese station square, Bandai Plaza will not be occupied by bus and taxi parking zones, instead allowing people to sit and enjoy the plaza from under the forest of willow trees. The station intends to incorporate a bridge across the top of the plaza, linking the station to the city. Following his principles in 'place making', the plaza's design has incorporated the results of community participation workshops, resulting in a design that is truly built for its citizens.

Today's landscape architects face the issue of creating a 'sustainable environment through collaborative systems that are not confined to just one specialized field,' Sasaki explains. 'The future of landscape architecture means a profession which creates places which form a fun and attractive environment created through landscape, infrastructure and architecture working together.' In addition to Sasaki's legacy of creating incredibly poetic landscapes that respect nature while providing socially engaging spaces, he would also like to establish a landscape architecture professional education programme.

Through decades of practice, Sasaki has mastered the ability to balance the manmade with the natural. Designing with coloured pencils and a Pentel Sign Pen, Sasaki creates complex spaces that capture the invisible moments within nature set to a backdrop of geometric planes of materials and forms, and in doing so he gives nature an audible voice just heard over the noise of today's densely populated cities.

Favourite plants

1 Sawara cypress (*Chamaecyparis pisifera* 'Filifera Aurea')
2 Mondo grass (*Ophiopogon japonicus*)
3 Sacred bamboo (*Nandina domestica* 'Otafukunanten')
4 Baby's breath spirea (*Spiraea thunbergii*)
5 Camellia (*Camellia japonica*)

Favourite trees

1 Cherry (*Prunus cerasus*)
2 Japanese maple (*Acer palmatum*)
3 Madake (*Phyllostachys bambusoides*)
4 Zelkova (*Zelkova serrata*)
5 Maidenhair (*Ginkgo biloba*)

Favourite materials

1 Quartzite
2 Japanese roof tile
3 Shirakawa sandstone
4 White granite
5 Impala black granite

Hannam the Hill is a luxury apartment and condominium complex located in the heart of Seoul. Using the design concept of 'showing invisible nature', this project converts a steep embankment into a water wall made from strata-like rock formations to create a landscape with sensory qualities. Art sculptures situated inside and outside of residential buildings convert the entire site into a sculpture park.

Located in the woodlands of a suburban neighbourhood of northern Singapore, this design incorporates the naturally sloping site to establish a new 'campus in the park' identity for Republic Polytechnic's 14,000 students. Sasaki developed Fumihiko Maki's 2002 competition-winning design in collaboration with Maki and Associates.

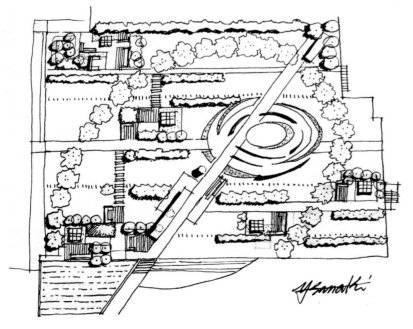

Sakuradia Condominium, Saitama-city, Japan (2008)

This rooftop garden courtyard creates a central green gem for the overlooking condominium complex. With limited loading conditions, and therefore reduced soil depth, large trees and structures had to be avoided. In order to keep the landscape dynamic, the design took a layered approach; by creating overlapping levels of landscape character, areas are defined for various uses.

Favourite plants

1 Japanese mugwort
   (*Artemisia princeps*)
2 Japanese plantain
   (*Plantago asiatica*)
3 Japanese geranium
   (*Geranium thunbergii*)
4 Heart-leaved houttuynia
   (*Houttuynia cordata*)
5 Thistle

Favourite trees

1 Camphor
   (*Cinnamomum camphora*)
2 Bamboo
3 Dogwood (*Cornus*)
4 Cherry (*Prunus*)
5 Maple (*Acer*)

Favourite tools design with

1 Heart
2 Brain
3 Ballpoint pen

Upon graduating from Kuwasawa Design School in Japan, Eiki Danzuki went on to attend Environment Art Studios in Japan, headed by the artist Nobuo Sekine, before founding his firm EARTHSCAPE in 1999. The firm's award-winning projects create experiential works that heighten the connections between humans and nature. These include non-profit projects that seek to give back to society, reclamation projects and public squares.

One such public square is the Jingumae Residence in Shibuya-ku, Tokyo. The 5,176-square metre (55,714-square foot) square is nestled into an area of southwest Tokyo that features restaurants, boutiques and cafés. Designed as 'the living room of the city', complete with a lamp set within a bench, the square provides a peaceful landscape set apart from the city's surrounding bustling activity. The residential gardens are designed with ten different spaces, defined by the themes of trees, wind, light, colour, shadow, soil, sky, water, harvest and smell, allowing visitors to have sensorial connections with nature while providing a luscious setting for the residents to use for outdoor dining, socializing and play.

Taking inspiration from 'the principles hidden in nature and the natural phenomena', Danzuka's designs evolve from 'words', which then go on to form the base of his design concepts. These nature-derived 'conceptual words' inspire his designs and evolve into landscapes that instigate a connection with nature in an almost poetic way. Indeed, Danzuka himself defines his style as 'A prose poem. I design so that infinite imagination is born between words.' This is certainly the case with most of Danzuka's projects. Exploring the interactive quality of landscape architecture, his projects, like poetry, are designed to evoke a feeling that is retained as a memory of that experience. Built to evolve through time, as Danzuka's projects mature and adapt so too will the experiences users have with them, offering a multitude of experiences as seasons, weather and materials change.

Danzuka believes that one of today's most pressing design issues is a lack of 'sensitivity/feeling'. To cope with this issue he has developed the Medical Herbman Café Project (MHCP), initially in Niigata, Japan. Designed in part with EARTHSCAPE, the project travels the globe to teach people about the relationship between humans and nature. The 'Herbman' is literally a human-shaped garden with a variety of herbs planted over different areas of its human form, organized according to how each plant might benefit that part of the human body; for example, 'herbs that aid digestion are planted in the stomach area'. The herbs are updated to suit the needs of each region's culture and climate while all proceeds go to funding the Herbman

project's travels worldwide and to educational, social and environmental projects.

But providing users with memorable experiences of his projects doesn't always coincide with educational elements. With Danzuka's Urban dock LaLaport Toyosu, located in Tokyo, his concept of seeing the landscape as an 'ocean' and the visitors as 'voyagers' created a project which saw the conversion of two dockyards into a playful landscape packed with experiences. The project includes a café, museum and radio station – dotted around so as to resemble islands – set within a graphic landscape that includes white coral-shaped benches seemingly floating among the 'waves'. Without defining specific routes through the landscape, the voyagers 'travel freely through the space, experiencing new discoveries and encounters, sometimes letting their bodies be swept [by] the current, and sometimes navigating through with purpose'. Overlooking Tokyo Bay, the landscape's ground plane undulates above the ground in an almost wave-like form, providing informal seating areas and play spaces for children. The site was designed to conjure memories of the dockyard while providing playful experiences of the present.

When asked about the future of landscape architecture, Danzuka believes that 'landscape architects need to become "water"'. Alluding to the fact that a large percentage of the adult body is made up of water and that water is an element that starts from rain and flows down rivers, through mountains and hills and over valleys before finally reaching the sea, making a 'marvellous natural landscape [through a] natural process'. Always in a state of 'flux', water evolves through various processes and so too, he believes, should landscape architects. In another analogy, Danzuka describes the harmonious balance in which tree roots and leaves function and depend on one another. And so, like trees, landscape architects need to connect 'the divided things in our senses' and make creations from these connections. This, he suggests, will lead designers to good design.

Using his 'heart and brain [and] a ballpoint pen' to design his works, it is no wonder his word-derived concepts create projects which offer visitors a poetic experience of urban spaces. Danzuka's designs, themselves in a constant state of change as their extensive planting plans evolve through seasons, weather and annual life cycles, give users the opportunity to 'feel something individually from [his] design works that will continue forever to the next generation and beyond ...'

Eiki Danzuka, EARTHSCAPE Tokyo, Japan

'Eiki Danzuka's designs reveal a radical and humorous approach to nature and society without being caught up in the power of the market economy. His attitude towards design has given a stimulus to modern society.'

Yoji Sasaki on Eiki Danzuka

Eiki Danzuka, EARTHSCAPE

Sekitei Parking, Shinagawa-ku, Tokyo, Japan (2013)

This unique motorcycle and moped parking garage in the southern part of Tokyo presents a simple, yet effective arrangement of horizontal lines interrupted by various-sized circles, which are allocated as 'parking bays'. Patterned as a black and white striped arrangement, when viewed from either above or at ground level, the graphic qualities of this site's design are compelling.

250

Eiki Danzuka, EARTHSCAPE

Urban Dock LaLaport Toyosu, Tokyo, Japan (2006)

This project's concept presents the site's entire ground plane as an ocean surface, complete with paved undulating 'waves', floating coral seats and water walls. A former shipyard, the site's new design respects its historic use while creating surprise elements for the voyagers, or pedestrians, to experience, such as the playful ground plane that rolls up and out of the ground.

<u>The Jingumae Residence</u>, Shibuya-ku, Tokyo, Japan (2014)

This residential project applies the concept of creating an outdoor living room, including setting a lamp within a bench. This design provides ten different spaces, each themed to provide residents with a sensorial experience on their doorstop. The extensive planting plan, including flower gardens, lush shrubs, grasses and trees, evolves with the seasons to provide a radiant landscape.

Mario Schjetnan,
Grupo de Diseño Urbano
Mexico City, Mexico

Inspired by the work of Modernists such as Mexican architect, Luis Barragán, Brazilian landscape architect, Roberto Burle Marx and American landscape architect, Garret Eckbo, Mario Schjetnan has spent the last thirty-seven years creating award-winning projects in landscape architecture, architecture and urban design. Through the work of his firm Grupo de Diseño Urbano, Schjetnan has created a wide range of projects, of which his most celebrated have been his works in the public realm, such as the Parque Tezozomoc in Mexico City, winning the President's Award of Excellence from the American Society of Landscape Architects. In addition to his design work, Schjetnan has devoted his life to teaching, giving workshops at the Harvard Graduate School of Design and lecturing in universities in the Americas, Australia and China.

'The future of landscape architecture is immense,' Schjetnan exclaims. He believes the future role of the landscape architect is two-fold: they need to proactively protect and conserve 'the natural and built patrimony in our communities, countries and world regions', as well as to take part in a 'new urban agenda of greener, more sustainable, more egalitarian cities'. Schjetnan's own designs address these future ambitions. Often working with low budgets, basic materials and modest details, his projects give much needed improvements which capture the imagination of the community while restoring ecological balance and 'allowing the city to breathe'.

Existing since the 1460s, and receiving over 16 million visitors a year, Chapultepec Park in Mexico City is an example of such an achievement. Schjetnan's involvement saw the enhancement of specific areas of the masterplan developed over two phases. The first phase included improving the water quality and its amenity and irrigation uses, tree maintenance, lighting and services such as food courts and street vendor locations. The second phase included adding a new botanical garden, a fountain promenade, a museum and visitor centre and archaeological restoration to Moctezuma's baths. Choosing this park as one of his most recent projects he would like to spend the day in, Schjetnan reveals that 'within the park there is a particular inner secret garden where you can bring your CDs and play music (jazz or classical) to share'.

Inspiration for Schjetnan's designs comes from the site, 'in all its natural and artificial complexity', he explains. It is in the site's surroundings that Schjetnan finds the 'clues to the needs and aspirations of the users'. His creative process evolves through working with internal teams as well as collaborations with professionals such as scientists, botanists, artists and engineers.

Copalita Eco-Archaeological Park, on the Pacific coast of Mexico, is an example of a project with such a collaboration. Set within an outstanding archaeological site and located within an ecologically rich environment, in addition to the site's archaeological restoration, the park will be built over three phases. Phase one features a visitor centre and café, while phase two includes an archaeological site museum with management and research offices for archaeologists, botanists and administration. The final phase will incorporate an ethnobotanical garden, bird lagoon, crocodile station, an observation tower and a camping area among other services and attractions.

Highlighting what he thinks are today's most pressing design issues: 'water – recycling, harvesting, infiltrating – and the human right to urban quality', Schjetnan would like to 'humanize public space (natural and urban) and make it accessible to all in the city'. An excellent example of how Schjetnan resolves these issues can be found in his Canal de la Cortadura. Located in the port city of Tampico in Tamaulipas, Mexico, this project demonstrates 'that landscape architecture is a transformative, regenerative, aspirational human activity that can integrally improve conditions of marginality, territorial appropriation (safety) and environmental conditions (water pollution, public space, recreation ... and beauty)'. The project is located on a canal near the Tampico's historic centre that connects a large lagoon with the Panuco River and the Gulf of Mexico. The project was part of a larger effort that included cleaning up the badly polluted lagoon and the canal itself, which was trash-filled, polluted and un-navigable with unsightly concrete abutments and adjacent housing. The project's goal was to recover the waterfront space for public use and to create a navigable waterway from the lagoon to the ocean. In redesigning the canal edge Schjetnan created pedestrian-friendly promenades, water features, gardens, plazas and terraces. The refurbished canal promenade now provides opportunities for residential and commercial use, including markets, hotels and restaurants. In improving the water quality, the canal was drained, widened and dredged, which allowed the water to flow in and out with the tide. The impressive design now grants multiple points of access to the water, some stepped and some sloped, some architectural and some planted, providing the community with an inspiring urban landscape for all to enjoy.

Summing up how he would like to influence future generations of landscape architects, Schjetnan explains he 'would like to remind landscape architects and architects that our goal is to achieve imaginative and contemporary solutions to old, new and everyday design problems. These solutions have to be feasible, buildable, efficient and aesthetic with the conviction to conserve and improve the environment.'

Favourite plants

1 Century plant (*Agave americana*)
2 Swiss cheese plant (*Monstera deliciosa*)
3 Ocotillo (*Fouquieria splendens*)
4 Spider plant (*Aralia elegantissima*)
5 Orchids

Favourite trees

1 Flame coral (*Erythrina americana*)
2 Frangipani (*Plumeria*)
3 Fiddle-leaf fig (*Ficus pandurata*)
4 Orchid (*Bauhinia*)
5 Sweet gum (*Liquidambar styraciflua*)

Favourite materials

1 Basalt
2 Decomposed red basalt
3 Concrete
4 Steel
5 Red cedar wood

This project saw the cleaning and redesign of the city canal, enabling a stronger connection between the people and the water's edge. During the cleansing process the canal was widened, dredged and drained, allowing the water to flush in and out with the tide. The new layout sees a livelier promenade edge, incorporating new walkways, gardens, plazas and commercial opportunities.

This project merges an ecologically rich environment, with over thirty-five species of trees, seventeen birds and nineteen reptiles, and an important archaeological site to create an eco-archaeological park. Created over three phases, the project includes a visitor centre and archaeological site museum. Phase three will include the creation of an ethnobotanical garden, bird lagoon and crocodile station.

This high-tech office complex incorporates contemporary open spaces, gardens and water features to provide areas for workers to relax and communicate in a high-quality working environment. The adopted ecological concepts include rainwater harvesting, storm water infiltration and the treatment of grey water on site for use in feature pools and irrigation.

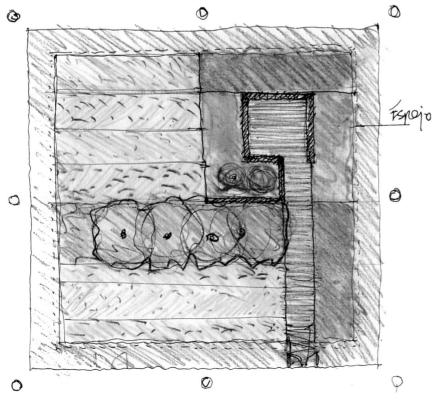

Rehabilitation of Chapultepec Park, Mexico City, Mexico (2010)
With over 16 million people visiting yearly, this fifteenth-century park's rehabilitation saw areas redeveloped over two phases. The first phase involved water quality improvement for irrigation and amenity purposes, as well as new seating areas, improved lighting and the inclusion of food courts and street vendor locations. The second phase saw the addition of a new botanical garden, fountain promenade and visitor centre.

Favourite plants

1 Ocotillo (*Fouquieria splendens*)
2 Mexican aster (*Cosmos bipinnatus*)
3 Red dahlia (*Dahlia coccinea*)
4 Mexican shellflower
  (*Tigridia pavonia*)
5 Aztec lily (*Sprekelia formosissima*)
6 Copper zephyrlily
  (*Zephyranthes longifolia*)
7 Morning glory (*Ipomoea purpurea*)
8 Zakaton (*Muhlenbergia macroura*)

Favourite trees

1 Oak (*Quercus*)
2 Mexican swamp cypress
  (*Taxodium mucronatum*)
3 Copal (*Bursera cuneata*)
4 Red-hot poker
  (*Erythrina abyssinica*)
5 Elephant's ear
  (*Enterolobium cyclocarpum*)

Favourite materials

1 Stone
2 Wood
3 Palm
4 Sascab
5 Concrete

Pedro Guillermo Camarena Berruecos specializes in ecological restoration, green infrastructure and mobility through his work at LAAP, the firm he co-founded in Mexico City. Studying both landscape architecture at the National Autonomous University of Mexico (UNAM) and sustainable development at the University of Lanús, his work is focused on landscape architecture with urban interventions and proposals working at a territorial scale. Camarena Berruecos teaches landscape architecture at UNAM, is a Visiting Professor at Universidad Marista of the Merida, Yucatan, and is the current president of the Landscape Architects Society of Mexico.

'Night insects in the rainforest, mixed birds, Sunday in a happy neighbourhood, water in any presentation, silence in the desert night, the waves under a shiny moon and a crowded restaurant' describe a fitting selection of Camarena Berruecos's favourite sounds. Merging the needs of a sustainable development with optimal social outcomes, his designs draw both from 'the genius of the place' and from understanding a site's ecological and social patterns. People who study ecosystems and the impact humankind has had on them, such as American marine biologist Rachel Carson in her book *The Silent Spring*, have influenced Camarena Berruecos's work. His focus on understanding places and their culture leads him to design spaces that consider time and a project's budget, and are low maintenance while also improving local biodiversity and optimizing water management. 'I prefer a simple design for easy application, like a toolkit for people in any landscape. I believe more in long-term processes rather than single and isolated projects.'

Camarena Berruecos believes that, like him, you would want to spend more than a day enjoying a visit to his project Gardens of Native Flora: 'In this magical place we can see every detail of the plants as they change, different colours and shapes according to whether it is the drought or rainy season.' Completed in 2007, the garden is situated over 2.4 hectares (6 acres) inside the UNAM campus in Mexico City and was designed to demonstrate the potential of using native flora in a specific ecosystem, in this case xerophytic planting in a lava field. The garden's simple design is evocative of Camarena Berruecos's style: divided into a series of rectilinear plots, a central paved road divides the site's forty-two rectilinear plots into twenty-one on either side of the path. Linear low walls clad in stone further delineate the individual plots. In explaining why he would choose this project to spend the day in, he explains: 'I would like to be working here when I'm sixty-four ... doing the garden, digging the weeds ...

and staying involved in the care and maintenance, explaining to those who visit the use of native flora, the way to reduce maintenance costs and saving water while we increase biodiversity inside an urban area.'

Although Camarena Berruecos collaborates with numerous specialists on his projects, it is from the sociologists and scientists that he has learned the most. However, his collaborative relationships are not limited to specialists, he loves to work with people who want to change their neighbourhood who have 'intelligent, revolutionary and ... innovative ideas'. He believes that landscape architects need to include not only the normal list of collaborators, but also academics, public officials and potential users in order to make good teams, and therefore good solutions.

In his response to the question of the future of Mexican landscape architecture, Camarena Berruecos believes that it is headed in two different directions. The first is the one influenced by styles from outside Mexico, which provides more of a decorative landscape vision. The other tends to be focused on resolving the issues of sustainability through using native plant mixes that are less water-demanding. He believes there is a movement towards developing landscape projects that take into consideration ecological, geographical, anthropological, sustainable, artistic and restorative values. 'I think that is where there is the greatest opportunity for landscapers, not only Mexicans but Latin Americans, since we have a great cultural diversity which is derived from an equally rich biodiversity, which rests in a huge diversity of landscapes that we have to protect and in which we must learn to live.'

Camarena Berruecos believes that design issues faced by landscape architects today are both environmental – climate change and the effect on biodiversity – and social – the effects of urban densification – and he equates 'chaotic urban development' with an increasing social fragmentation. To address such issues, he believes landscape architects should 'work more like advisers, promoting creative ideas'. He also talks about giving 'free recipes' for citizens to apply directly themselves, thus taking action in helping to promote and maintain a healthier relationship with the environment. Speaking about his future legacy, Camarena Berruecos explains: 'My goal is that future generations will make a genuine effort to better understand the environments, not only natural, but social and economic environments they will design, so that projects become "life projects". Landscaping is a slow process: dynamic, alive and in constant evolution.'

Pedro Camarena Berruecos, LAAP
Mexico City, Mexico

Pedro Camarena Berruecos is a young landscape architect with many abilities; having worked at the University Ecological Reserve of the National Autonomous University of Mexico, he has become a specialist in the volcanic ecosystems characteristic of this menacing yet beautiful landscape.

Mario Schjetnan on Pedro Camarena Berruecos

Pedro Camarena Berruecos, LAAP

Gardens of Native Flora, UNAM campus, Mexico City, Mexico (2007)

This demonstration garden illustrates the potential of using native flora, xerophytic plants, on a lava field. Located on the UNAM campus, the garden's design is based on rectangular plots organized around a central pedestrian spine. The forty-two plots, twenty-one on each side, are divided by low linear walls and include native plants with ornamental value.

Pedro Camarena Berruecos, LAAP

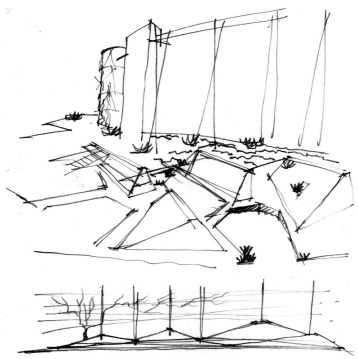

<u>National Laboratory of Sustainability Sciences (LNCIS)</u>, UNAM campus,
Mexico City, Mexico (2014)

This design creates a series of patterned surfaces, based on the superposition
of two scientific forms, the molecular Borromean rings and the Sierpinski triangle.
The graphic shapes have been in-filled with lava rock and plants that thrive in
the dry environment, creating a wildlife corridor near a protected, natural area
inside the Ciudad Universitaria UNAM campus.

Rainer Schmidt,
RSLA
Munich, Germany

Rainer Schmidt is a landscape architect and urban planner who established his firm, Rainer Schmidt Landscape Architects and Urban Planners (RSLA), in 1991. With offices in Munich, Berlin and Bernburg, Germany, over the last twenty years his firm has created numerous award-winning projects through Schmidt's practical and theoretical approach of 'working from location – the spirit of place'. Inspired by philosophers such as Henri Lefebvre and Jean Gebser, Schmidt's designs explore space as it relates to the natural and human scale. Lecturing extensively, including at the University of Beijing in China and University of California, in Berkeley, Schmidt maintains the relationship between nature and culture as the main focus in his teaching and practice.

When asked which one of his recently built works he'd like to spend the day in, Schmidt suggests Park Killesberg, situated in Stuttgart, Germany. In addition to enjoying the artificial topography and water movement, he remarks that he would also like 'to watch people adapt to the new conditions in terms of enjoying landscape and perceiving "nature" from a new point of view'. By presenting new perspectives and manipulating a sense of scale 'the skilful illusion of the new topography intensifies the feeling of being completely absorbed in the landscape and generates a surprisingly playful experience for the park user – a new sensation'.

The site was previously an industrial quarry, which, according to Schmidt, 'informed one of the two themes characterizing its design: a soft, near-natural landscape and manmade quarries as hard topographies'. The 'hard forms' of typical quarry topography are, over time, softened by the regrowth of landscape. This park's design, as Schmidt describes, simulates 'the long natural process of smoothing out irregularities by creating a new topography of lawn "cushions" between path systems'. A new mixed-use development entitled Think K provides another element to the project. Here, the concept of sustainable and ecological development is an underlying theme, with rainwater from Think K's roofs collected underground before being piped through to the new lake in Park Killesberg.

The inspiration for Schmidt's striking designs comes from, in his words, 'knowledge about the history of a location, continuing the history into the future by telling a spatially perceivable "story". The story then becomes "space" [where] space is understood as "use, image, concept", according to Henri Lefebvre.' Developing his creative process further, the 'structural conditions of time in place and the culture behind are studied, explored and almost intuitively turned into a holistic concept which combines space (use, image, spatial organization of uses), function and form as well as atmosphere'. The resulting design concept forms 'an art-like position of "nature by culture" towards the structural conditions'.

In 2005, Schmidt participated in the Federal Garden Show (commonly referred to as BUGA) in Munich. The project saw the creation of differently themed gardens based on the concept of 'the basic organic structure of every form of plant life', with the connecting thread of 'change in perspective, from micro to macro'. Zooming into different areas of a plant's cell structure inspired the form of the four gardens Schmidt designed. The microscopic pattern at the human scale revealed itself as paths and planting, reflecting the patterned images' positive and negative spaces. Interweaving these elements created new perspectives of space, inviting all to play, discover and relax. As Schmidt describes, the 'overall concept is a critical and creative commentary on horticultural shows in general. It is a distinct artistic dissociation from the fair, compartmentalized planting bed as a common and indeed almost archetypal constituent of such shows, proposing its own kind of "educational" aesthetics in the allocation of surfaces, in spatialization, in the creation of atmosphere and meaning for a novel way of experiencing nature.'

Discussing today's most pressing global issues, Schmidt suggests 'meaning, instead of function, gains importance in overcoming the monotony of industrial routines and their spatial phenomena. This needs to be founded, derived and bridged structurally within regional and local conditions.' This is why Schmidt applies the design approach of 'working from location' or 'based on the spirit of the place'. The future of landscape architecture will need to work 'on a distinction of locations, building new "living systems" of structures and elements in the environments of "people and nature"'. In order to make better cities of the future, Schmidt believes 'future spaces need to be conceptualized and implemented holistically in cooperation with engineers, architects and urban planners'. In fact, landscape architecture, he feels, is an important consideration that should be tackled at the beginning of the design process.

Schmidt's advice to future generations of landscape architects is 'to learn from history (Renaissance and Baroque) how open spaces have been shaped and differentiated (public and secret gardens … flower and vegetable gardens) for different social demands and cultural routines.' Accordingly, he feels, 'they need to learn [to develop] a contemporary grammar of building and enriching open spaces [through the addition of] topography, vegetation and materiality in landscapes, parks and gardens, [allowing] for a "freedom" of behaviour in inner and outer open space, merging privacy with the public realm.' However, this 'freedom', he remarks, needs to be balanced with the 'obligations' of integrating the 'spatial organization of the public realm's respective context'.

Favourite plants

1 Maiden grass
 (*Miscanthus sinensis*)
2 Sunflowers (*Helianthus*)
3 Delphiniums
4 Hostas
5 Roses (*Rosa*)

Favourite trees

1 Empress (*Paulownia tomentosa*)
2 Caucasian walnut
 (*Pterocarya fraxinifolia*)
2 Indian bean (*Catalpa bignonioides*)
3 Magnolia (*Magnolia acuminata*)
4 Tulip (*Liriodendron tulipifera*)

Favourite natural landscapes

1 Sahara, Africa
2 Himalayas, South Asia
3 Alps, Europe
4 Rocky Mountains, USA
5 Tuscany, Italy
5 Ticino, Switzerland

Favourite sounds

1 Whispering of leaves
2 Singing of birds

Federal Garden Show, Munich, Germany (2005)

Part of the Federal Garden Show (BUGA), this project included a series of gardens based on the concept of revealing a plant's organic makeup, zoomed-in to show minute details, and thus changing our perception of space. A garden show like no other, the project uses enlarged plants' microscopic patterns, such as the cell structure of marigolds, to create a design which, at the human scale, take the form of paths, planting areas and topography.

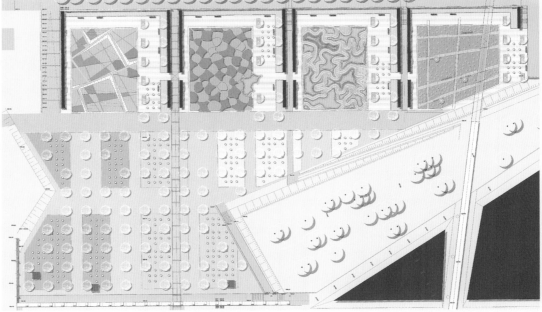

Bavarian National Museum – Entry Square and Courtyards, Munich, Germany (2011)

This project takes inspiration from the design's original features. Influenced by the original square's sunken design, the sloping entrance parterre is defined by a linear stripe of paving and wedge-shaped boxwood hedges. The inner courtyard spaces have been inlaid with stone slabs arranged in floral patterns, echoing the building's scrolled gables.

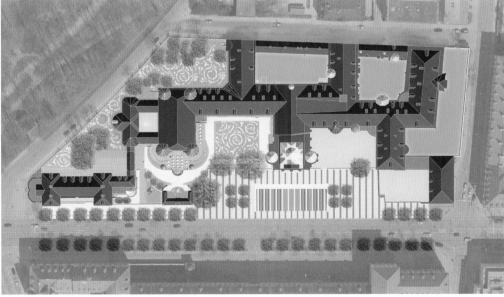

Park Killesberg and Think K, Stuttgart, Germany (2013)
This project comprises a park and a new mixed-used development, Think K. The former quarry site has been transformed into a soft, sinuous park with hard topographic edges, referencing its historic past. Its metamorphosis into a landscape of topographic 'cushions' and paths simultaneously offers privacy and gathering areas. A sustainable development, Think K recycles rainwater into the park's central lake.

Favourite plants

1 Red bistort 'Firetail' (*Persicaria amplexicaule*)
2 Burnet (*Sanguisorba*)
3 Ramsons (*Allium ursinum*)
4 Chives (*Allium schoenoprasum*)
5 Ferns

Favourite trees

1 Old apple
2 Hackberry (*Celtis*)
3 Serviceberry (*Amelanchier*)
4 Sycamore (*Acer pseudoplatanus*)
5 Common olive (*Olea europaea*)

Favourite materials

1 Shell limestone
2 Concrete
3 Oak
4 Steel
5 Syenite

Favourite contemporary artists

1 Egon Schiele
2 Cy Twombly
3 Joseph Beuys
4 Josef Hader
5 Konstantin Wecker

Born in Salzburg, Austria, Christian Henke studied at the Vienna Universities of Applied Arts and of Natural Resources and Life Sciences and the University of Dresden. His designs reflect his dual interests of 'precise engineering' and 'atmospheric conceptualization', creating projects that combine 'sensuality with precise craftsmanship' while responding to the landscape's 'individual heritage'. After several internships, Henke went on to work with Rainer Schmidt, where he met his future collaborator and business partner Elisabeth Lesche, with whom he set up the firm el:ch in Munich in 2005. Since 2008 el:ch has expanded to include an office in Berlin, run by Lesche, where she 'contributes an inclination towards narration and concept, the written word and design employing plants'. Ranging in works from district masterplans to private gardens, the firm's area of expertise is design proposals entered in architectural competitions. These range from purely landscape architecture commissions to architectural and urban projects.

One might expect that 'nature' would come high on a landscape architect's list when asked 'where do you take your inspiration?', and it does in Henke's response. However, as he points out, 'landscapes, in contrast to landscaping, are not a hodgepodge of diverse and unrelated materials, shapes and ideas'. Landscape design features 'logical' structures and 'simple concepts', but designers, he believes, can 'dilute' a landscape and in doing so destroy 'the original landscape's appeal'. This belief is something that inspires Henke to create designs with a limited number of 'features', allowing the strength and quality of the design to create a high-quality landscape. 'I do not try to imitate nature or landscape, but I strive to apply a conclusive design language to our projects.'

This is certainly true with Landhauspark and Promenade in Linz, Austria, where el:ch created a design in which the main goal of the Promenade was to 'purge'. Before being redesigned, the loss of 'spatial coherence' and clutter of materials distracted from the landscape and surrounding buildings. The new design, completed in 2009, features a careful selection of materials, allowing the buildings to stand out, and an open expanse of elongated portions of paving. The Promenade now provides a setting from which to stroll, take in the sights and enjoy the uncluttered facades of the surrounding buildings'. In contrast, the Landhauspark retained many of the park's mature trees, connected by a 'ribbon of turf', and is framed by a long linear bench. In removing the garbage bins and car-parking spaces, this project is a successful example of stripping back to the basics while retaining the historic elements; the park and promenade now provide areas for children to play, 'couples to kiss' and functions to be held.

In describing his creative process, Henke explains that 'intuition arranges a playful texture of possibilities (structures, shapes and materials) and imperatives (functions) … and these parts are combined into a conception.' He states the importance for him of creating landscapes with a sense of 'well-being' and, consequently, that 'sensuality' and 'atmosphere' play key roles in his design process. He is also keen to stress the idea that these concepts must form an essential focus for design issues today. When suggesting urban development as one of the most pressing issues for today's landscape architects, he insists that the key to success can be found in considering landscape on a large scale as an 'atmospheric design process' rather than a process 'based on structures and rules'.

Henke's response to Rainer Schmidt's question of what he'd like to 'conceptualize and get built' exemplifies his treatment of some of his own built and unbuilt projects: 'I would like to design a project involving a restrictive range of economic and environmental specifications, such as a major hotel complex or resort. The aim would be to demonstrate that aesthetics do not have to contradict ecological and economical issues; as they usually are treated [as something] nice to have as opposed to a basic need.'

The Housing project Urbanstraße 11 in Munich built by el:ch in 2008 demonstrates their desire to create spaces which meet both ecological and economical issues through a select group of materials: wood planks for horizontal and vertical surfaces combined with sturdy groundcovers and shrubs. This design creates a series of spaces ranging from a central, multiuse meeting area to more private areas in front of the individual townhouses. Modular furniture allows residents to determine the amount of privacy they desire. The overall design allows for social interactions set against a backdrop of clean-lined, elegant spaces.

The work of el:ch is clearly focused on designing projects which create ecologically rich, economically sustainable and socially interactive spaces set within an atmospheric backdrop. When asked about the future of landscape architecture, Henke's response that landscape architecture 'should play a bigger and more central role in the development of existing and future settlements' comes as no surprise. He further believes that 'diverse topics such as functionality, atmosphere, aesthetics, social and ecological processes must be assessed as a whole, creating synergies and generally more viable structures'.

Christian Henke, el:ch landschaftsarchitekten Munich and Berlin, Germany

'Having started as employees of RSLA, el:ch have successfully developed the creative power necessary to implement durable, quality designs, enabling multidisciplinary cooperation in response to everyday tasks.' Rainer Schmidt on Christian Henke

Wine Garden, Cantina di Terlano, Terlan, Italy (2009)

This roof garden celebrates the surrounding vineyards and mountains by merging the garden space with the extended horizon line through the use of a transparent, glass balustrade. Inspired by local field patterns, rectilinear wooden decks and planting areas organize the roof spaces. Planting includes grasses, bulbs, fragrant herbs and a central pomegranate tree, while pathways are made from local porphyry stone.

Christian Henke, el:ch landschaftsarchitekten

Christian Henke, el:ch landschaftsarchitekten

Landhauspark and Promenade, Linz, Austria (2009)

This project comprises a park and promenade that have both been renovated to create coherent spaces for the town of Linz. The promenade's design saw it stripped back to the essentials, and now features a cohesive paving pattern that unifies the project from curb edge to building facade. The park's design saw it de-cluttered, reorganized and better framed, creating a versatile city park.

Housing project Urbanstraße 11, Munich, Germany (2008)

Through the selection of basic, yet elegant, materials and lush vegetation, this green gem at the centre of a Munich housing project provides a densely populated residential block with both private and communal garden spaces. Here, repeated themes of horizontal and vertical wood surfacing define specific spaces, while sturdy groundcover plants have been chosen to yield seasonal interest.

Martha Schwartz,
Martha Schwartz Partners
London, England, UK

'I love to see new ideas that challenge how we see and think,' Martha Schwartz responds when asked what inspires her award-winning projects. 'I have always been thrilled by visual inventions that are generated by the art world and the works of artists such as Robert Smithson, Walter De Maria, Robert Irwin, Sol LeWitt and Olafur Eliasson.' A landscape architect and an artist, Schwartz focuses her interests on cities, communities and the urban landscape. Over the last thirty years, Schwartz has created highly celebrated works, from site-specific art installations to working with cities at strategic planning levels. Her focus is on environmental sustainability and the creation of awareness about how the urban landscapes underwrite sustainability through functioning as the connective platform for a city's environmental, social and economic health. In addition to her design work, Schwartz is also a tenured Professor in Practice of Landscape Architecture at the Harvard Graduate School of Design and a founding member of the Working Group for Sustainable Cities at Harvard University.

In designing her highly evocative projects, Schwartz attempts 'to hear what is needed to address a site'. 'My mind organizes itself graphically,' Schwartz explains, 'so I go to the plan first to be able to gather my thoughts.' This is carefully analysed, 'like an academic exercise', and then she visits the site, which, in her words, 'pretty much wipes out all memory of the previous stages. The spatial qualities, details and feeling of the site come in at a visceral level. From then on it is a struggle between the visceral and the intellect to synthesize what we know, what the issues are and how to approach this so that we have an aesthetic strategy that can organize and tie together the variable.' For Schwartz, it is unclear where an 'aesthetic direction or inspiration' comes from, but, she explains, 'I often come up with ideas as I am about to fall asleep.' Schwartz's more recent project, Fengming Mountain Park, located in Chongqing, China, presents a design that is orchestrated around the site's prevailing features combined with her characteristic graphic intuition.

The park is set against a backdrop of mountainous peaks, the Sichuan Basin valleys, rice paddy terraces and the Yangtze River located beneath an atmospheric Chongqing grey-white misty sky. These elements inform the design behind the mountain-like pavilions, zigzag-patterned pathways and terraced terrain, while vivid colours are used to contrast with the milk-coloured skyline. The dynamic pavilions provide a stunning navigational component to the design, illuminating the skyline – as bright orange sculptures by day and glowing lanterns by night – leading you through the sloped terrain. The zigzag path ensures the extreme level change is accessible for all while referencing trails winding down a steep mountain. The presence of water is an important element of the site's design and is expressed as a continuous flow leading from the arrival plaza to the lower level, incorporating various effects, including channels, pools and jets, to create a cool, atmospheric backdrop.

In response to what she feels are today's most pressing design issues, Schwartz replies 'climate change and urbanization', she emphasizes the need to improve cities, and in particular to 'support densification and the efficient use of resources'. As she explains, 'Cities are our future and the open spaces must now play an increasingly important role on numerous levels so they function environmentally, socially, culturally and economically.' To achieve this goal and to create successful urban open spaces, Schwartz insists that these spaces must be high quality and beautiful – attracting people and creating value. In her words, 'Design and sustainability cannot be separated. Design is critical in achieving a better quality of life for those in cities.'

Beiqijia Technology Business District, a mixed-used development in Beijing, China, does just this. In 2014 Schwartz and her team completed the demonstration zone and associated show garden. The design includes sunken gardens, bespoke seating elements and gateway structures with integrated lighting. The masterplan, which comprises three different zones – commercial-retail, residential, and a central park – incorporates sustainable urban drainage systems complying with LEED (Leadership in Energy and Environmental Design) Gold-certification. The project locates high-quality, energetic urban space at the forefront of urban development, highlighting the value in including landscape architects early on in the design process of new building development.

When asked about the future of landscape architecture, Schwartz believes that 'as projects are becoming more complex, more clients and institutions are becoming increasingly aware of the importance of the role of public space in the creation of successful projects', highlighting that the role of landscape architects is now often considered in advance of building design. Schwartz concludes that as the rate of urbanization expands, and the desire to achieve 'quality of life' balanced with the 'needs of creating and protecting our ecosystems' strengthens, so too will the landscape architecture profession: 'I would like to have future landscape architects embrace landscape as an art form and a means of expression … We must organize and give shape and meaning to what we make. What we see and how we experience our landscapes shapes us as individuals and citizens of a city, or even a country. I would like landscape architects … to find their own voices when they design, as an individual voice can make a change and a contribution to the world.'

Favourite trees

1 Lombardy poplar
  (*Populus nigra* 'Italica')
2 American elm (*Ulmus americana*)
3 Acacia
4 Willow (*Salix*)
5 White oak (*Quercus alba*)

Favourite contemporary artists

1 Anish Kapoor
2 Richard Artschwager
3 Tara Donovan
4 Olafur Eliasson
5 Jeff Koons

Favourite design tools

1 Pencil
2 Niji Stylist – narrow felt tip
3 Tracing paper – white
4 Rolling ruler
5 Equal space divider
6 Clay

Favourite natural landscape

Marconi Beach, Cape Cod
National Park, MA, USA

Martha Schwartz, Martha Schwartz Partners

This public space design takes inspiration from the square's existing landscape and Studio Daniel Libeskind's theatre. Overlooking Dublin's Grand Canal, the project features a 'cracked glass' theme with a central 'red carpet' connecting the canal to the theatre, broken with pedestrian 'desire lines' and speckled with sticks of light. A 'green carpet', connecting the hotel and office development, features planters with marshland vegetation framed by seating.

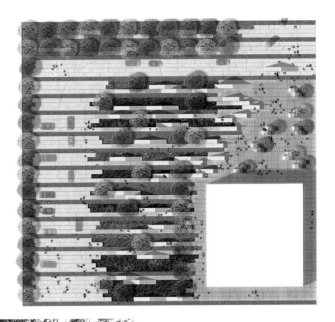

Beiqijia Technology Business District, Beijing, China (2014)

Built as a show garden for a mixed-used development, this demonstration zone incorporates gateway structures with integrated lighting, bespoke seating elements and planting areas. Here, linear lines of staggered planting beds, boardwalks and paving create seating areas and discreet parking bays. Incorporating sustainable strategies, the complete masterplan will include commercial and retail areas, residential zones and a central park.

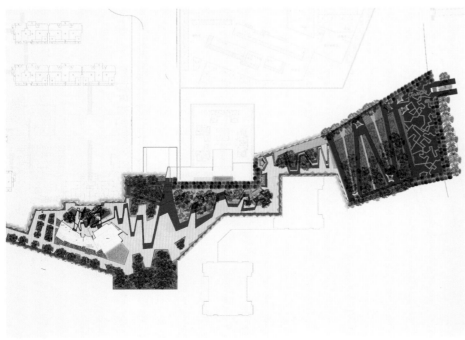

Fengming Mountain Park, Chongqing, Sichuan Province, China (2013)

This park connects the upper arrival area to the plaza below through a zigzagging path system reminiscent of a winding mountain footpath. The fully accessible path introduces a strong graphic language used throughout the project. Vividly coloured sculptural pavilions act like beacons, guiding visitors through the site, while water moves from the arrival space to the valley below, presented as channels, pools and jets.

Favourite plants
1 Agaves (*Agave americana*, *Agave tequilana*, *Agave attenuata*)
2 Mexican feather grass (*Stipa tenuissima*)
3 Blue finger (*Senecio mandraliscae*)
4 Mexican bush sage (*Salvia leucantha*)
5 Lavender (*Lavandula angustifolia*)

Favourite trees
1 Southern live oak (*Quercus virginiana*)
2 Jacaranda (*Jacaranda mimosifolia*)
3 Common olive (*Olea europaea*)
4 Shaving brush (*Pseudobombax ellipticum*)
5 American sycamore (*Platanus occidentalis*)

Favourite natural landscape
Muir Woods National Monument, CA, USA

Born in Mexico City, Claudia Harari first studied architecture before her interest in landscape architecture led to an internship with Peter Walker's office in 2001. After obtaining a Master in Landscape Architecture from Harvard University Graduate School of Design, where she studied under professors such as Michael Van Valkenburgh, Gary Hildebrand, George Hargreaves and Martha Schwartz, she then went on to collaborate with Peter Walker and Martha Schwartz before returning to Mexico. In 2005, together with her partner Silverio Sierra, she set up the firm HLA in Monterrey, Mexico, receiving their first ASLA Honor Award from the American Society of Landscape Architects for Horno 3 – Museum of Steel in Monterrey, NL, Mexico, 2009. When designing spaces, Harari will visit a site at different times of the day, on different days, and undertake personal 'interviews' with clients whereby she discerns exactly what they want. This, together with understanding the site's sense of place, its surrounding context, its users and its programmatic needs, pushes the design forward with conceptual sketches evolving into 2D and 3D explorations from which one or two of the best solutions are selected.

This design process has led to the award-winning project Horno 3 – Museum of Steel, described by Harari as a 'once in a lifetime [opportunity where] you get to design a landscape around an iron furnace by recycling its pieces'. This project takes a formal industrial site and transforms it into a museum and learning centre where visitors can relax, play or even have lunch. Done in collaboration with Grimshaw Architects and with her friend, the designer James A Lord, the new museum's design blurs the boundary between exterior and interior with 1,700 square metres (18,298 square feet) of green roofs blanketing both the structure and the museum's central symbol, a pleated steel structure that features an extensive green roof. It is perhaps Harari's multidisciplinary background which has led to a project that celebrates the '... steel-making process and artfully dissolves the borders between architecture and landscape'.

The museum's sustainable strategies, including rainwater harvesting, recycling of site materials, energy-efficient fountains and green roofs, are all examples of how Harari deals with what she feels are pressing global issues. 'Climate change, natural resources depletion and contamination, sprawl, fast urban population growth, immigration. In developing countries we face [these] issues magnified everyday, while at the same time we work to educate our clients to value landscape design as a way to address these issues.' Harari's work and education in the United States have led her to embrace international trends in technologies and techniques and use them to push the boundaries of contemporary landscape architecture in Mexico. With influences such as Brazilian landscape architect, Roberto Burle Marx, and past collaborations with internationally celebrated landscape architects, it is no wonder that Harari would like 'to inspire more talented Mexican and Latin American designers to choose landscape architecture as their way of expression'.

In 2016, together with architects from Populous and VFO, Harari will unveil Latin America's first LEED (Leadership in Energy and Environmental Design) certified soccer stadium located in Guadalupe, NL, Mexico. The Monterrey Soccer Stadium Park's location, sited on a former landfill site next to the La Silla River, lends itself to being a new urban park and plaza for the city of Guadalupe. According to Harari, the project's LEED certification is 'due to the landscape intervention transforming the huge parking area into an urban forest with a web of rain gardens that will treat storm water on site'. Harari's experience with working in urban environments, and her work with talented designers, whose buildings' geometries she takes inspiration from, leads to projects which 'translate it all into some artful expression that is very graphic/visual and meaningful for its users, but which works at all other levels'. This is certainly is the case with the soccer stadium park which seems to be an extension of the stadium's organic lines, bending and arching towards the La Silla River where it links up to a 20-kilometre (12.4-mile) riverbank park.

In creating better cities for the future, Harari believes that with an increasing number of people living in urban centres it is becoming ever more important to create 'high-quality, safe and vibrant' parks and plazas, which bring people together despite 'social, economic and racial differences'.

Harari's driving force of providing city dwellers with a better quality of life and creating resilient, exciting and sophisticated sustainable open spaces comes as no surprise. Her work is able to span the fields of architecture and landscape architecture, allowing her to collaborate with (and understand the needs of) architects and engineers in order to maximize a landscape's potential for the creation of exciting and sustainable urban projects on a large scale. Considering the future of landscape architecture, Harari would like to see it become 'the leading discipline in the design and planning of the most sustainable and meaningful cities in the future'.

Claudia Harari, HLA Harari Landscape Architecture San Pedro Garza García, NL, Mexico

'Claudia utilizes her adventurous nature to create highly memorable landscapes. Her artistic approach is based on a strong sensibility for materials and colours, giving her designs a strong visual language with graphic qualities.'

Martha Schwartz on Claudia Harari

Monterrey Soccer Stadium Park, Guadalupe, NL, Mexico (2016)

A former landfill site, this project takes inspiration from flowing water patterns, visible in the forms of the planting beds, paving patterns and fluid rows of trees and plants. Transforming the site into a large urban forest, complete with rain-water gardens and on-site storm water treatment, the project is set to make a dynamic new urban park while revitalizing the surrounding area.

Claudia Harari, HLA Harari Landscape Architecture

Claudia Harari, HLA Harari Landscape Architecture

<u>Horno 3 – Museum of Steel</u>, Monterrey, NL, Mexico (2008)

This reclamation project celebrates the steel-making process and blurs the boundaries between architecture and landscape architecture. The design transforms a former steel foundry into a museum incorporating sustainable strategies such as storm water harvesting, recycling site materials and green roofs. The new museum gallery's pleated green roof provides a distinctive identity for the museum.

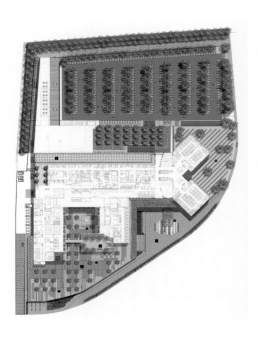

<u>CMZH – Zambrano Helion Medical Center</u>, San Pedro Garza García, NL, Mexico (2012)

This project comprises a series of patios and terraces built on top of concrete slabs, necessitating minimal soil depths and therefore drought-tolerant plants, such as agaves, lavender, rosemary, sedums and grasses. The building's geometry inspired the repetitive lines of planting, paths and water, orientated to frame views of the surrounding landscape.

Günther Vogt,
VOGT Landscape
Zurich, Switzerland

As a child, Günther Vogt was surrounded by huge gardens, those of his mother and his two grandmothers. 'Growing up in [gardens] like [these] as a child was certainly decisive, and it also shaped my perception of scale which still interests me so much, right up to the present day and plays an important role in our projects,' Vogt explains. Today, Vogt is a landscape architect with a passion for and extensive knowledge of plants and literature. Establishing VOGT Landscape in 2000, Vogt develops global projects through analytical and model-based design. In 2010, he opened Case Studio VOGT in Zurich as a platform for research and exhibition. In 2012, Vogt was award the Prix Meret Oppenheim for his projects and surveys both in landscape architecture and urban development and his constant work with architects and artists.

Evolving his work through teamwork, Vogt explains that 'discussions among ourselves, designing by discussion, the discursive design, plays a central role' in his creative process. 'For the project teams, I am primarily a discussion partner, you could say a kind of sparring partner – and sometimes also a killjoy.' Vogt intentionally tries to avoid the project's day-to-day design issues. In this way he doesn't get 'too involved' and become 'trapped' by issues. 'From a certain distance and with a clear overview,' he explains, 'I can radicalize much more effectively as well as contribute critical questions.' Vogt also places value on the purpose of the existing landscape. Concluding that two 'approaches are needed: a scientific, knowledge-based approach as well as an aesthetic one. Without the former the design becomes too superficial.' Clearly inspired by teamwork, Vogt also feels that he learns a lot from collaborating with other professionals. Using collaboration with artists as an example, he explains, 'What fascinates me, is their very intense analysis leading up to a work, through research and by acquiring knowledge of a subject area they originally knew nothing about.'

Design principles

'With which principles and tools do we design the landscapes of the city? Between the task itself, natural conditions, scientific parameters, social issues and design questions, the search moves to the right design for the specific location.'

Scientific studies

'Field trips to certain landscapes work as a series of scientific studies … at the beginning, mostly unintentional interest in certain phenomena, whether geological, biological or manmade, become specific work.'

Pedestrian experience

'The view of the pedestrian is of fundamental importance for the planning process … the sequence of all the rooms we pass through before and after the designed space.'

In 2008 VOGT finished the first phase of Novartis Campus Park, in Basel, Switzerland, a park that, as Vogt describes 'sequentially reconstructs the natural phenomena of the surrounding Rhine terraces', both geologically and botanically, merging them by means of design into an atmospheric park landscape. The park's alluring planting concept situates, furthest from the Rhine shore, a forest of indigenous woody plants where huge glacial boulders have remained as the oldest evidence of glacial activity. Deeper into the wood, lime trees are arranged at uncomfortable angles, the bases of their trunks hidden by pebbles, creating a landscape frozen in a moment of devastation. The park's middle section comprises large expanses of lawn. Here, paths bifurcate into raised terrain, reconstructing another Basel phenomenon whereby a narrow track cuts into the earth, forming an overgrown tunnel of dense shrub. Visitors then reach the lower terraces adjacent to the Rhine where reeds are intermittently interrupted by groups of birch and cottonwood trees. Taking advantage of natural circumstances, this design creates a sublime park with a dynamic, if not educational, planting and landscape narrative.

Vogt believes that the difference between city and landscape, 'no longer exists, … and if this is the case, then we must discuss landscape in an entirely different way. Urbanized landscape means that the city has spread extensively into the landscape and taken possession of it.' It is this separation of functions that Vogt believes is one of the 'major deficits of Modernism: people live in one area, work in another and spend their leisure time in a third area of the city. This is actually an unbelievable system and today you ask yourself why in the first place separate everything in order to connect it again by means of an extremely expensive transportation infrastructure?' With the distance between home, work and 'what are termed local recreation areas' expanding, Vogt explains, so too will 'mobility'.

When asked about the future for landscape architecture, Vogt explains that 'ultimately society will generate the directives for us … All the new tasks and themes in our discipline such as sustainability, ecology or a natural kind of design did not emerge from the specialist discipline itself, but from the social and political processes and developments by which we are driven, and are borne to a far greater extent than by developments within our own discipline. Then, like seismographers, we landscape architects must record these social developments and themes, develop them and find answers.'

Rectory Farm, his project located in London's green belt, has been identified as a sustainable gravel resource. Here, the construction of a framework below ground supports the creation of a park above, allowing for gravel to be extracted without disturbing the visible landscape. As well as providing functional space below ground that can accommodate future uses, the design enables excavation to continue while minimizing the impact on the green belt. The masterplan offers a vision and guiding framework for how the park may be developed over time in parallel with the gravel extraction process. As Vogt explains, 'Rectory Farm features two entirely different landscapes as a result of the different time frames on which the project is based – the gravel extraction underground and the creation of a park on the surface.'

Rectory Farm, London, England, UK (2021)

Rectory Farm has been identified as a strategic gravel resource for the London area. Mining will take place underneath a constructed slab, creating space below ground for gravel extraction, while above ground the public park maintains London's green belt, improving local connectivity and biodiversity. The masterplan illustrates how the park can develop in parallel with the gravel extraction process.

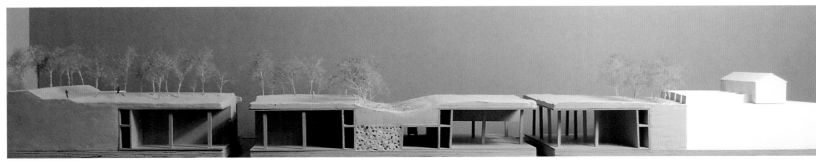

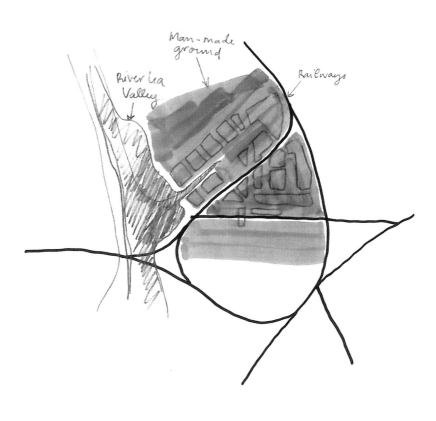

Athletes Village, London, England, UK (2012)
Located between the River Lea and Leyton, a residential area in East London, this project's open space design references the area's urban context and natural characteristics. Originally used as the Athletes Village in the London 2012 Olympic Games, the site's surrounding topography, plants and watercourses informed the character of the public squares and open spaces. The site is now a residential community that forms part of the Stratford City development.

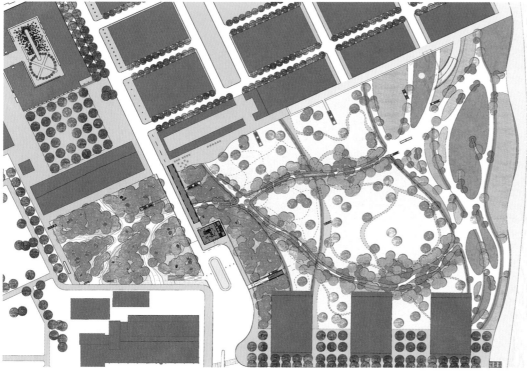

Novartis Campus Park, Basel, Switzerland (Phase 1: 2008 / Phase 2: 2016)
This park sequentially reconstructs the natural phenomena of the surrounding Rhine terraces. The area furthest from shore is designed as a forest with huge glacial boulders. Deeper in the wood, lime trees stand tilted at uncomfortable angles, almost frozen in time. Lawns define the park's middle section, interrupted by paths bisecting the rising terrain, while the lower terraces feature reed beds punctuated with trees.

Favourite plants

1 Ivy (*Hedera helix*)
2 Common box
   (*Buxus sempervirens*)
3 Red fescue (*Festuca rubra*)
4 Common holly (*Ilex aquifolium*)
5 Common privet
   (*Ligustrum vulgare*)

Favourite trees

1 English oak (*Quercus robur*)
2 Common hornbeam
   (*Carpinus betulus*)
3 European beech (*Fagus sylvatica*)
4 Field maple (*Acer campestre*)
5 Cedar of Lebanon (*Cedrus libani*)

Favourite natural landscape

1 Salar de Uyuni, Bolivia
2 Zabriskie Point, CA, USA
3 Mima Mounds, WA, USA
4 Fern Canyon, CA, USA
5 Lake Manicouagan,
   Québec, Canada

Rémy Turquin forms one half of the firm Bassinet Turquin Paysage, based in Paris, France. Together with his partner, Grégoire Bassinet, they established their firm in 2010 and have since built a dynamic team, believing that 'each new project should be an occasion to build a wholesome, meaningful universe, born from its environment but also a testimony of multiple references'. While each is equipped with a palette of skills – Turquin comes from a illustration background and Bassinet from gardening – they approach each project with the necessary creative and technical skills needed to enable them to create inspiring and holistic designs.

Their projects have included various collaborations with big and small architecture firms, including Shigeru Ban, LIN Architects, Boidot & Robin Architectes and Kubota & Bachmann Architects. Each collaborative partnership has given them the opportunity to learn from diverse working methods and points of view, allowing them to acquire new creative ways of working. In their design work, they very much welcome these new opportunities to enhance their range of skills and 'expand their creative horizons'.

The roof garden Cité Musicale in Boulogne-Billancourt, Paris is an example of such a collaboration. The roof garden is situated on top of a vast music complex designed by Shigeru Ban and Jean de Gastines Architects on Seguin Island overlooking the Seine River. The design will form part of the urban complex by architect Jean Nouvel and landscape architect Michel Desvigne. According to Turquin, their concept aims 'to answer the technical challenge of the project by finding solutions blooming with poetry'. Using an endangered ecosystem in the Île-de-France region of France, calcareous grasslands, the gardens will provide a dynamic backdrop from which to enjoy the Seine River valley. The planting hierarchy has been defined by the 'popularity' of spaces, with more delicate plantings placed in areas with minimal pedestrian access and sturdier plants located in zones with a higher footfall. With particular attention paid to colour gradients and seasons, the design will provide experiential journeys of the passing seasons enhanced by the topography, the building's stunning architecture, the views and the garden's proximity to the Seine River.

Their design for a cemetery in the small town of Ermenonville is, in their words, 'a place where everything overlaps'. A mix of new and old headstones, 'it's a place that's alive'. Centrally located, near to the city hall, school and church, in addition to designing new stelae made from local limestone, Bassinet Turquin's plan allows the existing pine woodland and the gravestones to coexist while creating spaces for all.

The duo believes that 'to seek inspiration means to give up all forms of rest', and they are always looking for ways in which to 'update' their knowledge, whether it involves the arts, architecture, botany, science or any other discipline. This 'search' for inspiration takes the form of a comprehensive archive whereby pictures of projects are categorized and retained for future inspiration. Their most 'complete' version of this comes in the form of the 'landscape book', a three-volume manuscript, each concentrating on a single theme: nature, urbanism and infrastructures. The book includes more than 3,000 titles all represented by four pictures over two pages. According to Turquin, the book represents 'different patterns of inspiration for landscape architects'. Their inspiration comes from everywhere and everything: artwork, roads, maps and sculpture – and merging these contrasting inspirations often informs the studio's designs.

'The goal is to balance our capacity to apprehend the site with all its complexities while trying to listen to our intuition,' Turquin explains. 'We aim to find plans that will ring true, rather than try to leave our stylistic signature.' Their thorough research into a site's potential combined with their constant search for inspiration creates incredibly unique and site-specific designs.

Their 12 quai Henri IV project, located in Paris, takes its inspiration from Parisian public squares and their 'blatantly' natural aesthetic. The garden's design creates a space with dense planting that helps to create a successful dialogue between the human scale and the residential building, designed by LIN Architects. Using the concept of the classic Parisian public square and updating it with curves inspired by artists Robert Mangold and Jean Arp, Bassinet Turquin Paysage created a garden that features meandering paths and luscious planting, offering visitors a sensorial experience of texture, scent and colour. A nod to the rockeries in Buttes-Chaumont Park in Paris, an arching, in-situ concrete structure creates a sculptural shelter for residents.

According to Turquin, their diverse repertoire of projects and designs always 'endeavours to achieve a demanding attitude towards every aspect of our projects – composition, architecture of space and general meanings'. Their use of inspirational imagery combined with sophisticated planting strategies and ecological systems also plays an important role in their work, and their ability to balance strong concepts with the natural world is an achievement noted in most of their designs.

Rémy Turquin,
Bassinet Turquin Paysage
Paris, France

'I'll always remember Rémy as the guy who wanted to climb a glacier in red sneakers.' Günther Vogt on Remy Turquin

Rémy Turquin, Bassinet Turquin Paysage

12 quai Henri IV, Paris, France (2015)

This garden space uses luscious planting and tall trees to create an intimate garden surrounding the residential building by LIN Architects. A winding path curves through an atmosphere of densely planted groundcover and tall beech and maple trees, creating a sensory journey through a textured, colourful garden space. At the heart of the design sits a bespoke cavern-like, curving bicycle shelter.

Rémy Turquin, Bassinet Turquin Paysage

<u>Cité Musicale</u>, Boulogne-Billancourt, Paris, France (2016)

Enveloping this large music complex's expansive roof, this garden space is restricted by minimal soil depths and high wind and sun exposure. This led to the concept of creating a meadow landscape rich in plant species while also offering panoramic views. A complex planting palette was created, as highlighted in the illustration, offering seasonal interest through colour.

Peter Walker,
PWP Landscape Architecture
Berkeley, CA, USA

In a career spanning five decades, Peter Walker has exerted a profound influence on the field of landscape architecture. Identifying the source of his inspiration and how it has informed his work, Walker explains: 'I have based my practice on the design work of André Le Nôtre, Giacomo Vignola and Dan Kiley, as well as the Minimalist artists of the 1960s: Donald Judd, Carl Andre, Richard Long and Sol LeWitt, among others. I admire the former for their ability to craft landscapes of special boldness, sustaining beauty and refined scale. I admire the latter for their economy of means, use of industrial process and geometry, along with a clarity and refinement in craft and detail. These designers and artists inform our efforts to produce important and iconic works of landscape.'

Since training at the University of California, Berkeley, and at the Harvard Graduate School of Design, Walker has pursued a highly successful career as a professor, lecturer, advisor, author and leader of numerous design firms. Walker has designed landscapes all around the world, including the United States, Asia, Australia and Europe. Yet, regardless of the expansive range of projects he undertakes, from gardens to city masterplans, Walker has a 'dedicated concern for urban and environmental issues'. In addition to winning numerous high-profile awards for his projects, Walker's accolades include Harvard's Centennial Medal, the ASLA Medal, from the American Society of Landscape Architects, and the Honor Award of the American Institute of Architects. PWP is currently working on a 'once in a lifetime opportunity' at Barangaroo in Sydney, Australia (in collaboration with Rogers Stirk Harbour + Partners and Skidmore, Owings & Merrill); this project will transform a former container port into a mixed-use development including a public park in the form of a harbour headland.

Of his recently built projects Walker would like to spend the day in the National September 11 Memorial in New York City. 'First, I would enjoy its craft,' Walker explains. 'Second, I would like to observe the crowds, their movement and varied demeanour, because the completed design intends to serve both as a memorial and a public-park open space for the surrounding high-density neighbourhoods. Third, I would enjoy the plantings and the rows of trees. They are supported by a complex soil- and water-recycling system with retention basins seven storeys below. These basins store water collected in the spring and use it for irrigation in the summer and fall. The growth of the swamp white oaks will enrich and change the memorial over time,' he concludes. For this highly celebrated design, PWP joined architect Michael Arad in the memorial design competition's final stage with the aim of imbuing the project with a more welcoming atmosphere.

The memorial takes the form of two areas where square voids mark the sites of the former World Trade Center towers. Water flows down the walls of the voids. The names of the casualties from the attacks in 2001 and 1993 are listed on a bronze parapet. Set back from the busy Lower Manhattan streets, the landscape incorporates both lawn and paved areas, with granite slabs providing seating and a forest of swamp white oaks creating an atmosphere that encourages reflection. In order to define areas for contemplation and circulation, the forest of trees creates a landscape that is both formal and naturalistic. Viewed east to west, the oaks are aligned along a regular grid interrupted by granite slabs; viewed north to south, the planting is reminiscent of a natural forest.

Walker collaborates with 'all parties' from clients and architects to cultural historians. He explains that his design process always begins 'with an examination of the site within its context of orientation, ecology, location, weather range, water movement and its flora' and continues with discussions with collaborators. From here, the 'resultant design evolves from diagrammatic analysis to alternative concept sketches, through preliminary alternative designs, design development with material and plant selections, construction drawings and details, and, finally, careful supervision of construction'.

The competition-winning design for the Novartis Headquarters landscape masterplan transforms a 21-hectare (51-acre) site beside the Rhine River in Basel, Switzerland, from a former industrial landscape into a pedestrian-friendly research and administrative campus complete with outdoor art, trees and parks. Novartis commissioned the Italian architect Vittorio Lampugnani to create a new urban-design plan, which developed a central spine along historic Fabrikstraße, pedestrian arcades and a grid layout for future buildings by such world-famous architects as Frank Gehry, Renzo Piano and Tadao Ando.

Looking to the future, Walker admits, 'I have no idea what is to come, because it will be the product of future landscape architects and societies. I know that almost all my academic training has become obsolete over my time of practice (fifty-plus years). The exceptions are what I learned about history, grading and plant materials'. Asked how he'd like to influence future landscape architects, Walker explains, 'I hope that we will be primarily remembered first for our completed work, then for my twenty years of teaching and continuous design publication.'

Trees
'The trees on the majority of projects are by far the most important elements; they provide shade, the intermediate scale between the pedestrian and the architecture and cars. They also provide oxygen in our increasingly urbanized environment. They symbolically represent life.'

Plants and materials
'Next is grass, groundcover and pervious pavements that allow water to recycle back to the aquifer to then be re-used for irrigation.'

Spaces
'Finally, all of the above should define a series of elegantly scaled spaces for aesthetic effect and functional activity.'

This outdoor gallery provides a backdrop to a significant collection of modern sculpture. Responding to Renzo Piano's building, parallel 'archaeological' walls frame views from the Arts District's main street, through the building, towards the garden. Display areas are defined by rows of trees, holly hedges and stone plinths, while water features add to the ambience.

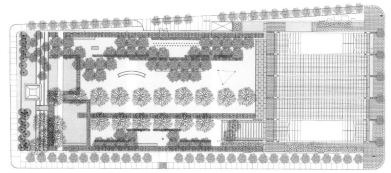

National September 11 Memorial, New York, NY, USA (ongoing)
This memorial's design features two large square voids lined with waterfalls. Around the edges of these voids the names of the victims of the 2001 and 1993 attacks are listed on a bronze parapet. Set back from the streets of Lower Manhattan, granite slabs and planting beds create an urban space where one can reflect and contemplate under a canopy of hundreds of swamp white oaks.

PWP won the 1999 design competition to transform a 21-hectare (51-acre) site running along the Rhine River from a paved, post-industrial landscape to a contemporary, pedestrian-friendly campus. Creating informal meeting areas and private areas for quiet contemplation, the research and administrative campus for Novartis Headquarters features art installations, tree-planted squares and walkways, parks and water features.

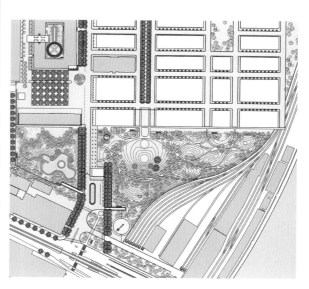

Barangaroo, Sydney, Australia
(Barangaroo Point: 2015 / Barangaroo Precinct: 2025)

This project transforms a former container port in central Sydney into a publicly accessible park and mixed-use development. PWP is leading the public domain strategy for the site's three redevelopment areas: Barangaroo Point, Central Barangaroo and Barangaroo South. The design is highlighted by the re-creation of the 1836 headland with a shoreline promenade constructed of sandstone blocks quarried on site.

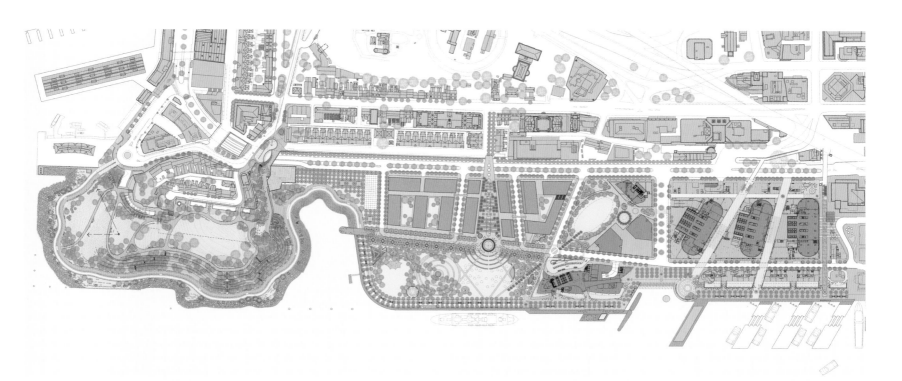

Tom Leader established his firm in 2001 after working with Peter Walker and Partners, where he designed award-winning projects both in the United States and internationally. Since then his practice has received Honor Awards from the American Society of Landscape Architects, and in 2012 received the Urban Land Institute's Open Space Award for Railroad Park. Leader's work seeks to create designs that are original but also pragmatic, complementing the studio's ambition to apply experimental and emerging ideas in a practical manner. Although experienced in large-scale projects, Leader does not shy away from small-scale works, as seen with his Pool Pavilion Forest project, located in Napa Valley, California, a landscape featuring work by the artist James Turrell.

'"Collaboration" stands for a lot of different ways of working with others,' Leader explains. Leader's studio tends to work in a 'team situation', collaborating with the usual groups such as architects and engineers where the 'collaboration can be a fairly practical search for solutions based on function'. However, with his Pool Pavilion Forest project, where he worked with architect Jim Jennings and James Turrell, 'it can be a real meeting of like minds with certain ideas that fit together well'. For future collaborations, Leader is keen to work with a writer 'where we could imagine a story unfolding about a community'. Stories are a medium that almost everyone understands; yet 'we're so limited in how we think about them'.

It is perhaps not surprising that Leader selected his award-winning Railroad Park in Birmingham, Alabama, as one of his most recent projects to spend the day in. Working with a large team of consultants, Leader completed this park and masterplan for the rail corridor in 2010. When Leader visits the site now, he enjoys spending time walking through the park, looping in different directions. He states 'that was one of the real revelations of that project – the importance of loops. But not like a flat running track, more like a web laid out over varying topography and water.' The park's new topography created a lake and a stream, and provides flood protection and biofiltration, as well as knolls offering visitors the chance to view the trains travelling along the 4.6-metre (15-foot) high rail viaduct on one side of the park. 'You ramp up to the level of the moving trains, around over a rain curtain, through forest, down through a Greek theatre – and there are just a lot of ways and combinations so it always feels interesting, different views and exposures to the city and the rail.' In consideration of this, and of all parks, Leader believes they are places to be 'in motion rather than in respite and repose'. His creative process for projects varies greatly. For each one, time is spent looking at the 'situation', 'thinking about it' and searching for the 'essential, endemic thing or dynamic' on which they base their work. For Railroad Park it was the eleven rail tracks. And in order to evolve his designs Leader takes time to understand the needs of the people and research their culture. He believes that gaining people's trust is essential to the success of this process, ensuring that the community can see that their interests are being represented. 'You start many projects where someone wants to import something they have seen somewhere else. Our job is to put them in contact with the fantastic thing or experience that may have been hiding in plain sight; we just need to re-frame it and make it visible.'

His future project, Making Ground/Farming Water, is a speculative proposal based on studies and research about the intersection of rising sea levels and seismic activity along the San Francisco Bay, California, shoreline. He describes the project as 'an odd combination because one factor is very incremental and the other is instantaneous', but aims to resolve both future dilemmas. The problems and the solutions concern the acceptance of the Bay's 'aquatic lifestyle' and 'living in partnership with water'. Reconnecting to a partnership that existed there 200 years ago, when the Bay provided a fertile and productive environment in terms of biodiversity and agriculture, his proposals 'dramatically alter the topography of low-lying urban edges such as the Corte Madera Creek waterfront'. This, combined with creating deeper tidal channels, will produce material that could be used to create 'large island mounds, much like their historic predecessor, Native American shell mounds', in turn providing more area for potential future development, as well as the possibility for saltwater farming of both biofuels and shellfish.

Leader would like to see an improved link in the future between the academic world and the practice of landscape architecture, believing there should be a complementary relationship between the two. He believes that 'the two really need each other, but when they don't interact enough, distrust and misunderstandings develop'. Leader himself trained at Harvard Graduate School of Design, where Peter Walker organized a 'good boot camp' in the first year, asking tough questions but respecting audacity. When working for Walker later, Leader continued his training in 'design based on material, physical ideas, especially through doing lots of grading and construction documents'. Importantly, he understands that his academic and practical experience has set him up to 'really evaluate his own work as well as others, based on what has been built and how well it works'.

Tom Leader,
Tom Leader Studio
Berkeley, CA, USA

'Tom Leader is one of today's most exciting landscape designers. His refined scale, his brilliant use of elongated dimension, his exploration of recycled and indigenous material are perfectly integrated within elegant spatial compositions.' Peter Walker on Tom Leader

Tom Leader, Tom Leader Studio

<u>Making Ground/Farming Water</u>, Corte Madera, CA, USA (2009)

This speculative proposal was created in response to San Francisco Bay's rising water levels in combination with seismic risks and proposes altering the topography of the bay's low-lying urban edges. This includes the removal of tilt-up structures and dredging deeper tidal channels, with superfluous materials re-used to make island available for development. Newly flooded areas will provide areas for saltwater farming of shellfish and biofuels.

Tom Leader, Tom Leader Studio

Railroad Park, Birmingham, AL, USA (2010)

Together with a large team of consultants, Tom Leader Studio created a unifying concept for this rail corridor and downtown central park. The park sits alongside a 4.6-metre (15-foot) railway viaduct that bisects downtown Birmingham. The park new topography creates knolls, allowing visitors firsthand views and the physical experience of multiple trains slowly rumbling through town, and forms water bodies, providing flood protection and biofiltration.

Kongjian Yu, Turenscape Beijing, China

Kongjian Yu's designs aim to reconstruct ecological infrastructures within an environmentally ethical aesthetic. His research and proposals about the pattern of ecological security and ecological infrastructure at various scales have fundamentally changed China's environmental and land use policies at a national level. In addition to receiving his Doctor of Design from Harvard Graduate School of Design, Yu is the founder and Dean of the College of Architecture and Landscape Architecture at Peking University. Yu's projects, through his firm Turenscape, have been widely published and internationally celebrated for their ecologically sound and culturally sensitive design.

Built on a former industrial site, Turenscape's recent project, Landscape as a Living System: Shanghai Houtan Park, is a regenerative living landscape on Shanghai's Huangpu riverfront that very much represents Yu's design ideology. As he explains, 'this park's constructed wetland, ecological flood control, reclaimed industrial structures and materials, and urban agriculture are integral components of an overall strategy designed to treat polluted river water and restore the degraded waterfront in an aesthetically pleasing way'. Selecting this park as a recent project which he would enjoy visiting, Yu describes it as 'a rich landscape that integrates various natural, industrial, agricultural and art elements that invite exploration. It is a peaceful and aesthetically beautiful [park] in the middle of the noisy big city that allows me to slow down and be a part of nature.'

Yu identifies his childhood farming experience as his main source of inspiration, and this, combined with 'the contemporary design of minimalism and ecological thinking, including the works of Peter Walker and Michael Van Valkenburgh, and the systematic and ecological planning of Ian McHarg, Carl Steinitz and Richard Forman', has very much informed his work. Turenscape's stunning Qunli Stormwater Park exemplifies this influence. As Yu explains, 'contemporary cities are not resilient when faced with inundations of surface water. Landscape architecture can play a key role in addressing this problem'. Located in Qunli New Town, Harbin City, in China's Heilongjiang Province, the project's full title is 'A Green Sponge for a Water-Resilient City: Qunli Stormwater Park', reflecting the principle that it acts as a green sponge, cleansing and storing urban storm water. This function is integrated with other ecosystem services such as habitat protection, aquifer recharge and recreational use, while offering an aesthetic value and fostering urban growth.

In describing his creative process, Yu explains in the first instance he sees 'the project, or the site, as problems that may be specific to the site such as storm water runoff, soil or water pollution, or exist beyond the site boundary, such as climate change and food security. I will then ask myself what my design can contribute to solve these problems.' From here, Yu takes the 'negative approach', a term he uses 'to describe the planning and design process, to identify what shall not be designed and what shall be preserved, and to minimize change, and then make transformative interventions in a creative way, to fix the problem or demonstrate a replicable solution to solve the bigger problem beyond the site'.

Yet, beyond what he understands as 'the commonly believed pressing issues of climate change, ecological security [particularly water-related ...], environmental degradation, food and energy security', Yu would like to put forward two issues which he believes are the most pressing: 'the segregated and single-minded engineering approach to problems of any kind ... and the wasteful lifestyle (driven by wrong values and aesthetics) depending on the consumption of fossil fuels and even other kinds of so-called green energy (including hydropower)'.

Yu believes that landscape architecture can make 'great contributions' to these issues through holistic and integrated design work that addresses 'big decisions'. As Yu explains, 'I define landscape architecture as the "Art of Survival" for Homo sapiens and for humanity' and he wants professionals 'to be aware of the mission of this profession in the new era'. In fact, he believes a revolution is needed, and what he terms, 'the Big Feet Revolution' comprises an important part of Yu's philosophy. Titled in reference to the unhealthy practice of binding a woman's feet so that their diminished form might convey an elevated sophistication and status that made her more desirable, 'Big Feet' is symbolic of Yu's belief that design must function for the wider society, not the ornamental pleasure of an elite. Yu wants to see 'a new aesthetic that values productive and healthy landscapes, low-maintenance and high-performance landscapes, makes friends with floods and works to improve ecosystems'.

When asked how he'd like to influence future generations of landscape architects, Yu would like them to be 'innovative and to explore all kinds of possibilities in solving the pressing issues that the world is facing today, related to resources, ecology and environment, food and energy security, cultural identity and social equity. Most of my projects are experiential, that test alternative solutions to various problems that we are facing today, allowing our young professionals to learn from [them], be they successes or failures.' Yu runs Turenscape as an 'open school', welcoming interns and young professionals from around the world.

Yu sees landscape architecture's future role as 'The Art of Survival', conducting human actions in healing the land and environment, globally, regionally and locally'. Yet, in order to be successful, Yu insists that 'this mission requires the transformation of a profession defined traditionally as gardening or park design, and requires fundamental changes to our programmes of education'.

Favourite plants

1 Produce crops (rice, corn and sunflowers)
2 Tall grasses (*Pennisetum* and *Miscanthus*)
3 Wetland vegetation (lotus, purple lythrum and cattail)
4 Self-reproductive flowers (*Coreopsis* and *Cosmos*)
5 Bamboo

Favourite trees

1 Chinese redwood (*Metasequoia glyptostroboides*)
2 White poplar (*Populus alba*)
3 Japanese persimmon (*Diospyros kaki*)
4 Chinese tallow (*Sapium sebiferum*)
5 Chinese sweet gum (*Liquidambar formosana*)

Favourite contemporary artists

1 Christo and Jeanne-Claude
2 Maya Lin
3 Richard Serra
4 Alexander Calder
5 Isamu Noguchi

A transformed brownfield site on Shanghai's Huangpu riverfront, Houtan Park incorporates existing industrial structures and lush wetland gardens as part of a restorative project for the area. Providing flood control and treating polluted river water in a visually stunning way, wooden walkways, platforms and folded sculptural shelters provide characteristic elements typical of Turenscape's work.

Turenscape's Qunli Stormwater Park provides a 'green sponge', effectively
cleaning and storing excessive storm water and enabling its reuse for multiple
ecological and recreational purposes. Raised wooden walkways provide routes
through the park, while elevated platforms offer pockets of shelter from which
to enjoy the surrounding vistas.

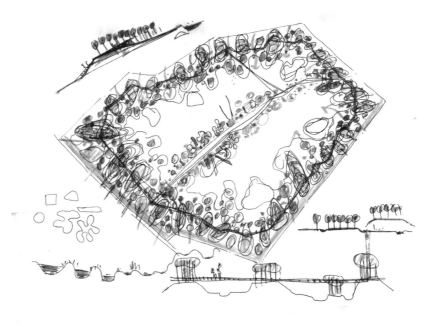

Kunming Dianchi Lake Water Remediation Farm is a large-scale landscape that uses farmland to cleanse the polluted lake. As well as food crops, the farm is expected to produce 830,000 cubic metres (219 million gallons) of clean water every day while providing an attractive landscape for recreation and a catalyst for land development around the farm.

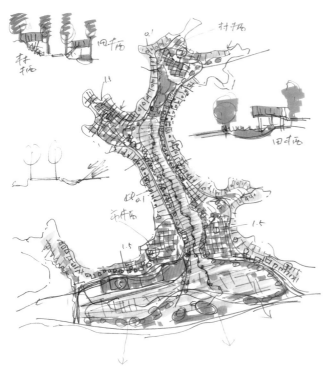

A Mother River Recovered: Qian'an Sanlihe Greenway, Qian'an, Hebei Province, China (2010)

A former sewage drainage and garbage dump, the Qian'an Sanlihe Greenway's once neglected landscape has been dramatically restored. Combined pedestrian and cycle paths are integrated with a continuous red sculptural element, a fibre-glass folded art form that offers shade and seating while revitalizing social identity by reflecting local paper-folding traditions. The project generates ecological and aesthetic benefit, catalyzing sustainable urban development in the region.

Favourite plants

1 Moso bamboo
  (*Phyllostachys edulis*)
2 Orchids
3 Reeds
4 White flowered iris (*Iris lacteal*)
5 Fragrant plantain lily
  (*Hosta plantaginea*)
6 Mao bamboo
  (*Phyllostachys heterocycla*)

Favourite trees

1 Chinese red pine
  (*Pinus tabuliformis*)
2 Camphor oil plant
  (*Cinnamomum camphora*)
3 Sweet gum
  (*Liquidambar styraciflua*)
4 Chinese scholar
  (*Sophora japonica*)
5 Smoke (*Cotinus coggygria*)

Favourite materials

1 Rubble
2 Rusted steel plate
3 Gravel
4 White concrete
5 Raw wood

Graduating from the School of Landscape Architecture, Beijing Forestry University in 1997, Yufan Zhu was awarded the first PhD in Landscape Architecture by the Ministry of Education of the People's Republic of China. Since 2000, Zhu has both taught and undertaken research in the theory and history of landscape architecture at the School of Architecture, Tsinghua University. Through the work of Zhuyufan Y³C Studio, Zhu has been exploring landscape theory by pursuing his own high-quality designs. Zhu lists his favourite natural landscapes as a 'bamboo-lined path at Yunqi, Hangzhou and lofty mountains and flowing water', qualities which are reflected in the tranquility and sinuous nature of his designs, as seen with his Quarry Garden in Shanghai Botanical Garden in China.

A renovated abandoned quarry, this garden has become a 'new landmark and calling card for Shanghai'. Once dangerous, inaccessible and abandoned land, Zhu has turned the site into an attractive tourist area. The park provides a dramatic transformation of a disused quarry and offers visitors the chance to experience the culture of the quarrying industry while surrounded by a serene backdrop of cascading water and sinuously constructed forms. The success of the project is illustrated in the successful creation of challenging spaces, which conquer difficult construction techniques while restoring ecological values.

Along with the influence of the site itself, experience of which he believes can bring the designer a 'true inspiration' that is rooted in context, Zhu reflects that his designs take a great deal of inspiration from the visual arts, 'especially traditional Chinese calligraphy and painting, because they express Chinese cultural ethos in their visual language and reflect the specific [style] of Chinese people, viewing nature and the world in an historical perspective'. Zhu then 'translates' this inspiration into a 'kind of ethos' and uses it in his own contemporary designs.

Indeed, the influence of some of his own favourite contemporary artists, like Eduardo Chillida, Richard Serra and Sui Jianguo, can be seen in the sculptural nature of his works. The Nuclear Memorial Park, Qing-Tibet Plateau, China, provides an example of such work. This park, constructed in 2009, is built on top of a former nuclear weapon research and development base. With the guiding principles of sustainability, this project innovatively responds to multiple challenges in the form of a serene landscape. The park, as Zhu explains, 'aptly demonstrates how sustainability could orchestrate every element into synergy, to unfold collectively abstract and individually concrete experiences, freeing itself from national boundaries to become a vehicle for something far larger and more universal – the pursuit of peace'.

Although he affirms that they do work with engineers, 'especially structural and hydraulic engineers', in order to resolve and further develop challenging design issues, Zhu's firm seldom collaborates with other architects or artists. If they do, they tend to 'keep a distance' and work independently. Zhu believes that 'design' can be defined as solving 'the problem creatively'. In taking on environmental challenges, Zhu proposes that the 'designer must regard the design as a functional factor and balance it together with aesthetic and economic factors', and in this way they make a creative and feasible design – 'the duty of any designer'.

This is certainly the case with Zhu's project, Hongshan Nuclear Test Command Centre, situated in the mountainous area of Xinjiang Uygur Autonomous Region, in northwest China. Here, Zhu took on serious environmental challenges with what was once an area for nuclear testing. This project sees the creation of a peace-themed tourist destination. In addition to the creation of a Gobi oasis and wetland landscape, the memorial park's design will preserve and use a large extent of the former layout, mountains, boulders and forest, and in doing so create a spatial order that narrates the events of the past and the historic meaning of the area.

Zhu cites 'the twitter of birds' and 'the murmur of a brook' as his favourite sounds, and considering the effective cohabitation of people and wildlife, his suggestion that cultural and ecological sustainability are the pressing global issues that landscape architects face today is telling. In today's globalized world, Zhu believes the issue of cultural sustainability is becoming an increasingly serious problem, and one which requires 'a long-term plan'. Although his own designs attempt to incorporate cultural values, he feels the ultimate goal for landscape architects is to 'cure the damage' caused by globalization and urbanization. This is in line with how Zhu would like to create better cities of the future, by 'spreading the significance of landscape architecture to the public'.

When asked about his future work, instead of naming a specific project, Zhu responds with what 'opportunity' he'd like to be presented with. Believing that the Song Dynasty (690–1279) represented the pinnacle of Chinese culture, he explains that he would like 'to translate the Song ethos into the contemporary age', referencing a period when culture and society supported the advancement of the arts, creating new opportunities for innovative, exploratory design trends.

Yufan Zhu, Zhuyufan Y³C Studio, School of Architecture, THU Beijing, China

'Yufan Zhu has an excellent sense of material, texture and colour, and is able to use them in a mastered way, giving him the capacity of creating artful landscapes that can touch humans' deep mind of affection.' Kongjian Yu on Yufan Zhu

Yufan Zhu, Zhuyufan Y³C Studio, School of Architecture, THU

<u>Nuclear Memorial Park</u>, Qing-Tibet Plateau, Qinghai Province, China (2009)
Built upon a former nuclear weapon research and development base, this park's design sustainably transforms the environment to create a serene landscape, evoking a sense of the peace it symbolically aims to promote. Curvilinear walls and steps define the space and soften the site's historic purpose, offering areas for seated reflection.

Yufan Zhu, Zhuyufan Y³C Studio, School of Architecture, THU

<u>Quarry Garden in Shanghai Botanical Garden</u>, Shanghai, China (2010)

Quarry Garden transforms a previously abandoned quarry yard into an iconic tourist attraction based on ecological and cultural restoration strategies. Cor-Ten steel constructions dramatically bisect the rock face, providing viewing platforms from which to enjoy the surrounding natural landscape, as well as providing a pedestrian route through the gardens.

The list of 'favourites' on each of the designers' introduction pages is derived from their response to a series of questions that provide further insight into how they work. The questions asked them to list their favourite plants, materials, natural landscapes, and so on, and to give examples of who inspires them or has influenced their work, as well as to explain the tools they most frequently use when designing. The vegetation responses were wonderfully diverse and varied and have consequently been streamlined as much as possible. As some of these plants are known by more than one common name, depending on where they're used, we've sometimes chosen to use the common name by which they are known in the designer's home country. If the Latin name and the common name are the same, only the common name has been used. It should be noted that the choice of materials and plants is contextual, and that lists have not been prioritized in any particular order.

01 Stig L Andersson, SLA
www.sla.dk
01 Luis Callejas, LCLA office
www.luiscallejas.com

02 Thorbjörn Andersson,
Sweco Architects
www.thorbjorn-andersson.com
www.sweco.se
02 Mattias Gustafsson, URBIO
www.urbio.se

03 Enric Batlle, Batlle i Roig Arquitectes
www.batlleiroig.com
03 Martí Franch, EMF landscape
architects
www.emf.cat

04 Andrea Cochran, Andrea Cochran
Landscape Architecture
www.acochran.com
04 James A Lord, Surfacedesign
www.sdisf.com

05 Sacha Coles, ASPECT Studios
www.aspect.net.au
05 Henry Crothers, LandLAB
www.landlab.co.nz

06 Claude Cormier, Claude Cormier
et Associés
www.claudecormier.com
06 Marc Ryan, PUBLIC WORK
www.publicwork.ca

07 James Corner, James Corner
Field Operations
www.fieldoperations.net
07 Christopher Marcinkoski, PORT
www.porturbanism.com

08 Herbert Dreiseitl, Rambøll/
Atelier Dreiseitl
www.ramboll.com/LCL
www.dreiseitl.com
08 Walter Hood, Hood Design Studio
www.wjhooddesign.com

09 Andrew Grant, Grant Associates
www.grant-associates.uk.com
09 Anouk Vogel, Anouk Vogel landscape
architecture
www.anoukvogel.nl

10 Juan Grimm, Studio Juan Grimm
www.juangrimm.cl
10 Karin Oetjen, KO Paisajismo
www.karinoetjen.com

11 George Hargreaves,
Hargreaves Associates
www.hargreaves.com
11 Chris Reed, Stoss Landscape Urbanism
www.stoss.net

12 Mikyoung Kim, Mikyoung Kim Design
www.myk-d.com
12 Karen M'Closkey, PEG office
of landscape + architecture
www.peg-ola.com

13 Martin Knuijt, OKRA
www.okra.nl
13 Ronald Rietveld, RAAAF [Rietveld
Architecture-Art-Affordances]
www.RAAAF.nl

14 Tilman Latz, Latz + Partner
www.latzundpartner.de
14 Diana Wiesner, Diana Wiesner
Arquitectura y Paisaje
www.dianawiesner.com

15 Perry Lethlean, Taylor Cullity Lethlean
www.tcl.net.au
15 Christopher Sawyer, Site Office
www.siteoffice.com.au

16 Xiaowei Ma, AGER Group
www.agergroup.com
16 Xiao Ying Xie, View Unlimited
Landscape Architecture Studio CUCD
www.viewunlimitedlandscape.com

17 Adrian McGregor, McGregor Coxall
www.mcgregorcoxall.com
17 Francisco Allard, Urbanica
www.urbanica.cl

18 Teresa Moller, Study of the Landscape,
Teresa Moller and Associates
www.teresamoller.cl
18 Chloe Humphreys,
The Landscape Studio
www.chloehumphreys.com

19 Catherine Mosbach,
mosbach paysagistes
www.mosbach.fr
19 David Besson-Girard, David
Besson-Girard paysagiste
www.davidbessongirard-paysagistes.fr

20 Laurie Olin, OLIN
www.theolinstudio.com
20 Toru Mitani, studio on site
www.s-onsite.com

21 Jacqueline Osty, Atelier Jacqueline
Osty & Associés
www.osty.fr
21 Bertrand Vignal, BASE
www.baseland.fr

22 Myungkweon Park, GroupHAN
www.grouphan.com
22 Yi Kyu Choe, Unknown Practice
www.unknp.com

23 Martin Rein-Cano, TOPOTEK 1
www.topotek1.de
23 Kate Orff, SCAPE
www.scapestudio.com

24 Yoji Sasaki, Ohtori Consultants
Environmental Design Institute
www.ohtori-c.com
24 Eiki Danzuka, EARTHSCAPE
www.earthscape.co.jp

25 Mario Schjetnan, Grupo de
Diseño Urbano
www.gdu.com.mx
25 Pedro Camarena Berruecos, LAAP
www.laap.com.mx

26 Rainer Schmidt, RSLA
www.rainerschmidt.com
26 Christian Henke, el:ch
landschaftsarchitekten
www.elch.la

27 Martha Schwartz,
Martha Schwartz Partners
www.marthaschwartz.com
27 Claudia Harari, HLA Harari
Landscape Architecture
www.hararila.com

28 Günther Vogt, VOGT Landscape
www.vogt-la.com
28 Rémy Turquin, Bassinet Turquin
Paysage
www.bassinet-turquin-paysage.com

29 Peter Walker,
PWP Landscape Architecture
www.pwpla.com
29 Tom Leader, Tom Leader Studio
www.tomleader.com

30 Kongjian Yu, Turenscape
www.turenscape.com
30 Yufan Zhu, Zhuyufan Y³C Studio,
School of Architecture, THU
www.arch.tsinghua.edu.cn/eng/faculty

Stig L Andersson: all images courtesy of SLA

Luis Callejas: all images courtesy of LCLA office

Thorbjörn Andersson: Jan Raeber pg 23 l; PeGe Hillinge pg 23 tr, pg 27 b; Thorbjörn Andersson pg 23 cr, pg 24 b; Beat Rösch pg 23 br; Sweco Architects pg 24 t, pg 25 tr, pg 26 bl, bc, pg 27 t; University of Umeå p 25 tl; Åke E:son Lindman pg 25 b, pg 26 br; Kasper Dudzik pg 26 t

Mattias Gustafsson: Himlafoto / URBIO pg 30 b; all other images courtesy of URBIO

Enric Batlle: Jordi Surroca pg 33 t, br, pg 34 tl, cl, bl, pg 35 b, pg 37; Batlle i Roig Arquitectes pg 33 bl, pg 34 r, pg 35 tl, tr, pg 36 l; Jorge Póo pg 36 bl, br

Martí Franch: Sergi Romero pg 39; EMF pg 40 tl, tr; Pau Ardèvol pg 40 b, pg 41 t, c; Esteve Bosch pg 41 b

Andrea Cochran: Vicky Sambunaris pg 43 t; Emily Rylander pg 43 c; Marion Brenner pg 43 b, pg 44 t, br, pg 45, pg 46 b, pg 47; Larry Ripple pg 44 bl; Bruce Damonte pg 46 t

James A Lord: Marion Brenner pg 49, pg 50; Smithsonian Institute pg 51

Sacha Coles: ASPECT Studios, CHROFI pg 53 t, c; ASPECT Studios pg 53 b, pg 55 tr, pg 57 br; Florian Groehn pg 54, pg 55 tl, b, pg 56 b, pg 57 bl; Adrian Boddy pg 56 t; Simon Wood pg 57 t

Henry Crothers: LandLAB pg 59; Waterfront Auckland pg 60 tl; David Straight pg 60 tr; Claire Hamilton pg 60 b; Jeff Brass pg 61 t, br; Patrick Reynolds pg 61 bl

Claude Cormier: Guillaume Paradis pg 63 t, bl, 64 tl, pg 67 br; Marc Cramer pg 63 br, pg 64 tr, b, pg 65; Eastern Construction pg 66; Jesse Colin Jackson pg 67 t; Nicola Betts pg 67 bl

Marc Ryan: all images courtesy of PUBLIC WORK

James Corner: James Palma copyright 2014 pg 73; Photo: Iwan Baan pg 74–5; Tim Street-Porter pg 76 tl, b; © Steve Proehl pg 76 tr; early concept rendering is courtesy of London Legacy Development Corporation pg 77 t; photographs by Robin Forster courtesy of LDA Design pg 77 bl, br

Christopher Marcinkoski: all images courtesy of PORT Urbanism

Herbert Dreiseitl: all images © Atelier Dreiseitl

Walter Hood: all images courtesy of Hood Design Studio

Andrew Grant: Photograph courtesy of The Hive, Worcester, University and public library, Worcestershire Archive and Archaeology Service, Worcestershire Hub. Managed in partnership by Worcestershire County Council and the University of Worcester. Photo: Ashley Mayes pg 93 t; Darren Chin pg 96 t, c, pg 97 t; all other images courtesy of Grant Associates

Anouk Vogel: Jeroen Musch pg 99 t, pg 100 tl, bl, pg 101 tr, b; all other images courtesy of Anouk Vogel landscape architecture

Juan Grimm: Renzo Delpino pg 103–6; Office of Development and Construction of Bahá'í Temple of South America pg 107 tl; Studio Juan Grimm pg 107 tr; Juan Grimm pg 107 b

Karin Oetjen: Augusto Domínguez pg 109–111

George Hargreaves: Kyle Jeffers pg 113; Bernward Engelke pg 114 t, bl, pg 115 b; © Robin Forster / LDA Design pg 114 br; LDA Design pg 115 t; 天津博维永诚科技有限公司 – 彭卓敏 pg 116 t; BUPD – 赵旭 pg 116 bl, br; Paul Hester pg 117

Chris Reed: photo by John December pg 119 t, bl; Stoss Landscape Urbanism pg 119 br, pg 120 tl, b, pg 121 tr; © Charles Mayer Photography pg 120 tr; Stoss + SHoP pg 121 tl, b

Mikyoung Kim: Christopher Baker pg 123 l; Charles Mayer pg 123 tr, br; Hedrich Blessing Photography pg 124 t, George Heinrich pg 124 bl, br, pg 125; Mark La Rosa pg 126 tl, b; Mikyoung Kim Design pg 126 tr, pg 127

Karen M'Closkey: all images courtesy of PEG office of landscape + architecture

Martin Knuijt: Greenwich Council pg 133 t; Annie Beugel pg 133 bl, br; all other images courtesy of OKRA

Ronald Rietveld: Allard Bovenberg pg 139; Rob 't Hart pg 140; Ronald Rietveld pg 141

Tilman Latz: Serge Brison pg 143 tl, b; Bernard Capelle pg 143 tr; Ornella Orlandini pg 144 t, pg 145; Andrea Serra pg 144 bl; Latz + Partner pg 144 br, pg 147; Markus Tollhopf pg 146

Diana Wiesner: Bart Hoes pg 149; Diana Wiesner Ceballos pg 150 t, pg 151 t; Daniel Olarte pg 150 b; Francisco Jaramillo pg 151 b

Perry Lethlean: John Gollings pg 153 t, bl, pg 156, pg 157 t; Brett Boardman pg 153 br; Simon Devitt pg 154 t, pg 155; Jonney Davis pg 154 b; Peter Hyatt pg 157 b

Christopher Sawyer: Andrew North pg 159 t; John Gollings pg 159 bl, pg 160–1; Site Office pg 159 br

Xiaowei Ma: Green Townscape Design Ltd. pg 165 tr; all other images courtesy of AGER Group

Xiao Ying Xie: VULA Studio pg 169; Xie Xiaoying pg 170 tl, tr; Zhou Xinmeng pg 170 b, pg 171

Adrian McGregor: visuals by McGregor Coxall and Parramatta Council pg 173; photography by McGregor Coxall pg 174–5; Simon Wood Photography pg 176–7

Francisco Allard: all images courtesy of Urbanica

Teresa Moller: all images courtesy of Study of the Landscape, Teresa Moller and Associates

Chloe Humphreys: all images courtesy of The Landscape Studio

Catherine Mosbach: © mosbach&rahm pg 193; © mosbach pg 194–5; © Kazuyo Sejima + Ryue Nishizawa / SANAA, Tim Culbert + Celia Imrey / IMREY CULBERT, Catherine Mosbach / MOSBACH PAYSAGISTES, photograph by Hisao Susuki pg 196–7 t, 196 b; © Kazuyo Sejima + Ryue Nishizawa / SANAA, Tim Culbert + Celia Imrey / IMREY CULBERT, Catherine Mosbach / MOSBACH PAYSAGISTES, photograph by Catherine Mosbach pg 197 bl, br

David Besson-Girard: Sergio Grazia pg 199 t; David Besson-Girard pg 199 bl, br, pg 200, pg 201 br; Artefactory Lab pg 201 t, bl

Laurie Olin: © OLIN / Sahar Coston-Hardy pg 203; © OLIN / Laurie Olin pg 204 t, pg 205 b; © Peter Eckert pg 204 b; © ZGF pg 205 t; © KieranTimberlake / Studio pg 206; courtesy of OLIN pg 207 tl, tr; © OLIN / Peter Stegner pg 207 b

Toru Mitani: © Makoto Yoshida pg 209, pg 210, pg 211 t, br; studio on site pg 211 bl

Jacqueline Osty: Atelier J Osty pg 213, pg 215 bl, pg 216, pg 217 l; Dubois Fresney pg 214, pg 215 br; Martin Argyroglo pg 215 t, pg 219 tr, br

Bertrand Vignal: BASE pg 219; Karolina Samborska pg 220–221

Myungkweon Park: all images courtesy of GroupHAN

Yi Kyu Choe: Colin Grover, Pike Projects pg 231 b; all other images courtesy of Unknown Practice

Martin Rein-Cano: Photos © Hanns Joosten pg 233 t, lc, lb, pg 234 br; © TOPOTEK 1 pg 233 br, pg 236 bl, pg 237; Iwan Baan pg 234 t, pg 235; © Mike Magnussen pg 234 bl; Photos © Gen Wang pg 236 t, br

Kate Orff: Ty Cole Photography pg 240; all other images courtesy of SCAPE

Yoji Sasaki: Jeong Jinwoo pg 243; Maki Associates pg 245; all other images courtesy of Ohtori Consultants Environmental Design Institute

Eiki Danzuka: Yusuke Komatsu pg 249; Koji Okumura pg 250; Tadamasa Iguchi pg 251

Mario Schjetnan: Francisco Gómez Sosa pg 253, pg 254 b, pg 256 t, pg 257; Hector Velasco pg 254 tr, tl, pg 255; Mario Schjetnan / Archivo GDU pg 256 b

Pedro Camarena Berruecos: all images courtesy of LAAP

Rainer Schmidt: picture alliance / dpa / Andreas Gebert pg 263 t; Rainer Schmidt Landschaftsarchitekten pg 263 b, pg 264 t, pg 265 br, pg 266 br; Raffaella Sirtoli pg 264 b, pg 265 t, bl, pg 266 t, bl pg 267 t, bl; Besco pg 267 br

Christian Henke: Elisabeth Lesche pg 271 b; all other images Christian Henke

Martha Schwartz: images and plans courtesy of Martha Schwartz Partners pg 273, pg 274 tr, pg 276 bl; Terrence Zhang pg 274 tl, b, pg 275, pg 276 t, br, pg 277

Claudia Harari: Harari LA pg 279, pg 281; James A Lord pg 280 t; Abigail Guzman pg 280 bl, br

Günther Vogt: VOGT pg 283, pg 284 br, pg 286 b; Mike Odwyer pg 284 t, bl, pg 285; Christian Vogt pg 286–287 t, pg 287 b

Rémy Turquin: Bassinet Turquin Paysage pg 289 b, pg 290 tr, bl, br; Denis Barçon pg 289 t; Shigeru Ban Architects Europe – Jean de Gastines Architectes pg 290 tl, pg 291

Peter Walker: all images courtesy of PWP Landscape Architecture

Tom Leader: Tom Leader Studio pg 299, pg 300 t, bl; Nate Dreger br; Miller Mobley pg 301

Kongjian Yu: all images courtesy of Kongjian Yu / Turenscape

Yufan Zhu: photograph: Jia Yue pg 309; photograph: Chen Yao pg 310–11; all © Zhu Yufan

Photographic sources are listed where possible, but the publisher will endeavour to rectify any inadvertent omissions.

Acknowledgements

Thank you to all the amazing designers who submitted superb projects and imagery and gave fantastically detailed responses and project descriptions, all of which brought a diverse and personal touch to the book. Thank you to Emilia Terragni for commissioning the book and, together with Senior Editor Virginia McLeod, skilfully guiding it through to completion. Thank you to PLACE Design + Planning for their support and MRG Studio for their superb advice. And finally, an extra special thank you to my sister, Corre Kombol, for her sublime wisdom and wit, and to my husband, Aidan, and my children, Finn and Nina, for supporting me through such an enormous, but exciting, undertaking!

Phaidon Press Limited
Regent's Wharf
All Saints Street
London N1 9PA

Phaidon Press Inc.
65 Bleecker Street
New York, NY 10012

www.phaidon.com

First published 2015
©2015 Phaidon Press Limited

ISBN 978 0 7148 6963 6

A CIP catalogue record for this book is available from the British Library.

Commissioning Editor: Emilia Terragni
Project Editor: Meaghan Kombol
Production Controller: Steve Bryant

Design: Studio Joost Grootens / Joost Grootens,
Dimitri Jeannottat, Hanae Shimizu, Elena Meneghini

Printed in China